EMERGING TECHNOLOGIES AND HOUSING PROTOTYPES

Salvador Pérez Arroyo
Rossana Atena
Igor Kebel

Berlage Institute, Postgraduate Laboratory of Architecture

Sponsored by:
Empresa Municipal de Vivienda y Suelo. Area de Gobierno de Urbanismo,
Vivienda e Infraestructuras. Ayuntamiento de Madrid.

Contributors: Andrea Fiechter, Alexandros Vazakas,
Eriko Watanabe, Jung-Jae Lee, Jasmine Tsoi,
Kiwoong Ko, Lorena Franco, Maria Mandalaki, Noa Haim,
Pieterjan Vermoortel, Seung Soo, Yorai Gabriel

CONTENTS

023 MATERIAL & TECHNOLOGY RESEARCH
Rossana Atena

099 SUSTAINABLE PERFORMANCE

123 INTEGRATED PERFORMANCE

PROLOGUE

Promoting quality and sustainability in public housing is one of the priority action vectors of Madrid City Council's Public Housing Enterprise (The EMVS: Empresa Municipal de Vivienda y Suelo). Therefore, an extraordinary, innovative effort is being made, supporting initiatives based on the use of safe materials and the incorporation of new technologies that lead to unconventional processes and products that improve building quality and optimise sustainability in the houses promoted by the Municipal Administration.

We understand that the incorporation of Reasearch and Development in building technologies is a future environment that will lead us to more rational and efficient building systems, because the experimental application of new, unconventional materials to public housing will open the door to a new market of highly industrialised products that favour greater environmental respect for buildings and greater comfort for consumers.

In this context, special importance is generated by the initiatives being carried out in the European Union framework, initiatives such as the publication of this book, *Emerging Technologies and Housing Prototypes*, done within the Financial Instrument for the Environment (LIFE) programme, which is an important contribution to the promotion of sustainable development-oriented technologies.

Previously, research was carried out on new materials and construction systems which—being in principle, applicable to a number of different uses other than housing—could, at the same time, be used to improve the quality and sustainability of public housing promotion. Definitively, then, it has been a question of studying the possibilities for re-conversion and technological transference from other conventional productive sectors, with the aim of ameliorating public sector building processes.

This research, the fruits of which are collected in this book, was carried out by Professor Salvador Pérez Arroyo and the postgraduate students of the Berlage Institute in Rotterdam, under the coordination of the EMVS Direction of Residential Innovation Projects, in the framework of the agreement signed between the Institute and the EMVS.

Throughout this book, written in the model of an official manual for the use of new systems and materials, professionals in the fields of architecture, urbanism, and construction are able to find detailed information on new options for advancing sustainability in their projects and the environments in which they work.

In parallel with this investigative and publishing initiative, the EMVS will continue working to achieve the best quality and sustainability for buildings, via many other projects, such as the establishment of a good practice protocol promoting sustainable building in all municipal projects related to housing; fomenting ecological rehabilitation by using adequate environmental techniques and models, and the development of sustainable communities that combine bioclimatic architecture, efficient energy management, and self-supplying energy strategies.

This permanent EMVS initiative to foment quality and sustainability looks beyond public housing promotions and at the same time seeks to create a reference point for the private sector, providing it with the same creativity, innovation and desire for excellence that the EMVS applies to its construction activity. Without a doubt, this book, and its proposals and alternatives, constitutes an extraordinarily effective instrument designed to achieve such an aim.

Pilar Martínez
Government Council Member in charge of the Area of Urbanism, Housing and Infrastructures
President of the Empresa Municipal de Vivienda y Suelo.

INTRODUCTION: THE LIGHTNESS OF TECHNOLOGY

After the ideological battle of the Cold War and all the events of capitalist invasion that followed its proclaimed triumph, a sense of lightness fell over most cultural manifestations of the West, a lightness that proclaimed the non-necessity of a solid critical posture, since it appeared that the force of a counter-ideology was no longer a threat nor a thing to be dealt with in the near future. For many architects and artists, this meant the beginning of a time of pure experimentation, a time without a strong political obligation, a time to relax, play and explore.

"Don't think, look! Today we need to stop thinking so as to start again to see what we can't yet describe since we think too much. We need an art of description.... Art itself must become experimental". John Rajchman's 1993 declaration epitomises a specific and prolific attitude that began in the 1990s and continues to strongly influence today's discourse; an attitude of dedication and commitment toward design and building technologies yet to be tested; an absolute focus on shape and material innovation; and with it, the belief in the possibility of a new architecture. Salvador Pérez Arroyo, Rossana Atena and Igor Kebel are exemplary personalities in this discourse and their efforts, along with the Berlage Institute researchers that authored some of the prototypes presented, helped achieve a scientific but sensible understanding of the capacities applicable to the technological inventions in the first part of this publication. It becomes clear that their premise was, not only to catalogue the contemporary architectural obsession with new surfaces and materials, but also to project out of the precise knowledge of these composite materials a new fable for designing housing prototypes for the future.

The experimental spirit displayed in this book could not have been achieved without the authors' perceptual lightness of the time. Technology itself is understood as the ultimate product in the recycle of modernity and the urban production of its future; the object of technology becomes architecture, and architecture morphs towards a fictional machine of per-formative capacities. For the authors, consuming sustainability, performance and optimisation as technology advances is a reflection and a need of the contemporary market. In this body of work, we can sense their faithful consideration to actively involve the architecture profession in this regime of constant change and begin to address building efficiencies, climatic alterations, ecological environments, intelligent systems and serialised optimisation. The housing prototypes show us possibilities in the prediction of future market needs and therefore accord us a glimpse of what we can expect.

It is precisely this predictive quality that makes this research a valuable addition to the postmodern pallet of comprehensive material search tools we have as architects. The performance display of the materials investigated in this book incite our imagination toward indefinite descriptions and realities of their application, teasing us with fantastic dwelling prototypes, and it makes a statement for the need of more exploration and more tests in the production of architectural objects. It is a manifest that flows with today's liberal system that understands the lightness of technology and the serious playfulness with which architecture should be practiced in the establishment's ceaseless quest for the new. We have to be very thankful to the City of Madrid and the EMVS to enable us to explore the possibilities.

Alejandro Zaera-Polo
Dean of the Berlage Institute

SECOND HAND TECHNOLOGY

They had moved into a house in one of the large geodesic dome—G23—that surrounded the old medieval city, and had chosen a humid, temperate climate. Frequently, they went shopping in the city. They loved the old, organic smell of materials in constant decay, the incessant noise, and above all, the absence of nature. The few plants grew in ceramic containers that the inhabitants bathed with water. The architecture, the streets and the environment were hard and aggressive, there were few windows, the streets were narrow and dark. They used to record smells and sounds on their mini-atmosphere recorder. Then they would play them back at home. She liked to make love whilst reproducing these stolen noises and images, these smells. She was aware of her depravity, of wanting, perhaps, to see herself enveloped in a time in which relations were different. The recordings made her remember Paul Bowles' old stories, *The Sheltering Sky* or *A Distant Episode*, among others. The unconscious contact with the archetypes that man had developed in the past, in a land full of natural beauty, which was, however, cruel and uncontrollable. The contrast with the void that the total absence of cultural references could produce, the unpredictable, random life of the natural world. Daybreak with no other knowledge than that of your own body.

Their current home, that of our protagonists, was of the average kind. It was on level 40, and was equipped with high quality components, but they had made a bad choice. The exterior envelope, made of a gelatinous polymer, was not state-of-the-art and had few information and memory services. The interior of the dwelling also suffered from some erroneous choices. The wrong textures, slow layout programmes that were badly suited to their tastes. The food handling systems were extremely bulky. It was a highly rigid construction that could not respond to stimuli from the geode's artificial nature.

Recycling techniques were increasingly sophisticated, maintaining constant levels of materials at all times. The entities in charge of constructing and relocating housing moved with great speed. In the past, all of the old components of dwellings had been taken to rubble collection parks. Building had been carried out with very expensive materials: brick and concrete. Metal materials had gradually brought in a new era. Aluminium was the first material that had been intensively recycled. Afterwards, regulations had penalised all materials that could not be recycled. Increasingly light buildings had been demanded, and, of necessity, cleaner and quieter environments. The old cities had been kept as entomological remains of a world that had reached the limits of ecological survival.

The two of them had considered renewing many of their home's components. To this end, they had posted an announcement on all possible networks. By paying a little more, they could acquire state-of-the-art components or used parts that were of better quality and had more features. Opting for the latest technology always bore an extra cost and was not worth it. They looked at virtual models, they got in touch with other people who wanted to sell, but everyone was looking for more modern systems. They had definitely made a mistake in their choice: veined wall faces were no longer in fashion, nor were luminescent pieces of furniture that imitated wood. If they could not find buyers, they would try to sell components for recycling. They could not decide whether to change the exterior envelope for a completely virtual view or whether to partly accept the green, ordered view under the great geode in which they lived. Recently, a major market in components had arisen. Data storage systems had noticeably improved and everyone wanted to adapt to the new opportunities. Even the skin of the G23 was going to be renewed; it was going to simulate a sheet of fog, creating a special interior climate.

Some architects had begun to work with structures that were made lighter with gases and had very flexible supply supports. The dwellings sometimes responded with a gentle movement to the wind inside the geode. Even the lightest breezes could be reflected in their stability.

The different geodes were linked by material transport networks. These veins were connected to recycling parks for obsolete articles that were not accepted in the second hand market. The country was a great veined fabric for transporting molten aluminium, titanium, and all kinds of polymers. Even the transport of fibres or fluids had been perfected with special, pre-crystallised molecules; like a purée that was about to solidify. Construction made use of the transport of fluids suitable for putting parts together in situ. This had created a certain continuity in construction. Mechanical joints had been replaced by low melting point solders, pressure welding or induction welding. Building was becoming increasingly like blowing up a balloon or unfolding a self-opening umbrella. The location, the most appropriate support and the compatibility of the fluids had to be chosen—but little more.

However, these solutions were also becoming old-fashioned. Both of them had information about new technologies. Deep down, the current systems of creating spaces made them feel a certain degree of claustrophobia, a perceptual limitation. The most appealing building began to be—for people like them who wanted to travel and had been brought up in a culture in which possessing objects no longer meant anything—the dwelling designed to be formed out of aerogels. White clouds that provided isolation and transparency when needed. These were produced with many options for the layout and exterior form.

Basically, this new technology had brought about a return to primitive nakedness, contact with the exterior that enabled you to feel the cold breezes of the night, isolate yourself in the interior, or disappear. The lightness gave back the most natural meaning to a race that had become used to taking refuge in the architecture of large volumes. As Paul Bowles said, "The day dawned with the promise of change, but when it had reached its peak, the observer suspected that it was yet again the same, the same day that had been lived for a long time, again and again, this blinding day that time had not darkened." These were generations that were used to potential, permanent contact with nature. A great effort had been made to halt the crazy race to disaster: the non-recyclable construction without restrictions, remains and more remains everywhere, archaeological strata in unsustainable quantities, cities based on old defensive relations or on systems of power symbols. Water consumption that was impossible to maintain once the climate had changed.

Currently, the world was polarised between nature, a local universe, and the infinite, which was full of communication systems. It was impossible to understand the old accommodation systems, which could not exchange elements, could not keep up with the constant improvements in domestic technology. It was incredible that buildings had been created for centuries without a second hand market. In the past, buildings were made to endure. It was said that objects and houses had to last for ever. This was a strange phenomenon that was almost incomprehensible, there was a conceptual contradiction between the pressure on mutable nature and the desire to become attached to objects and immutable spaces. Now, that false stability had been replaced by richness and multiplicity.

The concept of home could no longer be the ancestral idea of other times. Those buildings had been created to protect people from the climate; now the climate was completely controlled. The only way to avoid destroying the atmosphere was to create inserted, protective layers. Each environment had its large external geode. Between the geodes was neutral, unpopulated land in which genetic archaeology techniques had been used to recover extinct species.

The house was a base for sensations. A medium in which to form relations and have children. A communication system, work and learning. Architecture had been broken up into a much more potent reality: mobility and constant mutability linked to technology operated from the 'living room', and the natural reality of a planet that had to be carefully looked after to prevent it from entering into irreversible processes. The so-called houses could be moved to other supports or even broken down into pieces with a memory, which sometimes stayed in the same support or were moved to a new location. Salvation had come from ideas. In a world like this, architecture meant everything. Everything was architecture dissolved in the reality and in the environment. However, architecture was inspired by many other factors. Otherwise it could not be as closely linked as it was to the most immediate life.

Salvador Pérez Arroyo
Visiting professor of the Berlage Institute

MATERIAL& TECHNOLOGY RESEARCH

Rossana Atena

INTRODUCTION

During the last decade, the increase in new materials in conjunction with the availability of new production processes has resulted in an increasingly codified approach towards the use of materials and the traditions that attend them. In the past, a far deeper understanding of materials existed than does today. In many cases contemporary knowledge is superficial, content merely to reference the latest trend in the dominant discourse.

The phenomenon of information overload, the development of new ideas and parameters, in addition to the growth of innovative technologies, has led to a knowledge glut. Because much of this knowledge is inconsistent, there is no abiding protocol around the use of materials.

Designers sometimes find themselves suddenly forced to make decisions—hyper choices—about incorporating new materials into a design, even when the designer lacks the tools to properly make such a complex choice.

Part of the issue is a 'technology transfer' in which technologies and materials from one specialised field migrate to ordinary applications in another, as in the field of architecture.

When addressing designed materials (materials created for a specific functional demand, or even better, numerous functional demands), it is important for you to push the boundaries of our current understanding of materials by envisioning them in new contexts.

But there are obstacles to incorporating new materials, including the much-used argument in current discourses that few people understand these innovations and even fewer are actually using the materials. Several public and private research centres around the world, each with a slightly different approach, are attempting to address this problem, and contribute to a greater understanding of new materials and how they be used.

In addition to understanding the applications of the surfeit of new materials, it is also important to control the dissemination of this knowledge. It is necessary to find and use new control tools, classification methods, database and research software, all of which must be tested to ensure that these controls engender wider practical and creative understanding of the materials.

The above arguments were investigated during a research program entitled *Domesticating Technology Transfer*, conducted by Salvador Pérez Arroyo, Igor Kebel and myself at the Berlage Institute from 2003–2004.

This book addresses the topic on two levels. The first, more general, investigates each material and technology independently; the second, more specific, studies how these materials and technologies can be applied to specific design projects developed and/or researched by the students of the Institute.

In the first part of the book, specific materials are investigated by experimenting with a new classification method based on studies of each material's performance characteristics. By integrating and overcoming conventional standards of the engineering field, this section proposes an alternative reading of materials, while introducing technological processes in architecture and other technical/scientific fields.

The second part of the book shows several design projects that build on a research-based and theoretical, rather than technological, approach, to develop the creative potential of transferred technology, and the use of innovative materials for a variety of purposes.

All designed projects respond to a proposal by the EMVS, Empresa Municipal de Vivienda y Suelo de Madrid of Spain. The EMVS developed a case study for the examination and analysis of a high-rise apartment building in southern Madrid. This book is a work in progress, written as part of the cultural discourse on innovative materials. It will be further developed alongside the two themes that were investigated in parallel throughout the year: theoretical research, and the contextualisation of material investigation through design project experimentation. It uses the design project as a method for investigation, and as a tool for feedback and evaluation.

The book should thus be understood within the context of research methodology. Often it becomes evident that materials intervene with technological process and come to be deformed or domesticated. In other words: the materials become 'designed'. As a result, the material becomes a new component belonging to the design debate instead of being considered a 'given' tool at the final project stage.

MATERIALS, TECHNOLOGIES & INNOVATION

The material from which the objects are made appears... even less definable by easy categories... We should talk... about 'material' not by defining 'what it is' but rather explaining 'what it does'; it might be that we can discuss a product's material and observe what seems to have been done, but we cannot know in truth what it is.... The identity mechanism of production has been hindered and afterwards went through a crisis caused by the acceleration of technical development and introduction of new materials.

Among these, plastic materials took on an important role... declaring their high degree of artificiality and their absence of history... contributing to the breakdown of an entire system of values, images and hierarchy that were based on natural quality and formed by perceptive and symbolic tradition.

The possibility that the material itself might have identity and image quality is irreversibly defaced... with the new material recognisability leading towards a 'light recognition'. This raises a material world without names, producing 'Zelig' materials in which the true image is undefined possessing the capability to assume any image given by the designer's preference. The traditional relationship between designer and material is therefore subverted, replaced by a new freedom for the designer to project new cultural and physical meanings, formerly produced solely for the material itself. However, this new realm seems to be perceived only through surfaces, local and temporary relations, in other words, through appearances.

The Material of Invention, Ezio Manzini, Milan, Arcadia Edizione, 1986

Human history is often influenced by the introduction and use of new materials and technologies. In response, cultures usually change. Within the history of human social evolution, the consequences of the introduction of new technology have concerned how raw materials were worked.

Each age was marked by the evolution of techniques for working and using materials: the Stone Age, the Bronze Age, the Iron Age, etc.. No less important was the further development of new materials such as ceramics, glass and textiles.

Centuries, sometimes millennia, of experimentation were necessary in order to introduce new technologies, and progress in the use of materials was slow. The century-long industrial revolution referred mainly to a revolution in the use of alloys and metals, with the possible exception of hydraulic cement in Britain during the mid-seventeenth century.

Never before the twentieth century has the evolution and application of new materials been so accelerated and with such consistently broad dimensions. It is evident that there is a close relationship between economic growth and the progress of material science.

Currently in countries with advanced economies, activity in the field of innovative materials including electronic, magnetic and optic contributes, directly or indirectly, through product or process, to about 30 or 40 per cent of that country's gross domestic product (GDP).

Although the impact on economics and industry is visible, the research role within the innovative material field is not often acknowledged. Thus the adaptation of existing relationships between property, structure and design of new materials is the foundation for the modern science of materials.

Each age is marked by materials that identify social, cultural and technical aspects of the period. At the beginning of the twentieth century, the introduction of glass and steel for architectural purposes radically changed approaches to design. Although, contrary to other cases, these materials did not immediately achieve their own iconographic autonomy, they were used, since their introduction, to reproduce the iconography of other traditional materials. This inertial approach towards innovation is still partly visible today in architecture.

It should be noted that the Bauhaus Manifesto marked the first attempt to introduce experimentation on and with different matter, thereby introducing the study of materiality to several fields. Concurrently, Johannes Itten developed a different approach to the study of materials based on material quality and sensory aspects. In other words, within the Bauhaus movement, materiality started to attain new significance that included both physical and psychological aspects.

The beginning of the crisis of traditional material culture can be seen, quite obviously, in the early 1960s when plastics were introduced on a large scale. The cultural and technological changes that plastics caused were so consequential, they are still being felt today.

The idea of materials being 'natural' was removed by the possibility of creating matter that was entirely homogenous and isotropic. A new issue emerged, that of material recognisability: plastic material derived from a wide range of polymer families with different characteristics. As production costs went down, it became a mass product, so much so that plastics were attributed with the social qualities of a sort of 'consumer democracy'. A new object aesthetic was raised and developed into 'interfaces' that were produced first for electronic and then for communication tools. These interactive devices allowed for a different mode of object use by transmitting in a mediated rather than a direct way.

A similar phenomenon with metal alloys occurred at the same time, although this material had a longer incubation period due to the cultural and technical difficulties of creating lightweight metal alloys. Since these innovations, however, the growth of new materials has been exponential.

Within this ever-changing territory, the concept of 'composite material' (grounded in technological human culture ever since the term was first used for a green brick made of straw with binding functions) suddenly broke with the concept of 'matter'. This compromised the possibility of having a scientific approach to material classification. The phenomenon of composite production brought about the merger of multinational companies that had previously occupied different product fields.

The degree of complexity was raised on a large scale and the guarantee of control underwent an inversion. Added to this complexity, nanotechnology is derived from nanomaterials that, for the most part, can be classified as nanocomposites. This is a clear illustration of the current cultural and technological debate.

Research and speculation has given rise to a different approach within this discourse; to 'design' materials, generating material made to measure for specific applications. This process opens up a new category of designers and a different cultural approach towards knowledge of the material.

Materials for specific applications were designed ad hoc rather than in response to precise demands. This new approach found its technical definition coming mainly from other highly specialised fields and from scientific applications with high technical content. This was not limited to sophisticated applications: it also started to be employed in the mass production of consumer products.

The 'silent revolution' caused by the advent of new materials has radically changed our approach to knowledge. Jean-François Lyotard was the first, in 1985, to introduce the term 'immaterial materials', in reference to postmodern materials and virtual technologies with the ability to define a different domain of sensory experience and open up new possibilities for everyday life.

A material that has the capacity for multiple areas of performance has a higher aptitude to for 'communicating', simultaneously, data about itself and other information. These so-called 'smart materials' are interactive interfaces that create a dialectic relationship with the user. Despite belonging to the material, the newly-introduced properties fall under the sphere of information and communication; the surface of the object loses its connection with matter.

In terms of perception, the new materials are assigned an aptitude to continuously modify their appearance without the possibility of their being described using objective and finalised parameters. There is no question as to how a material is produced, rather the demand is that the material offers performance: what is it used for and how is it used? The material is no longer considered a simple element, but a system able to perform with rigour and sophistication.

It is important to clarify the meaning of a word that has already been used very often within this book: material.

Whenever one talks about 'material' it is, from some points of view, in fault. Rather, we should talk about 'semi-finish', or, more precisely, about 'product'. Today when one talks about material the reference is rarely to precise raw material. In most cases, the references are primarily concerned with composite materials in which classification becomes even more complicated, causing a migration from one family to another.

'Material' is such an imprecise term that it can have different meanings in different contexts.

It is also important to address a word used in this book that often accompanies the word 'material': innovative. Juxtaposing words such as 'material' with 'innovative' creates imprecise expressions that are particularly overused in current discourses. By using the term 'innovative materials' one often excludes references to scientific or laboratory discoveries, as well as neglecting to refer to specific technological innovations. Most of the time, the selected materials are already part of the production process and, using known raw materials in different ways, they provoke a certain degree of innovation.

Within this loose definition, a material can be considered innovative for the following reasons:

- · It is non-polluting during the production process
- · It has been realised with low cost-effect technology
- · It is fully tolerable, recyclable and biodegradable
- · It is easy to stock
- · It is lightweight while maintaining high mechanical strength
- · It adds together properties of several materials
  (composite and nanocomposite materials)
- · It is obtained through technological transfer coming
  out of application from a different field

Thus, continuing to speak about material in this section can be seen as a suggestive simplification.

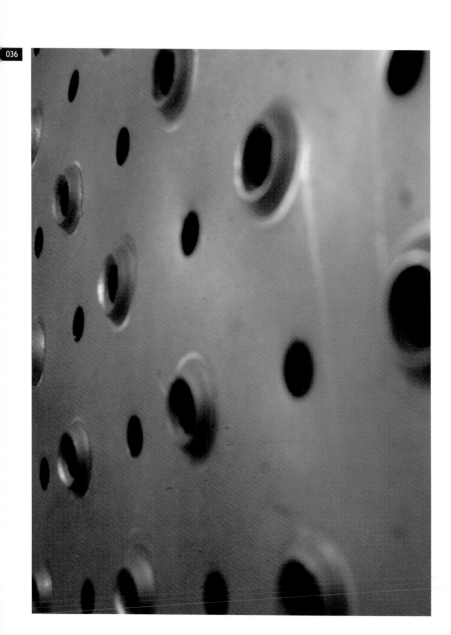

One of the scientific problems of taking materials as a research subject is the issue of material knowledge: this outlines the necessity of looking at it in terms of information and communication.

The previously mentioned increase in the availability of material has given rise to an increase in information. But this rapid redevelopment of its accessibility has caused an imbalance between material innovation and new knowledge within the cultural discourse.

As in other disciplines, the problem is not simply a lack of information. Rather the problem stems from an excess of information that is neither homogeneous nor properly addressed. This excess has created a language barrier between designers who deal with selected material culture and producers who generally have highly technical, specialised knowledge.

In order to address these needs, research and service centres that deal with innovative materials have become involved in the process. Private companies with commercial objectives first appeared in the mid-1990s and are now more widespread. Today, they act as mediators between designers, architects and manufacturers by collecting, organising, and systematising information.

From an architectural point of view, there is a growing trend for established manufacturers, who want their brand to be seen as a leader in research and material use, to finance experimental architects in testing out new materials and applications in design projects. Firms such as Herzog and de Meuron, Toyo Ito, Shigeru Ban, Kengo Kuma, and the Office for Metropolitan Architecture (OMA) are examples of this different cultural attitude towards the material domain.

However, this phenomenon has also engendered an elitist attitude toward material experiments, since these materials are not easily accessible to designers who operate with ordinary budgets. As a result, architects, who represent a field often considered inert in regards to technological innovation, are increasingly distanced from information.

One of the most difficult elements of design practice is, without doubt, acquiring and maintaining control of the project, the material and the technology. In other words, the challenge is to manage the project as well as to foresee any probable designed effects.

Since the field of architecture is slow to experiment, for reasons usually regarding either the scale of a project or economic concerns, it is important for architects to have access to information and instruments that can predict material behaviour and performances through the use of model simulations.

It is therefore necessary for materials to be tested, analysed and understood in order to establish their optimal use or predict their effects when production is completed. Obviously this process is even more complicated when dealing with materials that have not yet been frequently used.

It is necessary to note that there are many obstacles concerning the use of innovative materials in particular the lag between the invention of a material and the point when it is introduced to the market as a product. This lag period is usually dedicated to the testing phase.

This book will attempt to address and to reduce the technical and cultural distance between materials, producers, designers and consumers.

Working within the sphere of knowledge of innovative materials, the scope of the research herein maps out a new information system for architects and designers. It is proposed as an open system in which the point of entry for establishing a classification system is the performance of the materials.

Unlike technical material properties, performance behaviours have immediacy in showing the material's use in relation to its relevant properties. This is significant if we consider that the readers of this book will for the most part be designers and architects who necessarily have a pragmatic approach to materials for real-world applications and requirements.

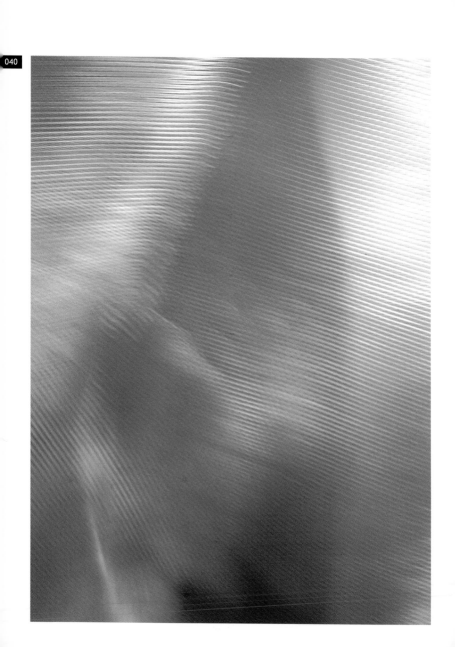

Within the research parameters established by the students, research which this book analyses in order to show its results, the 'material' is to be understood as 'everything that can be subjected to the technological process' and the concept of 'innovation' refers either to an application at variance with the one for which the material was initially tested and conceived, or to a precise material interpretation developed within each research project.

Thus, the main scope of the research project is based on 'technological transfer', which was considered one of the main operative tools for research developed by the students during the year.

This research approach elevates the practice of working in parallel with industries, manufacturers and field experts. It aims to shift the experimentation of the design and technological fields to real-world applications in order to validate this approach and to test the hypothesis of the design concept.

Several materials were selected for the research according to the criteria already described. The selected materials were divided into five categories: Shape Performance, Optical Performance, Sustainable Performance, Integrated Performance and Responsive Performance.

Materials are described in a chart illustrating the key properties of the materials and technical data. This includes different points of entry taken into consideration within specific case studies (case study applications) explored by the students, which are explained in the second section of the book.

A direct link is thereby set up between a theoretical research approach and the contextualisation of the materials that were explored in-depth within the applications for the case study: the high-rise building in Madrid. This classification, which is not exhaustive, shows how a methodological approach starts with a consideration of the performance aspects of material, aspects that move beyond the terms of a techno-functionalism. This approach is considered consistent with cultural aspects of the material domain in our era.

In this way, the relevant performance of each material is outlined and identified with a different colour. In association with this, and because it is impossible to unequivocally define material behaviour, it is important to acknowledge the possibility that materials may belong to other categories.

This not only demonstrates the non-linear and multi-directional means of classifying material that clarifies its original purpose, but transmits the potential for its use as a tool.

In addition, this limits the subjectivity of the reader and limits possible misinterpretation, and allows for more accurate feedback and evaluation. Following this methodology, the points of entry for the book come from two concurrent directions: the first considers the material performance within its more technical aspects, and the second refers to experimentation directly within the design projects.

Both mediate their definition through the concept of 'possibility', showing evidence of crossed research paths from materials to design and vice-versa. The research methodology is conceived as a process in which material interpretation is left open to further subjective outcomes.

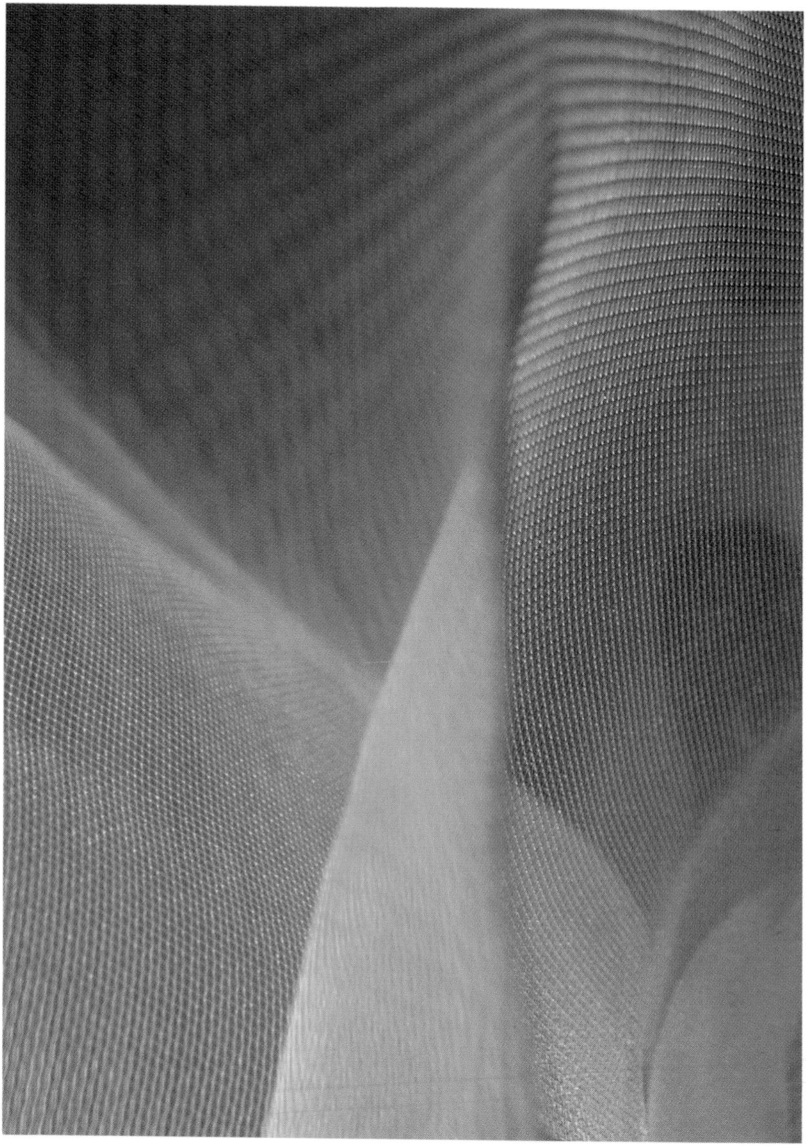

SHAPE
PERFORMANCE

SHAPE PERFORMANCE

Materials that are able to assume mechanical resistance due to a specific three-dimensional conformation.

Performance, and thus the use of these materials, is derived from their specific ability to develop in complex three-dimensional shapes.

Materials belonging to this category are very useful in terms of mechanical efficiency, for although they are reduced in volume, they also exhibit a higher mechanical resistance.

Materials that have honeycomb structures, a technology that was first applied in the aeronautics industry, belong to this order. When compared with their advanced mechanical resistance properties, these materials demonstrate considerable low weight levels. Their techno/aesthetic/functional characteristics give these materials substantial potential for many applications in the architectural field. The materials range from transparent to opaque, have shape resistance characteristics, and have insulation properties, achieved through specific three-dimensional moulding, which reduces the transmission of solar energy by creating mutual internal reflections within cells.

In addition, by combining the internal honeycomb structure with different coating materials on the exterior, they can have vertical/horizontal, planar/curved, indoor/outdoor applications, depending on the specific requirements. Metal meshes also produce transparent effects, and are adaptable to different forms and ruled surfaces while maintaining high mechanical resistance to tensile strength and weathering.

One well-known application of this method in design was by Dominique Perrault who, in several projects such as the French Library, used metal meshes for the faced system. These materials are produced by the GKD Metal Fabrics and, here again, we are at the cutting edge of a technological transfer: the material was initially used for constructing conveyer belts.

It is relevant to note that there were enormous economic benefits for this transference: due to open and experimental entrepreneurship, the company now occupies new market areas, thus enormously expanding their business.

SHAPE PERFORMANCE
PERFORMANCE/MATERIAL IDENTIFICATION

SHAPE PERFORMANCE	OPTICAL PERFORMANCE	SUSTAINABLE PERFORMANCE	INTEGRATED PERFORMANCE	RESPONSIVE PERFORMANCE
PARABEAM	PARABEAM			
FORMETAL	FORMETAL			
X-TEND	X-TEND	X-TEND		
SUPERFOAM ALUMINIUM		SUPERFOAM ALUMINIUM		
PRESSLOAD	PRESSLOAD			
WOVEN WIRE MESH		WOVEN WIRE MESH		
WEB PLATES		WEB PLATES		
STRUCTURAL PLATE		STRUCTURAL PLATE		
FLEXIBLE HONEYCOMB	FLEXIBLE HONEYCOMB	FLEXIBLE HONEYCOMB		
3D-TEX	3D-TEX		3D-TEX	
TORHEX HONEYCOMB		TORHEX HONEYCOMB		

· On the left page, the table shows a column with the list of materials that belong to the "shape performance" category in pink. In addition to this identification, and because it is impossible to unequivocally define material behaviour, the table shows the possibility that materials may belong to other categories: the material name is repeated under other categories.

· On the right page, the table shows a column that indicates the profile of each material and a column that shows the student who used each material, and the name of their case study.

MATERIAL PROFILE	PROCESS TECHNIQUE	CASE STUDY APPLICATIONS
GLASS		Eriko Watanabe/Tree Twister
		Soung Soo Shin/ Sustainable Interconnectivity
METAL AND ALLOYS		
POLYMERS		
COMPOSITES		Kiwoong Ko and Alexandros Vazakas/ Demand versus Geometry

PARABEAM
3-D GLASS FABRICS

Parabeam 3-D Glass Fabrics are woven with E-glass yarn and consist of two decklayers bonded together by vertical piles, which are woven into the deck layers to form an integral sandwich structure. The Parabeam is then impregnated with a thermoset resin, which is absorbed by the fabric and rises to its preset height due to the capillary forces of the piles. In this one-step process, a lightweight and strong sandwich laminate with excellent mechanical properties is formed. Parabeam offers several advantages in the building and construction industry; it is light, versatile and carries no risk of delamination, whilst offering the fast production of ready made panels with faces on both sides, and the possibility of fire-retardant panels (phenol or polyester based).

Parabeam has been used widely in the composites industry, with multiple advantages over traditional sandwich and solid laminates.

Manufacturer
  Parabeam bv
  PO Box 134
  5700 AC Helmond
  The Netherlands
  sales@parabeam.nl
  www.parabeam.nl
  t: +31 492591222
  f: +31 492591220
Introduction year
  · not available
Properties
  · excellent strength/
    weight ratio
  · integral sandwich
    structure with piles
    bonded in deck layers
  · no risk of delamination,
    corrosion or rotting
  · low resin-absorption
    resulting in lightweight
    and reduced
    styrene emission
  · translucent
Eco-efficient
  · made entirely of E-glass
  · lightweight
  · cost-effective processing
Current applications
  · building and construction
  · marine
  · transport
Case study applications
  · Eriko Watanabe,
    Tree Twister

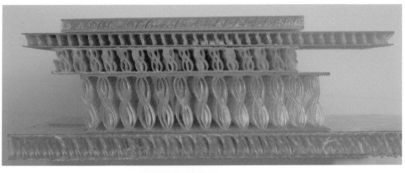

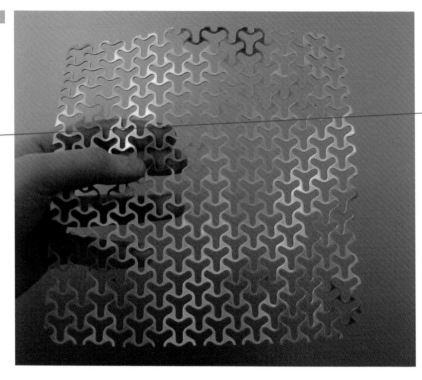

MATERIAL & TECHNOLOGY RESEARCH SHAPE PERFORMANCE

Manufacturer
Design For Metal
Damaschkestrasse 4
D-10711 Berlin
Germany
office@formetal.de
www.formetal.de
t: +49 3032705680
f: +49 3032705550

Introduction year
· **1999**

Properties
· **easily produced**
· **easily shaped**
  and customised

Eco-efficient
· **lightweight**
· **recyclable**

Current applications
· **interior design**
· **architecture**
· **clothing**
· **props and set building**
· **medical care**

Formetal is a flat metal sheet punched with a tri-lobal pattern, processed like wire grating, that was developed for copying three-dimensional forms. It can be shaped by hand, and enables the production, copy, repair and original design of very small and complicated forms. Once shaped it can be coated with fibreglass, gypsum, plaster or reshaped into its original form and reused. It is available in aluminium, copper, stainless and galvanised steel, in various thicknesses and custom sizes.

Formetal is used in costume, exhibition and interior design, and can potentially be used by artists, architects, restorers and orthopaedics.

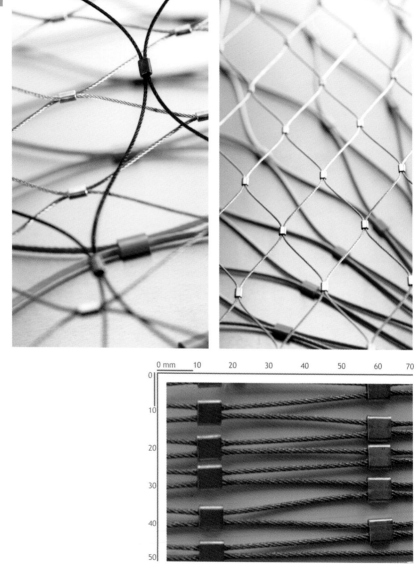

STAINLESS STEEL CABLE NET

Manufacturer

Carl Stahl GmbH

Postweg 41

D-73079 Süssen

Germany

derk.vos@carlstahl.com

www.carlstahl.com

t: +49 71624007184

f: +49 71624007968

Introduction year

· 1993

Properties

· flexible

· transparent

· stable

· long durability

· high corrosion resistant

· high load capacity

· weather resistant

· wide range of variations

Eco-efficient

· lightweight

· cost-effective processing

· no special maintenance
  after assembly

· long durability

Current applications

· indoor/outdoor

· design

· architecture

· bridges

· balustrade, facade, security,
  landing pad, design, enclosure

Case study applications

· Soung Soo Shin,
  Sustainable Interconnectivity

X-Tend is made of stainless steel cables that are linked together using corrosion-proof pressed ferrules to form a tensionable but flexible mesh structure.

Cable net constructions are light and transparent, they have a low inherent weight in relation to their load capacity and span. They are low-mass construction with minimum material costs, which offer cost effective building solutions.

The net can be manufactured endlessly: a length of over 20 metres made up of individual rolls can be joined in the transverse direction, without influencing strength.

X-Tend has been used for indoor and outdoor applications such as animals enclosures, balustrades, railings, seating helicopter landing pads, and interior design.

SUPERFORM ALUMINIUM

Superform aluminium is obtained through a hot-forming process in which a sheet of super plastic grade aluminium alloy is heated to 450–500 degrees centigrade and forced, using high air pressure, over or into a single surface tool.

The 'Superforming' process was initially developed to take advantage of 'superplasticity', a property of certain aluminium alloys that allows them to be stretched without breaking when they are heated to about five hundred degrees centigrade. The ability to stretch allows the alloys to be formed into complex three-dimensional shapes. Obviously, the degree of elongation that can be achieved dictates the complexity of the form for each alloy; where one alloy may be formed easily another may not be possible.

This process replaces welding or cold forming, and increases repeatability and strength whilst reducing weight. Superform aluminium has been used extensively in rail manufacture, on the Stockholm metro and Heathrow Express, in public architecture, notably at Waterloo station, Dorset House in Hong Kong and Tyne Bridge. It has also been used in electronics, aerospace and automotive manufacture, as well as by designers such as Ron Arad.

Manufacturer
  Superform Aluminium
  Cosgrove Close, Blackpole
  Worcester
  WR3 8UA
  UK
  sales@superform-aluminium.com
  www.superform-aluminium.com
  t: +44 905874300
  f: +44 905874301
Introduction year
  · 1974
Properties
  · high mechanical resistance
  · ability to stretch to many
  · times its original length
Eco-efficient
  · lightweight
  · recyclable
Current applications
  · aerospace, automotive
    and marine industries
  · civil and military
    industries
  · trains
  · cladding
  · electronics

MATERIAL & TECHNOLOGY RESEARCH SHAPE PERFORMANCE

Manufacturer
  Cellbond Composites Ltd
  5 Stukeley Business Centre
  Blackstone Road
  Huntingdon
  Cambridgeshire
  PE29 6EF
  UK
  sales@cellbond.com
  www.cellbond.net
  t: +44 1480435302
  f: +44 1480450181
Introduction year
  · not available
Properties
  · high torsion stress resistance
  · high bending ability
Eco-efficient
  · entirely recyclable
  · lightweight
  · excellent at absorbing energy
Current applications
  · interior design
  · architecture and construction
  · automotive, marine, rail
    and aerospace industries

PressLoad is a highly efficient and lightweight energy absorbing panel, which is produced by thermofolding and cold pressing aluminium alloys, thermoplastics (PP, PC, ABS/PC, etc.) thermoset plastics and other materials.

PressLoad is proposed as a cost-effective alternative to traditional aluminium honeycomb as a core material in composite panels or as an energy absorber. It is entirely recyclable, and it can be superior to aluminium honeycomb in bending and torsion between two skins. These sheets use a specially designed geometry to generate maximum absorption properties, and can be custom produced in any size up to 1.5 x 3 metre.

PressLoad can be applied in the automotive (occupant and pedestrian protection) and marine industries, in architecture and construction (cladding panels, structure, screen and space dividers, raised floors and partitions), rail, design and aerospace.

WOVEN WIRE MESH
METALLIC MESH

Due to its stability, unlimited service life, flexibility and the multiplicity of materials from which it can be made, woven wire mesh is used widely within architecture and construction. Stainless steel mesh can be fully recycled, and has a thin passive layer making it resistant to discolouration, weathering and corrosion. When in contact with light, the interplay between reflection and simultaneous translucency produces several aesthetic effects.

The capacity to fit stainless steel mesh to almost any constructional or tailor-made form, and the versatility of installation techniques that can be used with it, makes woven wire mesh exceptionally flexible and convenient.

Stainless steel mesh can be woven in widths of up to eight metres and up to almost any length.

Manufacturer
  GKD
  Gebr.Kufferath AG
  Metallweberstrabe 46
  D-52348 Duren
  Germany
  gb3@gkd.de
  www.gkd.de
  t: +49 242218030
  f: +49 2421803227
Introduction year
  · not available
Properties
  · long-lasting and fireproof
  · resistant to corrosion
    and weathering
  · flexible
  · can be produced in
    limitless dimensions
Eco-efficient
  · fully recyclable
Current applications
  · facade, ceiling, wall
    partitions, balustrade,
    balcony, shutters, screens,
  · used in the Bibliothèque
    National de France, Paris

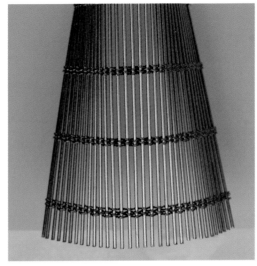

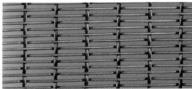

WEB PLATES
ALUMINIUM PLATE

Web plates are shaped two and three-dimensionally from aluminium, and can be easily and economically produced. When they are made, they can be stretched and extended horizontally and vertically, due to their close fold structure, to cover larger areas in interior design. Installation of web plates is made easier by their compatibility with flat materials and their flexibility in adhesion: they can be nailed, clipped and glued, and can be quickly installed in large areas.

The plate has been widely used in architecture and interior design, probably because of its capacity for carrying heavy loads, its flexibility, and its suitability for several different applications.

In 2004, Fielitz GmbH, the manufacturers of Web plates, opened a showroom in the vaults of the old fortification at Ingolstadt , to showcase the full range of their products and their potential applications. Web plates have been used to make ceilings, counter-panels, partition walls and lamps, amongst other things.

Manufacturer
  Fielitz GmbH
  Brunnhausgasse 3
  D-85049 Ingolstadt
  Germany
  info@fielitz.de
  www.fielitz.de
  t: +49 841935140
  f: +49 8419351413
Introduction year
  · not available
Properties
  · can carry heavy loads
  · easily produced
  · flexible, can be
    spherically shaped
  · anodising
  · screen printing
  · water jet cutting
Eco-efficient
  · economic use
    of raw material
  · recyclable
  · lightweight
Current applications
  · interior and outdoor design
  · architecture
    and construction
  · desk lamps, wall lamps,
    panels,ceilings, partitions

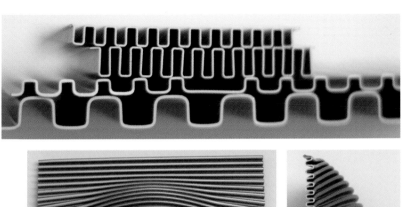

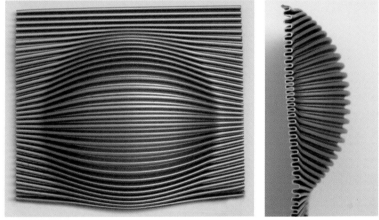

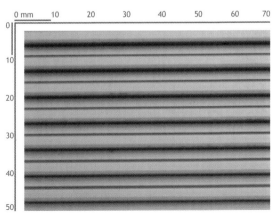

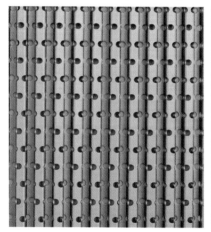

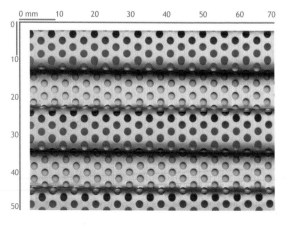

STAINLESS STEEL PLATE

Manufacturer

Fielitz GmbH

Brunnhausgasse 3

D-85049 Ingolstadt

Germany

info@fielitz.de

www.fielitz.de

t: +49 841935140

f: +49 8419351413

Introduction year

· not available

Properties

· **can carry heavy loads**

· **easily produced**

· **flexible can be spherically-shaped**

· **customisable**

Eco-efficient

· **economic use of raw material**

· **lightweight**

Current applications

· **indoor and outdoor design**

· **architecture and construction**

· **partition, automotive panelling, cladding**

Structural plates are lightweight construction plates made of three-dimensional stainless steel. In their initial state, they can be further modified by perforating, bending, welding, or combining them with wood, marble, glass and other materials to raise their resistance, and can be installed immediately.

The plates can be used to reinforce or structure large surface areas, and their geometry sets up a variety of possibilities for customisation. They are multi-functional, and applied in architecture and design to flat, unshaped element areas alternating with structural surfaces.

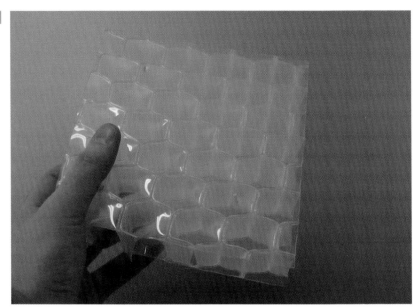

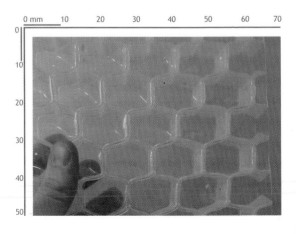

MATERIAL & TECHNOLOGY RESEARCH SHAPE PERFORMANCE

Manufacturer

Supracor Inc
2050 Corporate Court
San Jose, CA 95131-1753
USA
webmaster@supracor.com
www.supracor.com
t: +1 4084321616
f: +1 4084321975

Introduction year

· 1982

Properties

· indoor and outdoor use
· highly flexible
· excellent shock-absorption
· even distribution
  of weight
· anisotropic
· optimum strength
  to weight ratio
· lightweight

Eco-efficient

· lightweight

Current applications

· medical equipment
  and sports equipment
· equestrian
· automotive and
  aerospace industries
· cushions, mattresses,
  pads, skincare products,
  footwear, funrniture and
  bedding flooring

Supracor's flexible honeycomb is an engineered material produced from fusion-bonding technology. It is a matrix of elongated hexagons forming a complex pattern of alternating single- and double-walled cells. Each cell has eight interior and eight exterior radii.

Supracor Honeycomb is fabricated from an extensive range of thermoplastic elastomers (TPEs). These materials combine the best properties of rubber and plastics for superior durability and performance. They are noted for their exceptional tensile, tear and compressive strength, resistance to puncture, and their flexibility at low and high temperatures.

As a flexible and stable structure, Supracor honeycomb is setting high standards for shock-absorption in a wide variety of applications—from impact-absorbing components in athletic shoes to bumpers on amusement park rides.

TORHEX AND THERMEX HONEYCOMB

The folded honeycombs join the internal structure and properties of expanded honeycomb with the same efficient production principle and technology as corrugated cardboard.

Aluminium foils, Kraftliner paper and thermoplastic materials are used for the cores.

Their production concept is derived from corrugated cardboard production. Production from a single continuous sheet allows for a continuous process, resulting in high speed and low-cost production of this new sandwich core material.

The inner structure of folded honeycombs is similar to conventional expanded honeycombs, thus yielding excellent shear and flat-wise compression properties. Nevertheless, their production concept and their core-skin bonding concept are derived from the very efficient mass-sandwich production technology of corrugated cardboard.

The bonding of the skins can be fast and inexpensive due to a larger contact area with the skins, resulting in a more reliable bond, improved peel strength and enhanced after-impact performance.

Manufacturer
  EconCore NV
  Kapeldreef 60
  B-3001 Leuven
  Belgium
  www.econcore.com
  info@econCore.com
Introduction year
  · not available
Properties
  · excellent strength/
    weight ratio
  · lightweight
  · cost-effective processing
Eco-efficient
  · lightweight
  · cost-effective processing
Current applications
  · architecture
    and construction:
    structural application
  · packaging industry
  · automotive industry
  · furniture
  · cladding
Case study applications
  · Kiwoong Ko and
    Alexandros Vazakas,
    Demand vs Geometry

production principle and technology
of corrugated cardboard

folded honeycomb (Foldhex)

internal structure and proporties of
expanded honeycomb

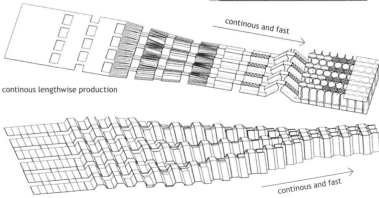

continous and fast

continous lengthwise production

continous and fast

alternative crosswise production

OPTICAL PERFORMANCE

OPTICAL PERFORMANCE

Materials that are able to perform in various conditions to produce optical effects: visual characteristics comply with material behaviours in order to disclose, to sign, to merge, to overlap and/or to add texture to the produced image.

Optical performance is introduced with the consideration of material perception under the sensory sphere.

Although optical properties have measurable parameters, defined by or relating to transparency, refraction, scattering or reflection, this chapter focuses primarily on perceptive material properties that are pertinent for the reader.

The approach here is subjective, commensurate with creative attitudes in dealing with the selected materials. In this category, we discuss complex effects achieved on the perceptive level through the optical performance of materials; as material transparency, texture and translucency set up a certain relationship between an environment and its users.

In many cases, these optical performances address the meaning of immateriality, which should be seen as material performance capable of modifying its subjective perception and its produced image.

The produced effects enable a dialogue between background and figure, wherein the concept activates a dynamic relationship with the matter and its ambiguity in self-representation.

Film has an important role in this field: it is made up of many layers of extremely thin membrane with multiple functions. Through this layering system, many different performances can be associated with a singular product. These performances range from solar control systems, security systems, mechanical resistance to optical properties, and viewer control systems.

OPTICAL PERFORMANCE
PERFORMANCE/MATERIAL IDENTIFICATION

SHAPE PERFORMANCE	OPTICAL PERFORMANCE	SUSTAINABLE PERFORMANCE	INTEGRATED PERFORMANCE	RESPONSIVE PERFORMANCE
SHIMMER	SHIMMER			
CRINKLE GLASS	CRINKLE GLASS			
	3D RADIANT COLOR FILM			
	PVC			
LEXAN	LEXAN			
STRALIGHT	STARLIGHT			
	REEMAY SPUNBONDED		REEMAY SPUNBONDED	
YST	YST			
	MICA LAMINATES			
PANELITE IGU	PANELITE IGU			
	LITRACON		LITRACON	

· On the left page, the table shows a column with the list of materials that belong to the "optical performance" category in blue. In addition to this identification, and because it is impossible to unequivocally define material behaviour, the table shows the possibility that materials may belong to other categories: the material name is repeated under other categories.
· On the right page, the diagram shows a column that indicates the profile of each material and a column that shows the student who used each material and the name of their case study.

MATERIAL PROFILE	PROCESS TECHNIQUE	CASE STUDY APPLICATIONS
CERAMIC		
GLASS		
POLYMERS		Maria Mandalaki/Housing Senses
		Lorena Franco/Accomodating Changes
FIBRES		Maria Mandalaki/Housing Senses
		Eriko Watanabe/Tree Twister
COMPOSITES		

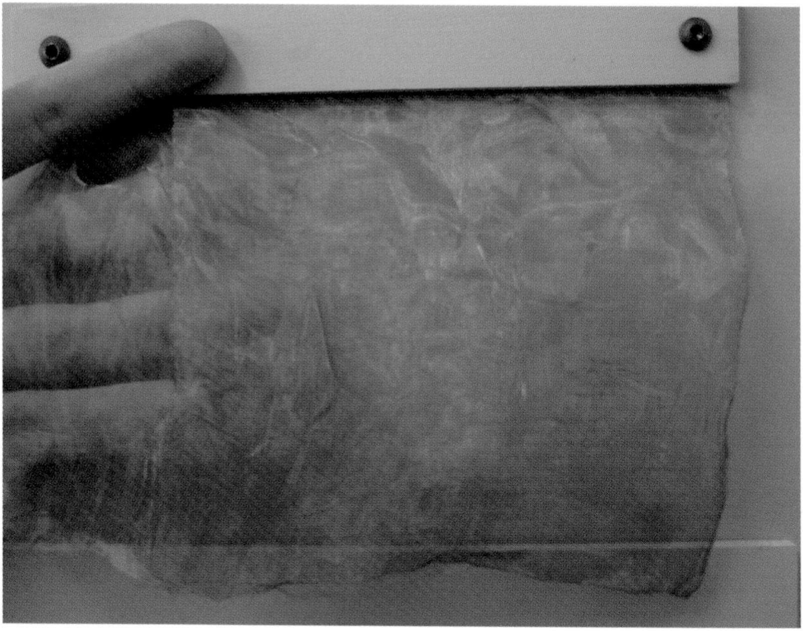

METALLIC FABRIC

Manufacturer
  GKD
  Gebr.Kufferath
  Artiengesellschaft
  Metallweberstrasse 46
  D-52353 Düren
  Germany
  info@gkd.de
  www.gkd.de
  t: +49 24218030
  f: +49 2421803211
Introduction year
  · 2002
Properties
  · breathable
  · transparent
  · UV resistant
  · scratch resistant
  · electro-conductive
  · abrasion resistant
Eco-efficient
  · recyclable
  · lightweight
Current applications
  · interior design
  · building and construction
  · home product design
  · clothing

Shimmer fabric is a finely woven metal mesh made from stainless steel and copper wire with uniform hole dimensions.

If produced with extremely thin metal wires, it exhibits high flexibility comparable to fabrics, and has a pleasant texture. It is abrasion resistant, can be transparent if very open-spaced, breathable and electrically conductive.

Two layers of mesh can be used together to produce Moire fringe effects. The fabric is available in rolls 30.5 metres long and 1.22 metres wide.

It is generally used for filters, dryers, reinforcement, protections, sieves, screens, and in pharmaceutical/chemical applications. It has also been used for interior applications such as architectural drapery and bed canopies. Recently, it has also been applied in new fields such as building, construction and sporting goods.

CRINKLE GLASS PANELS

Crinkle glass is made of a triple layer custom glass laminated composite. A panel of shattered glass is laminated between two outer sheets, which is then shattered again.

In this way, multifaceted glass fragments refract light to create a luminous effect.

The panels are available in custom colours and can utilise different glass types (patterned, textured, tinted), different thicknesses, and varying inter-layers; the glass can also be custom slivered.

The three-ply construct is offered in a choice of rectangles, squares, ovals, or custom shapes with flat polished, bull-nosed, and mitered edges. The pattern density can be customised from a more open to a compact texture. Current applications include, kitchen and bathroom sufaces, furniture and decorative door inserts.

Manufacturer
  Galaxy Glass & Stone
  277 Fairfield Road Fairfield,
  New Jersey 07004
  USA
  info@galaxycustom.com
  www.galaxycustom.com
  t: +1 9735753440
  f: +1 9735755235
Introduction year
  · 2002
Properties
  · transparent
  · can produce random
    visual effects
Eco-efficient
  · 100 per cent glass
Current applications
  · wall cladding
  · kitchen and bathroom
    sufaces
  · lighting
  · furniture

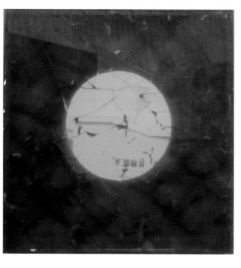

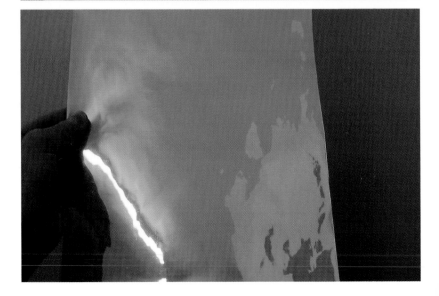

Manufacturer
  3M Corporate Headquarters
  3M Center Saint Paul
  Minnesota 55144-1000
  USA
  light_and_optics@mmm.com
  www.3m.com/about3m/
  technologies
  t: +44 18883643577
Introduction year
  · **2000**
Properties
  · **translucent**
  · **high reflective**
  · **flexible**
Eco-efficient
  · **lightweight**
Current applications
  · **indoor/outdoor**
  · **interior design**

3M Radiant Color Film is a high-performance film, non-metallic with iridescent colours that change with the viewing angle.

It consists of hundreds of layers of polymer or plastic that combine to produce different reflective qualities. The outer layers made of polyester, produce vivid colours in both reflection and transmission, which are so bright that objects made of these films appear to be lit from the inside. They are available in two versions that change colour according to the angle of observation: cyan/blue/magenta and blue/magenta/gold.

The film products can be embossed, die cut, sheer slit and cut into particles. The films can be coated either with adhesive or heat-sealant and can accommodate print.

PVC MEMBRANE

PVC membrane is polyester foil, coated on both sides with PVC. It is a translucent membrane for temporary, permanent and retractable structures, with an easy to clean surface, barely combustible, self-extinguishing, coming in various colours, and light transmission of up to 15 per cent.

Because it is weaker than other fabrics, with a life expectancy of only 15 to 20 years, it is only suitable for short spans, and therefore used most often for temporary, retractable and inflatable structures.

The material has been improved in recent years, to offer higher resistance to pollution and greater strength, and is being used more widely in temporary architecture.

Manufacturer
  Buitink Zeilmakerij Duiven
  Nieuwgraaf 210
  6921 RR Duiven
  The Netherlands
  info@buitink-technology.com
  www.buitink-technology.com
  t: +31 263194181
  f: +31 263194191
Introduction year
  · 1970
Properties
  · highly durable
  · highly malleable
    (offering almost infinite
    variation in shape and size)
  · 96 per cent transparent
  · flame retardant
  · can be supplied printed
    or white, to regulate light
    permeability
  · exceptionally resistant to dirt
Eco-efficient
  · lightweight
  · good insulation value,
    dependent upon
    the number of layers
  · permeable to UV light
Current applications
  · indoor/outdoor architecture
  · temporary installations
Case study applications
  · Maria Mandalaki,
    Housing Senses

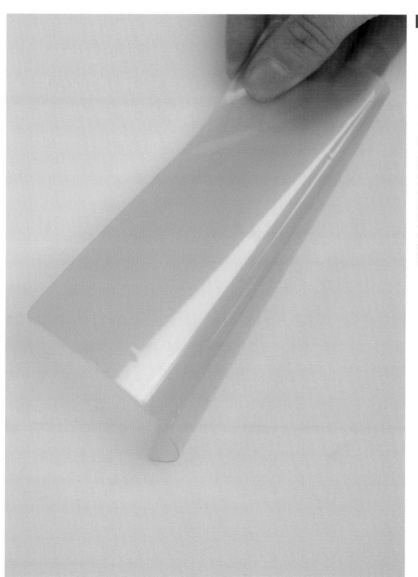

POLYCARBONATE RESIN

Manufacturer
  GE Global Headquarters
  One plastic Avenue
  Pittsfield
  Massachusetts 01201
  USA
  gelit@ge.com
  www.geplastics.com/resins/
  materials/lexan.html
  t: +44 4134487110
Introduction year
  · not available
Properties
  · inherent 'water-clear'
    transparency
  · resistant to high impacts
  · heat resistant-RTI up to 125
    degrees centigrade
  · dimensional stability
    at elevated temperatures
  · unlimited colours
  · produced to any degree
    of opacity
  · flame resistant
  · UV stable
Eco-efficient
  · very good processability
Current applications
  · indoor/outdoor
  · architecture
  · design
  · electronics equipment
  · objects
  · medicine
Case study applications
  · Lorena Franco,
    Accomodating Changes

LEXAN polycarbonate resin is an engineering thermoplastic characterised by its exceptional mechanical, optical, electrical and thermal properties. The resin is tailor-made for a range of conversion processes including injection-moulding, extrusion, blow-moulding and foam processing.

High-flow grades have been utilised in its manufacture, which make LEXAN ideally suited to thin wall, long flow-length applications. LEXAN resin can be reground and reused after its first application, and like other engineering thermoplastics it retains a high residual value. This means it can be recycled into similar applications within the same industry.

LEXAN resin is a naturally transparent, 'water clear' material, available in a many colours and opacities. It is capable of consistently reproducing mould surfaces with great accuracy, ensuring good quality high gloss or textured surface finishes for the designer. Its light transparency is similar to that of glass, with a refractive index of 1.586. For use in humid environments or those with intense sunlight, extruded LEXAN sheet can be additionally protected with clear UV cap layers, whilst injection-moulded parts can be protected with a range of GE Silicone hardcoats, to enhance their resistance to weathering and abrasion.

MATERIAL & TECHNOLOGY RESEARCH OPTICAL PERFORMANCE

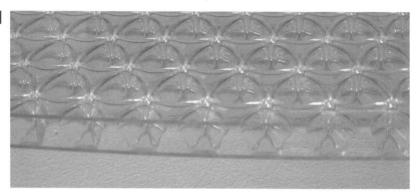

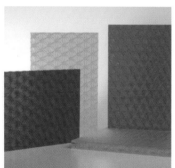

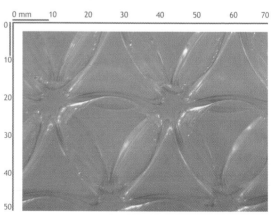

MATERIAL & TECHNOLOGY RESEARCH OPTICAL PERFORMANCE

Manufacturer
  Bencore srl
  Via S Colombano,
  9-54100 Massa ZI (MS)
  Italy
  info@bencore.it
  www.bencore.it
  t: +39 0585830129
  f: +39 0585835167
Introduction year
  · 2000
Properties
  · structural composite panel
  · translucent
  · available in a range
    of colours and finishes
  · easily workable
  · decorative
  · extra lightweight
Eco-efficient
  · lightweight
Current applications
  · indoor/outdoor design
  · sliding doors, light panels,
    partitions, table-tops,
  · reception desks, shelves,
    false ceilings,
  · raised flooring, display
    units, chairs
  · lighting systems
Case study applications
  · Eriko Watanabe,
    Tree Twister

The 'Birdwing' panel is called thus because of the similarity of its open macro-cone shaped cell structure to a bird's skeletal structure. Both benefit from an excellent, balanced strength/weight ratio. The panel, made from thermoplastics, can be filled with expanded foams or light concrete through its conic cell structure, and can be made from transparent or black polycarbonate, transparent PETG, coloured ABS, and white or grey polystyrene. It can be bent when heated, its curvature variable according to the thickness of the panel.

After surface treatment, the panel can be bonded, with any glue, to several different skins to create compound products.

The 'Birdwing' panel is soundproof, heat-insulated, non-vibrating, and unaffected by brine, mould and bacteria. Resilient, flame-resistant and water-resistant versions are also available. The wide bonding surface (nearly fifty per cent) makes the production of composite panels easier, and sandwiches can be made with plastic and metallic laminates, fibre-reinforced materials, stone and wood. The panel is particularly suitable for trade fairs, shop fittings, gyms, bars, restaurants, and set design, where resilience of materials is extremely important.

REEMAY SPUNBONDED POLYESTER
NONWOVEN SPUNBONDED TEXTILE

REEMAY is a non-woven fabric made of continuous polyester fibres arranged at random and thermally bonded at the filament junctions.

It is available in three product styles that use straight fibres with different filament densities and diverse thicknesses and unit weights. The crimped fibres have a soft, comfortable touch while the straight fibres have a firmer and crisper texture. Its on-site converting technology helps it to adapt to specifications and demands, lending itself to three-colour wide width printing, embossing, calendaring, point-boarding and laminating.

REEMAY has many uses in filtration systems, as interlining for clothes, furniture and bedding, as a fabric softener dryer sheets, seedbed and agricultural crop cover amongst others.

Manufacturer
   BBA Nonwovens,
   Flitration Business Unit
   70 Old Hickory Road
   Old Hickory
   Tenessee 37138-3651
   USA
   www.reemay.com
   t: +1 6158477000
   f: +1 6158477068
Introduction year
   · not yet available
Properties
   · highly tear resistant
   · highly flexible
   · moisture, rot and mildew
     resistant
   · sunlight resistant
   · excellent chemical
     resistance
   · abrasion resistant
   · difficult to ignite (ignition
     temperature 560 degrees
     centigrade)
Current applications
   · interior design
   · filteration systems
   · industrial and
     construction industries
   · furniture
   · agriculture
   · automotive industry
   · flooring
   · clothing
Case study applications
   · Maria Mandalaki,
     Housing Senses

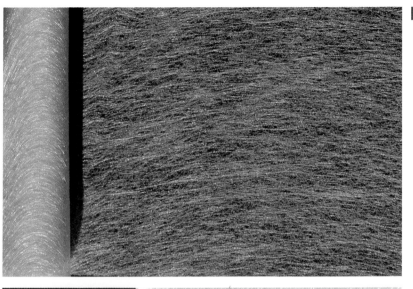

YST

MOULDABLE HONEYCOMB SHEET

YST honeycomb sheet is made from two deck layers of polyester with a honeycomb core of either aluminium or cardboard. The combination is exceptionally strong yet lightweight, and the honeycomb cells can be seen as flenses of an I-BEAM.

The YST panels can be fully integrated with typical floor and ceiling systems, and machined with standard tools. Metal angle profiles can mount the panels to the floor and ceiling slabs fasten them on either side.

YST panels can be used as stand-alone partition walls, by attaching them together and to walls with C-channel or angle profiles. For the vertical joint between two panels, C-channels or extruded H-channels can be used.

YST is used both commercially and domestically, in furniture, and for exhibition, retail and trade show displays.

Manufacturer
> Heideveld polyester vof
> Europaweg 24
> 8181 BH Heerde
> The Netherlands
> info@heideveld-polyester.nl
> www.heideveld-polyester.nl
> t: +31 578692058
> f: +31 578694651

Introduction year
· not available

Properties
· strong
· mouldable
· produces optical effects
· lightweight
· handmade

Eco-efficient
· lightweight
· handmade

Current applications
· interior design
· architecture
· furniture

Case study applications
· Eriko Watanabe,
  Tree Twister

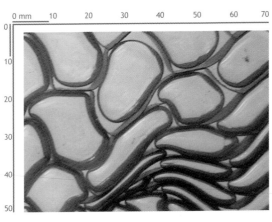

MICA LAMINATES

Mica is an alumosilicate mineral with a sheet or plate-like structure.

Mined mica is bonded through heat and pressure with a shellac resin into sheets that are workable even with standard carpentry tools.

Mica sheets can be used as translucent infill panels or mounted to a solid substrate like plywood for iridescent, opaque wall surfaces.

Mica can also be cold-curved or thermoformed on site.

The sheets are available in amber or silver, in thicknesses of 0.508, 0.762 and 1.524 millimetres, and panel dimensions of 914.4 × 914.4 millimetres. The mica sheets have proved to be popular with hotels, bars, offices and in domestic architecture.

Manufacturer
  Panelite llc
  315 West 39th Street,
  Studio 807
  New York
  New York 10018
  USA
  sales@panelite.us
  www.e-panelite.com
  t: +1 2129478292
  f: +1 2129478489
Introduction year
  · 2001
Properties
  · cold-curved on site
  · thermoformed on site
  · translucent
Current applications
  · interior design
  · architecture
  · furniture

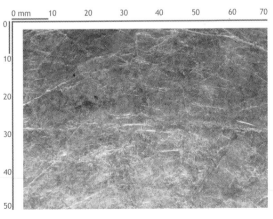

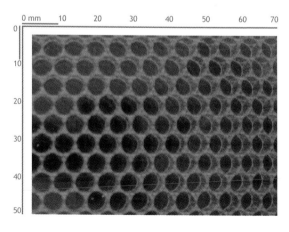

TUBULAR POLYCARBONATE HONEYCOMB CORE GLASS SANDWICH

Manufacturer
  Panelite
  315 West 39th Street,
  Studio 807
  New York
  New York 10018
  USA
  sales@panelite.us
  www.e-panelite.com
  t: +1 2129478292
  f: +1 2129478489
Introduction year
  · 2002
Properties
  · long durability
  · non-combustible rated
  · fire resistant
  · UV resistant
  · translucent when viewed
    from the front
  · adaptable
  · lightweight
Eco-efficient
  · lightweight
Current applications
  · interior design
  · architecture
    and construction

Panelite combines the transparency, durability and weather-resistance of glass with the adaptability of tubular polycarbonate honeycomb core for use in glazing and curtain walls. Its honeycomb core has tubular cells, which diffuse both light and sight lines.

Depending upon the angle and distance at which the panel is viewed, the Panelite IGU ranges from opaque to nearly transparent, which provides varying degrees of privacy whilst always being luminous. The panels can be used for sliding, pivoting and partition walls, ceilings and furniture, and can be cut, drilled and machined using standard wood-working methods and tools. Panelite IGU is compatible with all commercial store-front, glazing and curtain wall systems designed to accept insulating glass units. It can also be used to great advantage where fire-resistance and durability are priorities.

MATERIAL & TECHNOLOGY RESEARCH OPTICAL PERFORMANCE

LITRACON
LIGHT TRANSMITTING CONCRETE

LiTraCon is a combination of optical fibres and fine concrete. Thousands of fibres rub side by side transmitting light between the two main surfaces in each block. Because of their small size, the fibres blend into the concrete, becoming a component of the material like small pieces of ballast. As a result, the two materials are not just mixed—glass in concrete—but a third, new material is produced which is homogenous in its inner structure and on its main surfaces as well.

LiTraCon finds applications mainly in architecture and interior design. LiTraCon blocks are used like bricks or passable paving illuminated from beneath. A wall structure created out of LiTraCon blocks can be a couple of metres thick, as the fibres work almost without any loss in light up to 20 metres. Moreover, the blocks are load-bearing and provide the same effect with both natural and artificial light. Glass fibres lead light by points between the wall surfaces. Shadows on the lighter side will appear with sharp outlines on the darker one.

Manufacturer
LiTraCon GmbH
Tanya 832
6640 Csongrád
Hungary
info@litracon.hu
www.litracon.hu
f: +36 302551648

Introduction year
· **2005**

Properties
· **load bearing**
· **transmits natural and artificial light**
· **translucent**
· **can be used indoor/outdoor**

Eco-efficient
· **indoor/outdoor**
· **architecture**
· **interior design**

Current applications
· **illuminating subway stations, basements, pavements,**
· **trafficguide lights**
· **building blocks**
· **lighting**

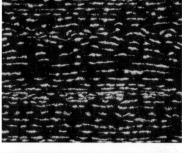

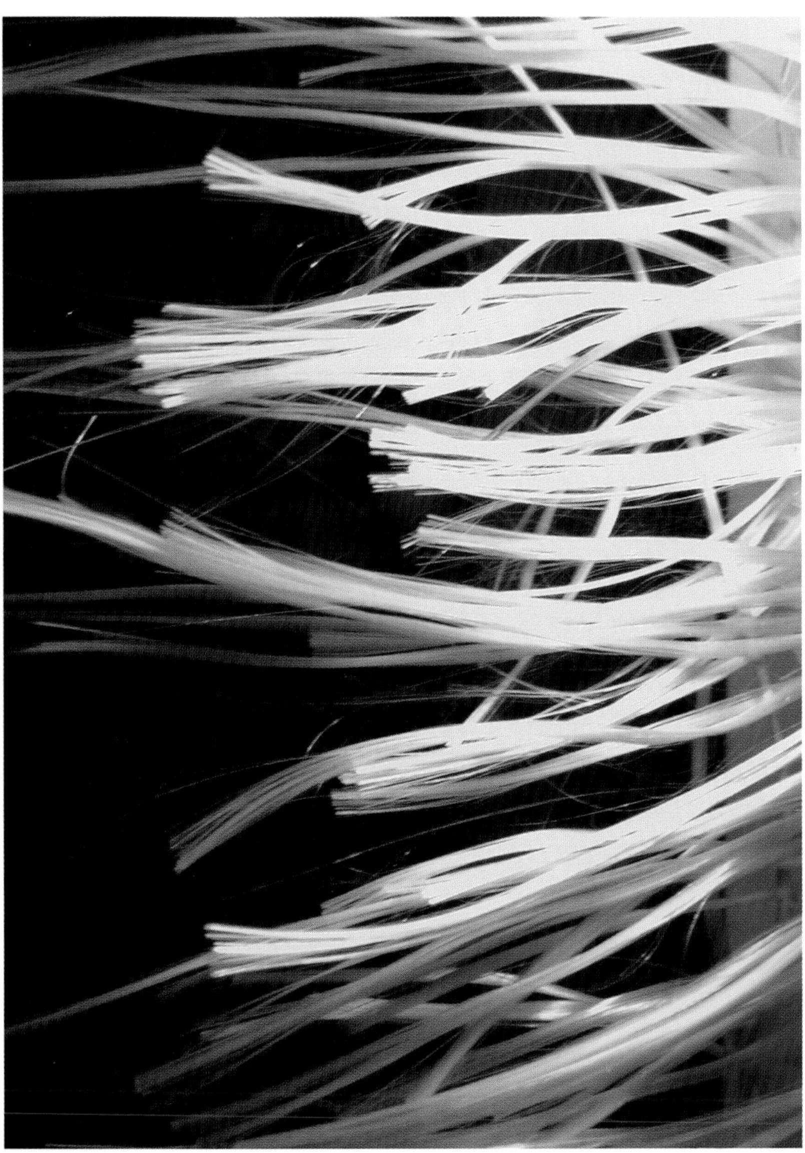

SUSTAINABLE PERFORMANCE

SUSTAINABLE PERFORMANCE

Materials that, firstly, provide products with one or more life cycle, and secondly, are advantageous in terms of production, workability, dissemblance, reuse, sustainability and environmental preservation.

The materials that belong in this category have claim to sustainability in any of the following characteristics:

- · they are produced mainly from raw materials that are easily renewable
- · their production has low environmental impact (pollution)
- · they are biodegradable
- · they have a 'closed life-cycle' (completely recyclable)
- · they are found locally to ensure low energy consumption
  for transportation to their place of production
- · they are lightweight and have high mechanical strength, saving energy
  by reducing their consumption, manufacturing and distribution costs

Particular attention was focused on two aspects. Firstly, the possibility, previously mentioned, of 'designing' a material that would meet specific performance targets. These would be targets that respond to the requirements of managing the environmental impact of the material during its entire life cycle and the possibility of recycling it. The 'dissolution phase' of the material is therefore planned for from the beginning, taking into account the possibility of recovery of energy or 'feedstock', and of mechanical recycling.

The second aspect is a consideration of the material's weight; one of the most relevant factors in the 'sustainability' criterion. Lightweight material is one of the most useful design strategies for eco-sustainability. For this reason, the demand for eco-efficient buildings increases the amount of research and experimentation into new lightweight, therefore and eco-sustainable materials.

Metal foam shows great technological potential for use due to its lightness, strength resistance and simultanous sound absorbency and heat insulation.

These materials are characterised by a porous core structure with different densities, ordered or irregular, with open or closed cells. The same structural composition can be realised with plastic-and ceramic-based materials, but the advantages of metal foam over plastic foam are its higher resistance properties and its longer working life.

SUSTAINABLE PERFORMANCE
PERFORMANCE/MATERIAL IDENTIFICATION

SHAPE PERFORMANCE	OPTICAL PERFORMANCE	SUSTAINABLE PERFORMANCE	INTEGRATED PERFORMANCE	RESPONSIVE PERFORMANCE
TENNAGE		TENNAGE		
3D-VENEER		3D-VENEER		
		FOAMGLASS		
	AEROGEL	AEROGEL		
POROUS CERAMICS		POROUS CERAMICS		
ALUSION AL.FOAM		ALUSION AL.FOAM		
	INSOLCORE	INSOLCORE		
	KAPILUX	KAPILUX	KAPILUX	
	ETFE MEMBRANE	ETFE MEMBRANE		
	3M OPTICAL LIGHT	3M OPTICAL LIGHT	3M OPTICAL LIGHT	
		CFAMC		

· On the left page, the table shows a column with the list of materials that belong to the 'sustainable performance' category in green. In addition to this identification, and because it is impossible to unequivocally define material behaviour, the table shows the possibility that materials may belong to other categories: the material name is repeated under other categories.
· On the right page, the table shows a column that indicates the profile of each material and a column that shows the student who used each material and the name of their case study.

MATERIAL PROFILE	PROCESS TECHNIQUE	CASE STUDY APPLICATIONS
NATURAL MATERIALS		
GLASS		
CERAMICS		
METAL AND ALLOYS		
POLYMERS		Maria Mandalaki/Housing Senses
COMPOSITES		Soung Soo Shin/ Sustainable Interconnectivity

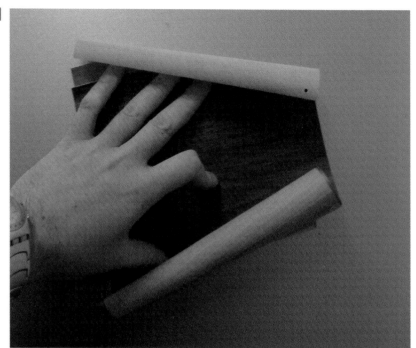

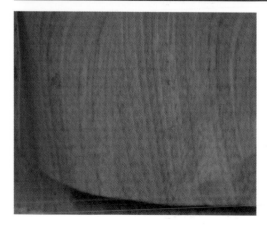

FLEXIBLE WOOD SHEETS

Manufacturer
Onlyone Products Inc
16428 Vista Roma Circle
Huntington Beach,
California 92649
USA
only1@onlyone-pro.com
www.onlyone-pro.com
t: +1 7148401014
f: +1 7148408462
Introduction year
· 2001
Properties
· customisable
· water resistant
· UV resistant
· flexible
Eco-efficient
· entirely recyclable
· lightweight
Current applications
· interior design
· home accessories
· home furnishings
· fashion accessories
· stationary
· automobile industry

Tennage is a flexible, thinly sliced wood sheet impregnated with biocompatible natural resin, making the wood flexible. It is processed with 100 per cent recycled lumber, and the sheets can be backed with paper, leather and natural fabrics for enhanced durability. They are water and UV resistant, and available in 26 different woods and textures.

The sheets can be sewn, laser-cut, or thinly sliced into yarn. Tennage can be used in the architectural field as an interior surface and for home accessories and other products.

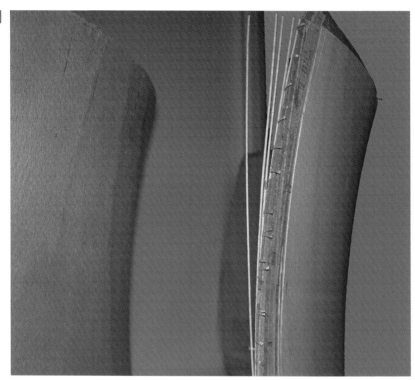

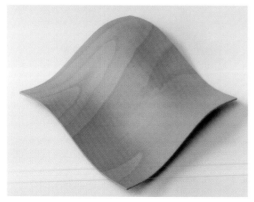

Manufacturer
  REHOLZ GmbH
  Sachsenallee 11
  D-01723 Kesselsdorf
  Germany
  www.reholz.de
  t: +49 35 204780430
  f: +49 35 204780450
Introduction year
  · 2002
Properties
  · three-dimensional
    moulding shape
  · lightweight
Eco-efficient
  · lightweight
Current applications
  · interior design
  · architecture
  · coating of three-dimensional
    surfaces and edges
  · homeware

3-D Veneer by Reholz is a three-dimensionally formable veneer for the industrial production of three-dimensional plywood mouldings.

Conventional wood veneers are treated in such a way that they can be 'deep drawn'. Texture of the wood is completely preserved. The three-dimensional shells can also be laminated, making use of well-known advantages of lightweight construction and three-dimensional sandwich structures. In consequence, material and weight reductions of up to 60 per cent, in comparison with mouldings of plastic or metal of the same strength, can be achieved.

Apart from the manufacture of moulded parts, it can be also used to coat three-dimensional components in a wide range of materials.

The 3-D veneer is available in a maximum width of one metre and a maximum length of two metres in various kinds of wood (beech, oak, walnut, cherry, maple). The standard thickness of the veneer is 1.2 millimetres.

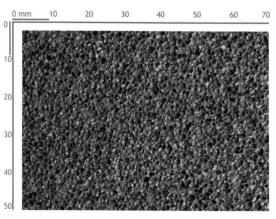

Manufacturer

Pittsburgh Corning Europe SA
Lasne Business Park-Building F
Chausée de Louvain, 431
B-1380 Lasne
Belgium
headquarters@foamglas.com
www.foamglas.be
t: +32 23510230
f: +32 23531063

Introduction year
· not available

Properties
· temperature limits: from
  260 centigrade to over
  +485 centigrade
· does not absorb water
· not hygroscopic
· not permeable
· not capillary
· impervious to common
  acids and their fumes
· non-combustible,
  emits no toxic fumes
· impervious to water
  and water vapour
· high compressive strength
· easily workable

Eco-efficient
· lightweight
· made from 50 per cent
  recycled glass
· perfect dimensional
  stability
· fire resistant
· high sound attenuation

Current applications
· architecture
· construction
· industrial

FOAMGLAS is a cellular glass, and a durable and ecologically sustainable form of thermal insulation, particularly suitable for the construction industry.

It is made from alumino-silicate cellular glass, of which more than 50 per cent is recycled. It is completely inorganic, and contains no binders. Cellular glass is both non-combustible and non-absorbent.

FOAMGLAS has a closed-cell structure, which guarantees that no wick effect will lead to spontaneous ignition. Its chemical composition from pure glass also ensures that no smoke or toxic gases can emanate from it. It is free from corrosive agents, and protects pipes and equipment for an indefinite duration. In addition, it is resistant to salt water, acids, petrol and organic solvents. Impervious to water and water vapour, this insulation material protects totally against corrosion, avoids ice formation and offers exceptional long-term thermal control. No vapour-barrier or gas-impermeable membrane is needed.

FOAMGLAS cellular glass is mainly applied industrially as piping, valves, fittings, tanks, chimneys, and in the building industry as roof, wall, floor, foundations, panels and parking decks.

AEROGEL
HYDROPHOBIC SILICA PARTICLES

Cabot's Nanogel aerogels have numerous potentialities for application; in the production of thermo insulation panels for daylight systems, insulation composites for transportation vehicles, thermo control agents for surface coating, and adhesives.

Aerogels are the lightest weight solids in the world, with only a five per cent solid content, the remaining ninety five per cent being air. The Nanogel aerogels can be customised according to specification, to make them opaque, translucent or almost glass-clear, and have 'permanent hydrophibicity': they are stable against hydrolysis and water damage over a wide range of pH levels. They have significantly low levels of extractables, so are ideal for applications that are sensitive even to traces of extractable ('free') siloxanes.

The aerogels are available with diameters up to 3 millimetres, and are used in the oil and gas, marine and building industries.

Manufacturer
  Cabot
  Interleuvenlaan 15
  B-3001 Leuven
  Belgium
  www.cabot-corp.com
  t: +32 16392400
  f: +32 16392444
Introduction year
  · 2003
Properties
  · translucent
  · highly stable
  · customisable opacity
    (from opaque to clear)
Eco-efficient
  · functions as
    an insulation system
  · reduces energy consumption
Current applications
  · interior/outdoor design
  · architecture
  · oil and gas industries
  · marine industry
  · windows

Manufacturer
  webmaster@msm.cam.ac.uk
  www.msm.cam.ac.uk/gordon
Introduction year
  · not yet available
Properties
  · low density
  · low thermal conductivity
  · low dielectric constant
  · high thermal shock
    resistance
  · high chemical resistance
  · low cost processing
Eco-efficient
  · low cost processing
Current applications
  · architecture
    and construction
  · civil engineering

Cellular ceramics are unique in their combination of valuable properties, with a low density, low thermal conductivity, low dielectric constant, high thermal shock resistance, high specific strength and high chemical resistance. This makes them useful for both structural and functional applications (thermal insulation, liquid metal filtration, impact absorption, catalyst supports, lightweight structures).

The process of obtaining silicone oxycarbide (SiOC) ceramic foams is simple, economical and versatile, and consists of co-blowing a homogenous solution of a thermosetting silicone resin with or without polyurethane precursors (polyols and isocyanates). The green porous bodies are converted into a SiOC ceramic foam by pyrolsis in nitrogen, and both open or closed cell macro cellular foams can be produced. This makes it possible to produce porous ceramics in any shape or design according to specification; rods, tubes, and thin plates are typically manufactured.

Porous ceramics are used in gas absorption, chromatography, vacuum holding plates and filtration for heavy metal ions in water.

Manufacturer
Alusion
6320-2 Danville Road
Mississauga
Ontario L5T 2L7
Canada
info@alusion.com
www.alusion.com
t: +1 9056962419
f: +1 9056969300
Introduction year
· **1992**
Properties
· **high mechanical resistance**
· **lightweight**
Eco-efficient
· **lightweight**
Current applications
· **indoor/outdoor design**
· **architecture**
  and construction
· **furniture**
· **flooring**
· **lighting**
· **ceiling**
· **signage**

Closed-cell aluminium foam products are made from a unique aluminium MMC alloy, produced in a continuous cast to make a lightweight foamed aluminium sheet. All three dimensions of the cast sheet can be controlled and the density of the foam can be varied from 4.5 per cent to 35 per cent—that of solid aluminium.

The sheets are available in their natural state, or the cells can be opened for improved acoustic performance via high pressure water blasting. The sheets can then be powder coated in any colour desired and/or resin coated. Resin coated foamed aluminium is typically used for table-top applications.

Aluminium foam can be used in highway noise barriers, as an alternative to existing fire-resistant materials and core materials for sandwich panels used in architecture.

INSOLCORE
TRANSPARENT INSULATION

InsolCore is a honeycomb transparent insulation, conceived at McGill University by KT Hollands and developed for commercial use by Advanced Glazings Ltd for use in passive solar, architectural glazing, and greenhouse insulation. The transparent insulation provides two functions: light transmittance and thermal insulation. Use of clear plastic for the cell structures allows for a high efficiency of light transmittance by reflection and refraction, even when the sun angle is not normal to the plane of the cell openings.

Material options are polypropylene for low cost and acrylic for high UV stability. InsolCore is currently available in widths up to 1.5 metres and lengths up to 40 metres. Its primary usage to date has been in passive solar applications (Trombe walls, de-salination) as greenhouse insulation, where it will save a grower as much as 75 per cent of their annual heating costs. It has also been used in architectural daylighting, inside Solera high-performance translucent glazing.

Manufacturer
  Advanced Glazing
  870 King's Road
  PO Box 1460
  Station A
  Sydney, Nova Scotia
  B1P 6R7
  Canada
  info@advancedglazings.com
  www.advancedglazings.com
  t: +1 9027942899
  f: +1 9027941869
Introduction year
  · 1999
Properties
  · high light transmittance
  · high insulation value of U=0.12
  · UV stable
  · structural
  · physically stable at temperatures up to 170 degrees centigrade
  · visible light transmittance averages 96 per cent across 180 degrees of incidence
Eco-efficient
  · long usable life
  · 100 per cent recyclable
  · lightweight
  · admits solar energy
  · prevents heat loss/gain
Current applications
  · indoor
  · architecture daylight
  · greenhouses

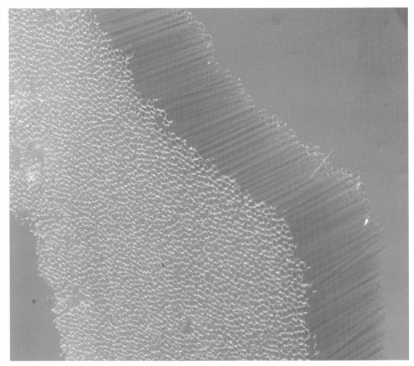

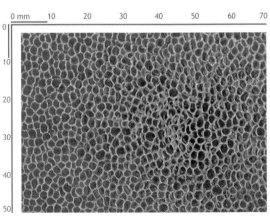

LIGHT DIFFUSING AND INSULATING GLASS

Manufacturer
  Okalux GmbH
  97828
  Marktheidenfeld-Altfeld
  Germany
  info@okalux.de
  www.okalux.de
  t: +49 93919000
  f: +49 9391900100
Introduction year
  · not available
Properties
  · light transmitting
  · thermal solar protection
  · glare protection
  · exceptional heat insulation
  · translucent
Eco-efficient
  · insulating system
Current applications
  · architecture, particularly
    buildings such as stations,
    airports, hospital,
    museums and libraries

Kapilux light diffusing and insulating glass units are conventional, hermetically-sealed insulating glass units, incorporating a capillary honeycomb structure within the unit cavity. The standard build-up (three pane) consists of a coated outer pane (cavity 1: 8 millimetres, with air or gas filling), and a middle pane with two offset Kapipane slabs of 10 millimetres thickness each. Kapilux offers excellent heat insulation, with UG values of up to 0.8 W/m²K; forward-directed light diffusion for improved in-depth illumination of the room; light transmission, thermal solar protection and glare protection, and partial throughvision, which gives the effect of depth. The capillaries do not only reduce heat loss, resulting in U-values as low as 0.8 W/m²K, but with their forward-directed light diffusion, the Kapilux capillaries also improve the in-depth illumination of the room. This effect is particularly valuable on overcast days and in rooms with side illumination.

Kapilux is suitable for use in both roof and facade areas of commercial, industrial, educational and recreational buildings. It may be installed in any architectural framing system, including windows, curtain walling, patent glazing, four-sided structural silicone glazing, point-supported structural glazing, and flat or sloping roof glazing systems.

3M OPTICAL LIGHT

3M optical lighting film (OLF) is a transparent plastic film with one smooth side and one prismatic side, manufactured using 3M Microreplication technology. OLF both reflects and transmits light. Its near-perfect 90 degree prisms enable OLF to reflect almost 99 per cent of light, striking it within a critical angle, while transmitting light above this critical angle.

A dot pattern added to the smooth side of OLF causes specular light to scatter when striking these white-pigmented regions. Dot-printed OLF not only reflects and transmits light, it also controls specularity and scatter. OLF is used to transport and distribute light uniformly with extreme efficiency.

In some applications, light from a point source is distributed through a tube creating a linear light source. It can also be used to create a uniform area light source from either a linear or a point light source.

Manufacturer
  3M Corporate Headquarters
  3M Center
  Saint Paul
  Minnesota 551441000
  USA
  light_and_optics@mmm.com
  www.3m.com/about3m/
  technologies
  t: +44 18883643577
Introduction year
  · 2000
Properties
  · irregular translucence
  · excellent uniformity
    in light-transmission
  · distortion of image
    reflection
Eco-efficient
  · lower energy usage
    for light transmission
  · lightweight
Current applications
  · lighting
  · interior design
  · architecture

CONTINUOUS FIBRE ALUMINUM MATRIX COMPOSITE

MATERIAL & TECHNOLOGY RESEARCH SUSTAINABLE PERFORMANCE

Manufacturer
  3M Corporate Headquarters
  3M Center
  Saint Paul
  Minnesota 551441000
  USA
  light_and_optics@mmm.com
  www.3m.com/about3m/
  technologies
  t: +44 18883643577
Introduction year
  · not available
Properties
  · low anisotropy content
  · very high strength
  · nonferrous
  · resistant to corrosion
  · high density per unit
    volume
  · low cost processing
Eco-efficient
  · low cost processing
Current applications
  · indoor/outdoor design
  · mechanical engineering
  · automotive industry
Case study applications
  · Seung Soo Shin,
    Sustainable
    Interconnectivity

Continuous Fibre Aluminum Matrix Composite (CFAMC) is a high strength material ideally suited to the design of high speed rotors. The material exhibits a strength and stiffness that are three times greater than monolithic metal alloys, and it is nonferrous and so it will not interfere with magnetic bearings. Its material properties are significantly less anisotropic compared to graphite/epoxy composites. The material has been successfully used in both flywheels and high speed electric generators (as a retaining ring on a copper rotor). The material is highly resistant to corrosion, and it will not give off gas in a vacuum.

The relatively low anisotropy allows for the design of thick-walled flywheels with an energy density per unit volume. CFAMC rotors may be cast with hubs and other features necessary to incorporate the rotor in the overall machine design. 3M has developed aluminum matrix composites using its high strength Nextel 610 alumina fibre. The fibre consists of high purity nanocrystalline alumina.
3M's CFAMC is produced using a process called pressure casting, in which a fibre preform is infiltrated with molten aluminum under inert gas pressure. Pressure casting is a cost effective method for producing CFAMCs because of the chemical compatibility between molten aluminium and the alumina fibre.

In the processing of CFAMCs, the inert gas pressure provides the energy necessary to produce wetting of the alumina fibre surface by the molten aluminum, and the result is a nano-scale reaction layer at the fibre matrix interface which is ideal for the properties of the finished composite.
The pressure casting process also allows for the efficient production of net-shape and bulk materials because the composite is formed in a single step.

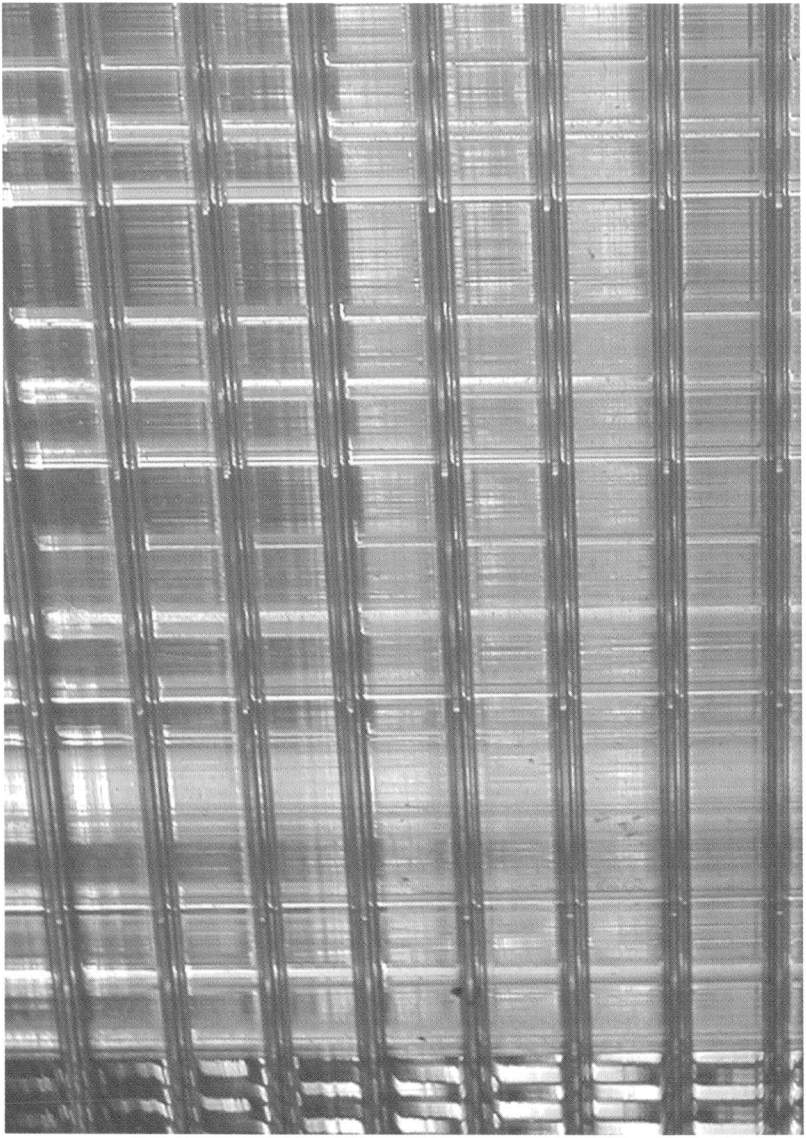

INTEGRATED PERFORMANCE

INTEGRATED PERFORMANCE

High-tech composite materials that integrate various technologies to improve performance in several different ways.

Investigation in composite material research leans increasingly towards materials capable of fulfilling multiple functions simultaneously, often using extremely thin materials. Nanotechnology is able to fulfil this specific requirement by using layering systems, and in the future, it will be able to assign technical content to 'poor' materials, allowing new potentialities for materials to be 'designed' from technical criteria in many different fields.

Textiles, fabrics and fibres are at the forefront of the development of new designed materials, and are increasingly relevant in the following chapter. Performance of these materials can be managed from two different positions. On the one hand, performance can be managed from a micro-mechanical perspective, dealing with the geometric level of fibre disposition within its volume; on the other, performance can be managed at a macro-mechanical level in the way fibres are oriented and overlapped in sequence within different layers.

Processing fibres such as carbon, glass, ceramics etc suggests new approaches in structural design: when volume is reduced to filaments and textiles, high tensile strengths are maintained, whilst lighter weights and transparency are simultaneously achieved. There are also significant improvements in the possibility of combining fibres with other materials in order to obtain thin structural 'assemblages' with consistent mechanical strength.

In addition, further developments are starting to be made in ink conductors that, by coating a material's surface, are able to transmit electronic input through hand contact. These inputs can control the on/off signals of lighting, sound systems, etc.. Although piezoelectric material, which converts mechanical input into electrical impulses, is being developed in the aeronautics industry, it is currently being tested in other broader applications.

Another relevant example is in micro-technology informatics, in which limits are overcome by integrating biological materials. For instance, one method integrates electronic circuits with cells in order to achieve and manage networks that are able to stimulate brain functions. Another example is the use of batteries to protect electrical circuits that have been previously researched.

INTEGRATED PERFORMANCE
PERFORMANCE/MATERIAL IDENTIFICATION

SHAPE PERFORMANCE	OPTICAL PERFORMANCE	SUSTAINABLE PERFORMANCE	INTEGRATED PERFORMANCE	RESPONSIVE PERFORMANCE
ENKARDIN			ENKARDIN	
	CUBEN FIBER	CUBEN FIBER	CUBEN FIBER	
	DIAX-LSP	DIAX-LSP	DIAX-LSP	
		CARBON-GLASS	CARBON-GLASS	
	TRAIXAL FABRIC	TRAIXAL FABRIC	TRAIXAL FABRIC	
FIBRE REINFORCED POLYMERS		FIBRE REINFORCED POLYMERS	FIBRE REINFORCED POLYMERS	
B-CLEAR GLASS	B-CLEAR GLASS		B-CLEAR GLASS	
		TYFO FIBREWRAP	TYFO FIBREWRAP	
			CORIAN	
			SIBU MULTI-STYLE	
GLASS CYLINDERS	GLASS CYLINDERS		GLASS CYLINDERS	

· On the left page, the table shows a column with the list of materials that belong to the 'integrated performance' category in red. In addition to this identification, and because it is impossible to unequivocally define material behaviour, the table shows the possibility that materials may belong to other categories: the material name is repeated under other categories.
· On the right page, the table shows a column that indicates the profile of each material and a column that shows the student who used each material, and the name of their case study.

MATERIAL PROFILE	PROCESS TECHNIQUE	CASE STUDY APPLICATIONS
POLYMERS		
FIBRES		Maria Mandalaki/Housing Senses
COMPOSITES		Andrea Fiecther/ How is Material Informing Architecture
		Eriko Watanabe/Tree Twister

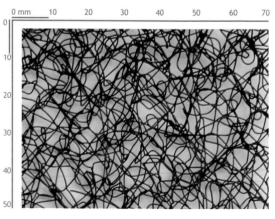

SUBSURFACE DRAINAGE MATTING

Manufacturer
Colbond bv
Westervoortsedijk 73
PO Box 9600
6800 TC Arnhem
The Netherlands
www.colbond.com
mari.fox@colbond.com
T: +31 263662677
F: +31 263665996

Introduction year
· 1975

Properties
· three-dimensional shape
· protects waterproof coatings
  and membranes from
  damage during back filling
· prevents sitting up
  of the collector drain
· high discharge capacity
  due to its open structure
· exceptional flexibility
· unaffected by chemicals
· fire resistant
· forms an insulating air
  gap between all and soil
· simple to install

Eco-efficient
· lightweight
  and easy to handle
· negligible waste
· rot proof so no risk of
  pollution of the subsoil

Current applications
· outdoor
· engineering and construction
· roads and rail
· landfills
· flooring

Enkardin is a geocomposite material which is lightweight, strong, flexible, easy to handle and quickly installable. It delivers high flow transmission per unit volume, with consistent, uniform and excellent longterm performance.

Enkardin is a three-dimensional composite that consists of a drainage core either connected to one, or sandwiched between two, non-woven synthetic geotextile fabrics. The drainage core is composed of tough, looped synthetic filaments that are fused together where they cross, forming an open structural material with a voids ratio of 95 per cent. The resulting product is chemically inert and durable. It has been used for a wide range of engineering works, such as roads, rail, basement walls and water drainage.

MATERIAL & TECHNOLOGY RESEARCH INTEGRATED PERFORMANCE

CUBEN FIBER TEXTILES

Cuben Fiber laminates use unidirectional prepreg tapes of in-line plasma treated Spectra 2000 fibers spread on mono-filament level films. (Spectra 2000 is a registered trademark of Allied Signal Inc) The Cuben Fiber process involves neither twisted filaments nor weaves and reduces 'creep' and 'crimp' to levels undetectable to standard sail makers' testing equipment. The result is excellent sail shape holding. Cuben Fiber is very thin and retains its strength even after much flexing. Aramid laminates lose 80 per cent of their strength after being folded 250 times while Cuben Fiber retains nearly 100 per cent of its original properties. Due to its characteristic of being moulded into complex shaped structures with compound curvatures, it has also been developed for architectural applications.

Cuben Fiber has great structural properties and is a lightweight material. It is available in a wide range of colours and is designed for a long life and resistance to the elements. It has been used in furniture, tension structures, tents and awnings, and inflatable and portable structures.

Manufacturer
  Cuben Fiber Corporation
  4511 East Ivy Street
  Mesa, Arizona 85205
  USA
  cubenfiber@cubenfiber.com
  www.cubenfiber.com
  t: +1 4806410438
  f: +1 4806410439
Introduction year
  · 1997
Properties
  · high structural properties
  · high breaking strength
    with a stretch resistance
    of over two times that
    of the aramids
  · high resistance
    to fatigues tests
  · very long working life
  · easily moulded to 3-D
    shapes
Eco-efficient
  · lightweight
Current applications
  · indoor/outdoor
  · marine, particularly
    sail cloths
  · architecture
    and construction
Case study applications
  · Maria Mandalaki,
    Housing Senses

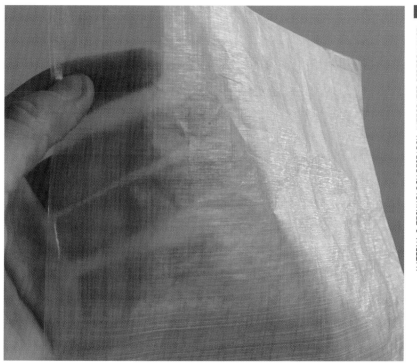

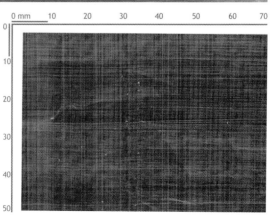

DIAX-LSP
HIGH PERFORMANCE LAMINATES

Diax is a mid-range laminate with great stability performance, tear resistance and lightweight durability, without the expense of higher tech constructions. DIAX-LSPs provide a reduction in warp stretch by utilising Pentex, a hybrid polyester fibre with 250 per cent higher modules (less stretch) than standard polyesters.

The blending of grey pigments with the adhesives gives increased UV resistance. and style and durability to sailcloth with proven outstanding performance. DIAX products are based on scrim component technology. Flat untwisted ribbons of fibre are formed into a number of scrims that maximise the performance of the yarn. In every DIAX fabric a zero crimp warp/fill scrim resists primary and secondary loading. This is combined with a 45 degrees diagonal axis scrim to reduce base stretch and to increase its structural performance. In addition, it has excellent light dispersion and is available in film.

DIAX-LSP, is used mainly for sailing, in a variety of craftys including dinghies, sports boats and club race yachts up to 14 metres.

Manufacturer
  Bainbridge International Ltd.
  Flanders Park
  Hedge End
  Southampton
  SO30 2FZ
  UK
  info@bainbridgeint.co.uk
  www.bainbridgeint.com
  t: +44 1489776000
  f: +44 1489776015
Introduction year
  · not available
Properties
  · stability
  · UV resistant
  · tear resistant
  · durability
  · outstanding low stretch
  · excellent light dispersion
Eco-efficient
  · lightweight
Current applications
  · indoor/outdoor
  · marine, particularly
    sail cloths
  · clothes
  · flags
Case study applications
  · Seung Soo Shin,
    Sustainable
    Interconnectivity

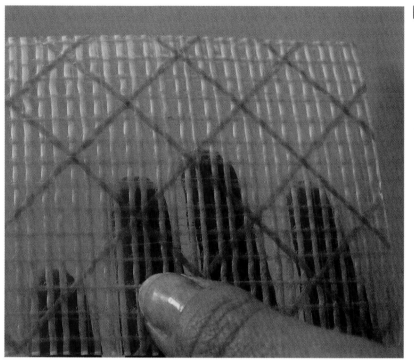

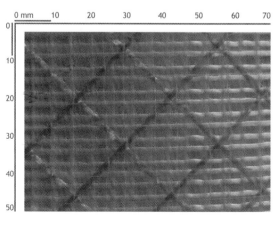

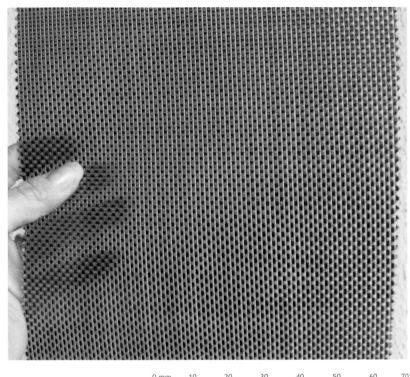

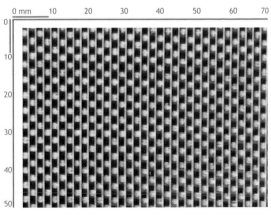

CARBON-GLASS FABRIC

MATERIAL & TECHNOLOGY RESEARCH INTEGRATED PERFORMANCE

Manufacturer
  Pidigi SpA
  Via della Meccanica
  29 ZA12 37139
  Verona
  Italy
  pidigi@pidigi.com
  www.pidigi.com
  t: +39 0459216888
  f: +39 0459216800
Introduction year
  · 2001
Properties
  · high mechanical strength
  · resistant to acids,
    to chemical, to moisture,
    to water, to wear
  · translucent
  · impermeable
Eco-efficient
  · lightweight
  · recyclable
Current applications
  · clothing and footwear
  · protection system
  · packaging

Carbon-Glass is a fabric made by layering carbon fibre, glass fibre and a final coating layer of PVC that makes the product resistant and reflective. It has a metallic effect, shiny on one side and opaque on the other, and can easily be cut, sewed, glued and fusion-welded.

The PVC ensures that the fabric has a long durability and high mechanical strength, while the carbon fibre contributes to its rigidity, compressive strength and lightness of weight. The glass fibre ensures it has a high breaking strength, and its tensile strength can be quantified as 3.000 N/mm squared.

The high-tech fabric is used mainly within the technical clothing industry and for security systems. It is also now used in footwear and packaging.

TRIAXIAL CARBON FIBRE FABRIC

Triaxial Fabric uses a weaving process in which three yarns—two warp and one weft—are interlaced at 60 to 70 degree angles. NASA developed this triaxial structure in the 1960s to fill the needs of space scientists for dimensionally stable and lightweight fabric to be used in aeronautics.

The triaxial structure allows maximum flexibility and strength for the material. The construction also requires fewer raw materials and is therefore lighter than conventional woven fabrics. The textile can be stretched in all dimensions without causing stress at any point.

It has been used to make antenna reflectors, solar panels, skis, fishing rods, speaker cones, and medical support for people who suffer from joint deficiency. It is also used for golf club shafts.

Manufacturer
   Sigmatex UK Ltd
   Fairoak Lane
   Whitehouse Industrial Estate
   Runcorn
   Cheshire
   WA7 3DU
   UK
   sales@sigmatex.co.uk
   www.sigmatex.com
   t: +44 1928790110
   f: +44 1928790074
Introduction year
   · 1991
Properties
   · high tensile strength
   · lightness and delicacy do
      not diminish their strength
   · texture finishing
Eco-efficient
   · lightweight
Current applications
   · architecture
   · sport
   · aeronautics
   · medicine

Manufacturer
  Gurit Holding AG
  Ebnater Strasse 7a
  CH-9630 Wattwil
  Zwitserland
  info@gurit.com
  www.gurit.com
  t: +41 719871010
  f: +41 719871005
Introduction year
  · not available
Properties
  · excellent strength/
    weight ratio
  · very good tensile strength
  · good mechanical resistance
  · resistant to corrosion and
    rotting
Eco-efficient
  · lightweight
  · cost effective processing
Current applications
  · marine
  · transport
  · interior design
  · architecture
    and construction
  · aerospace
  · automatic industry
  · marine industry
Case study applications
  · Andrea Fiecther,
    How is Material Informing
    Architecture?

Fibre-reinforced polymers or plastics (FRPs) are composites of polymer resin, usually epoxy, polyester, vinylester or polyester thermosetting plastic as matrix, reinforced with woven, knitted, stitched or bonded fibres, usually fibreglass, carbon or aramid, as reinforcement.

An FRP laminate is any FRP made from resin coated layers of fabrics or fibrous reinforcements which have been bonded together using FRPs which are not in distinct layers, such as filament wound structures and spray-ups.

The flexural stiffness of the FRP is proportional to the cube of its thickness. To increase the thickness, the core is introduced between two layers of laminates. Core types include Foam Cores (PVC, PU, SAN etc), Honeycombs (Aluminium, Nomex etc), and Wood (Balsa). The combination of fibres, resin, core, additives and coating to an appropriate system has to be carefully selected, usually with the help of the industry's material suppliers.

FRP laminate has very good tension and compression properties. The FRP sandwich shows similar properties regarding tension, but the compression properties are lower, whereas the flexural stiffness increases. The material's dimensions increase when the structure works mainly under high pressure. Geometries, where the FRP structure works mainly under tension, are favoured.

Fire-resistance can be achieved through reactive coatings, additives (for example aluminium trioxide) and selected (phenolic) resins. FRP is not suitable for building parts with a high fire load.

B-CLEAR GLASS
GLASS ALUMINIUM HONEYCOMB PANEL

B-Clear Glass is a composite material with an aluminium honeycomb core sandwiched between toughened glass, bonded together with clear epoxy resin. It combines lightweight durability with high resistance performance.

B-Clear Glass panels are incombustible, and so will not burn or ignite. An optional wearing layer of four millimetres heat-strengthened polycarbonate glass protects the structural sheet from accidental hard impact damage.

In the unlikely event that the glass should fracture, the composite structure retains the glass pieces, preventing the kind of shattering to which ordinary glass is prone and thus reducing the risk of injury. The panels are able to diffuse and reflect light, changing their aesthetic qualities depending on lighting conditions. They have been used for the most part in interior design, and can be used for flooring, tiles, stairs, bridges and tables.

Manufacturer
  Cellbond Composites Ltd
  5 Stukeley Business Centre
  Blackstone Road
  Huntingdon
  Cambridgeshire
  PE29 6EF
  UK
  emma@cellbond.com
  www.cellbond.net
  t: +44 1480435302
  f: +44 1480450181
Introduction year
  · 2002
Properties
  · high impact resistance
  · long working life
  · incombustible
  · safety system
  · lightweight
Eco-efficient
  · lightweight
Current applications
  · interior design
  · architecture
  · furniture
  · flooring
Case study applications
  · Eriko Watanabe,
    Tree Twister

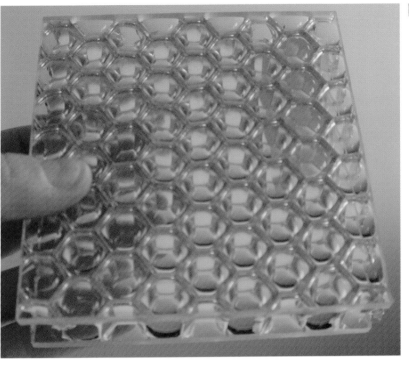

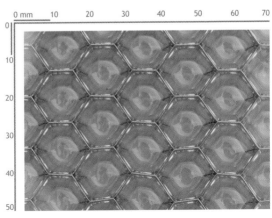

FIBRE REINFORCED COMPOSITE SYSTEM

MATERIAL & TECHNOLOGY RESEARCH INTEGRATED PERFORMANCE

Manufacturer
  Fyfe co LLc
  Nancy Ridge Technology
  Center
  6310 Nancy Ridge Drive
  Suite 103
  San Diego
  California 92121
  USA
  info@fyfeco.com
  www.fyfeco.com
  t: +44 8586420694
  f: +44 8586420947
Introduction year
  · 1988
Properties
  · high load resistant
  · economical in use of raw
    material
  · easy to machine
  · can be spherically shaped
  · customisable
  · lightweight
Eco-efficient
  · lightweight
Current applications
  · architecture
    and construction
  · civil engineering
Case study applications
  · Seung Soo Shin,
    Sustainable
    Interconnectivity

The Tyfo systems are a collective name for a variety of specialised carbon, glass, aramid and hybrid fabrics combined with resins. The composites have been tested at universities and private labs for structural applicability, durability, blast mitigation and fire-resistance since the founding of the Fyfeco company in 1988. They have also performed as designed (to mitigate blasts and minimise damage) in major urban earthquakes in Taipei, Los Angeles, Seattle and San Salvador. Research has also been carried out into the environmental impact and durability of Fibrwrap, simulating 50 to 100 years of its service life.

The Fibrwrap composites are usually used for strengthening, repair and protection work on buildings, but have a multiplicity of uses in the civil engineering and construction sectors.

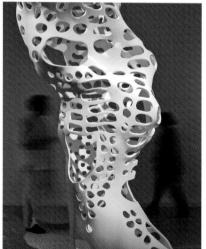

top: "Z. Island by DuPont™ Corian®", design Zaha Hadid (photo Leo Torri for DuPont™ Corian®) bottom left Resi-Rise, design Kolatan /Mac Donald, (photo Leo Torri for DuPont™ Corian®) bottom right Led Roulette table, design Moritz Waldmeyer (photo Rabih Hage Gallery-DuPont™ Corian®) Photos courtesy of DuPont.

COMPOSITE OF ALUMINIUM TRIHYDRATE AND ACRYLIC (PMMA)

Manufacturer

DuPont El du Pont
de Nemours and Company Inc
1007 Market Street
Wilmington,
Delaware 19898
USA
corian@coduaq.nl
www.corian.com
t: +1 80042674261

Introduction year

· 1967

Properties

· stain resistant
· solid
· discreet joints
· easily repairable
· thermo-formable
· translucent
· workable like wood

Current applications

· interior design
· architecture
· furniture

Corian is an advanced composite made by pouring a mix of aluminium tri-hydrate and Acrylic (PMMA) resin onto a moving steel belt. During polymerisation, heat is released, which is controlled in a cooling tunnel. Once cooled, the sides of the continuous sheet are trimmed off and the length is cross-cut to obtain Corian sheets. It is a remarkably durable and versatile material, which can survive the impacts, nicks and cuts that can occur with daily use. Colours and patterns can run through its entire thickness, to create luminescent surfaces.

Corian is solid and cannot delaminate. Joints can be glued inconspicuously, making it possible to produce virtually unlimited surfaces, which are hygienic because they are non-porous. Also Corian is inert, non toxic and hypoallergenic, and the aluminium tri-hydrate means it is highly flame-retardant. It is available in a range of colours and sizes, with the lighter six millimetre plates being more translucent.

The sheets can be thermoformed and treated like wood. Corian can be applied domestically, as durable surfaces in kitchens and bathrooms, but it also has the potential for other uses in public spaces, such as hospital operating rooms and intensive care facilities, cruise ships, airport check-in counters and as a design material for lamps, homeware and furniture.

SIBU MULTI-STYLE
METAL COMPOSITE

SIBU multistyle is a composite sheet made from a highly impact-resistant polystyrene base layer covered either by a metal-coated, polyester film or a printed surface. The material is held together entirely by the adhesive layer on the underside. It is available in two patterns; a "Diamond" slitted, finely scored style and a "CLASSIC" grid, with clearly visible score-lines, and various colours.   ·

It adheres to rounded surfaces and bends to fit any shape and is therefore, ideally suited to be bonded onto columns, as well as arched and flat surfaces.

For the most part. This is an interior design material, but it is also used for shop and trade fair design, display areas, theatre and stage sets, and furniture.

Manufacturer
 SIBU Design GmbH & Co KG
 Jupiterstrasse 8
 A-4452
 Ternberg
 Austria
 info@sibu.at
 www.sibu.at
 t: +43 725660250
 f: +43 72567020
Introduction year
 · 1984
Properties
 · highly impact resistant
 · reflective
 · highly flexible
Current applications
 · interior design
 · furniture
 · panelling

Manufacturer
  Schott AG
  Hattenbergstr 10
  D-55122 Mainz
  Germany
  info@schott.com
  www.schott.com
  t: +49 061316600
  f: +49 06131662000
Introduction year
  · 2003
Properties
  · high degree of precision
  · excellent resistance
    to corrosion
  · thermal shock resistant
  · chemical resistant
  · smooth surface
  · transparency
Current applications
  · architecture
    and construction
  · chemical, food, paper,
    automobile industries
  · engineering, measurement
    and control technology
  · laser technology
  · aviation
  · waterconditioning

Transparent and highly resistant to chemical and thermal stresses, Schott's glass tubes provide a weight-reduced alternative to steel or concrete elements in building construction. In order to make the tubes shatter-resistant, and to be able to withstand high-compression loads, an outer glass shell is laminated around an inner-core glass pipe.

Borosilicate glass, used for the glass tube, has outstanding properties: transparency, colour neutrality, chemical resistance, thermal shock resistance and a high level of homogeneity, essential for coping with mechanical stress.

In addition, tubular geometry provides a statically optimal profile for buildings with economical use of materials.

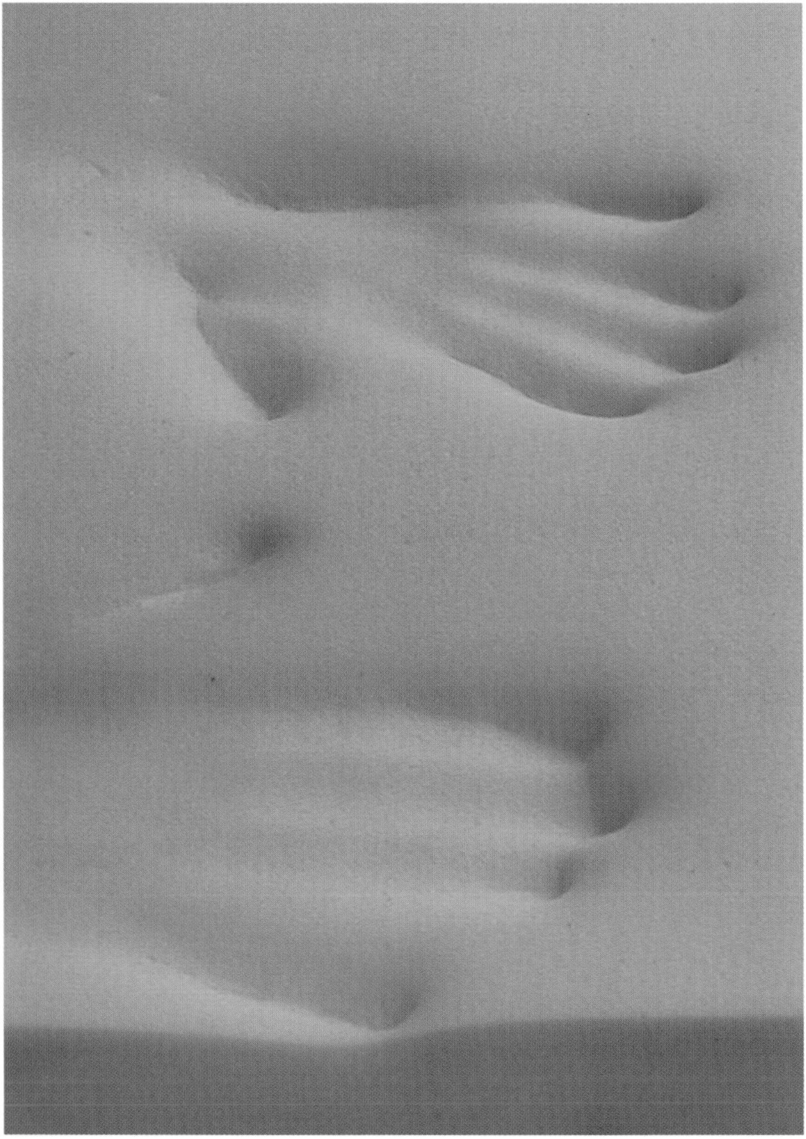

RESPONSIVE PERFORMANCE

RESPONSIVE PERFORMANCE

Materials with the built-in ability to evolve while interacting with users or external input, hence becoming an interface that reacts to stimulus that changes the material's physical state.

In this category, we find 'thermo-chromatic' materials, which react to UV rays and thus to temperature by modifying their colour; 'orthodromic materials', which are similar to thermo-chromatic ones but react under magnetic fields; and 'memory shape materials', which have the ability to interface with human actions and the environment, thus evolving dynamically in time.

Also very interesting are 'phase changing materials'. In Japan, for instance, researchers are experimenting with intelligent systems in the construction of building foundations which are able to resist earthquake tremors by applying sensors. These sensors amplify any such waves, producing a change in the material elasticity in order to absorb the shockwave impact.

Also included in this category are specific nanotechnologies such as thermo-regulator materials. These are impermeable textiles and/or transpiring foams that can affect factors such as temperature and humidity by maintaining certain optimal values; thus operating directly on potentially uncomfortable thermo-changes. Thermo-regulator materials act dynamically to react to the temperature variations of the body. Although the fabric is very thin, it is a very efficient thermo-insulation tool. These materials are used in the field of design for mattresses, pillows and covers; while in architecture they are used as insulation systems because of their capacity to uniformly appropriate, maintain and return heat.

Finally, materials with biological characteristics are also relevant. Because they have a provisional nature, they are able to catalyse, to 'process' impulses and to react by adapting to changes. For this reason, their resistance properties over time are much more consistent—even more so when reduced human intervention is taken into consideration.

RESPONSIVE PERFORMANCE
PERFORMANCE/MATERIAL IDENTIFICATION

SHAPE PERFORMANCE	OPTICAL PERFORMANCE	SUSTAINABLE PERFORMANCE	INTEGRATED PERFORMANCE	RESPONSIVE PERFORMANCE
	TECHNOGEL			TECHNOGEL
	LUMISTY			LUMISTY
				TEMPUR
	AQUACLEAN		AQUACLEAN	AQUACLEAN
			OPERATOR GLASS	OPERATOR GLASS
	GLASS SOUND		GLASS SOUND	GLASS SOUND
	POWER GLASS		POWER GLASS	POWER GLASS
	LUMINEX			LUMINEX
	RE LIQUID CRYSTAL SHEET			RE LIQUID CRYSTAL SHEET
SHAPE MEMORY TEXTILE				SHAPE MEMORY TEXTILE
		OUTLAST		OUTLAST

· On the left page, the table shows a column with the list of materials that belong to the "responsive performance" category in orange. In addition to this identification and because it is impossible to unequivocally define material behaviour, the table shows the possibility that materials may belong to other categories: the material name is repeated under other categories.
· On the right page, the table shows a column that indicates the profile of each material and a column that shows the student who used each material, and the name of their case study.

MATERIAL PROFILE	PROCESS TECHNIQUE	CASE STUDY APPLICATIONS
POLYMERS		
GLASS		
COMPOSITES		Jasmin Tsoi/Hybrid Living
		Maria Mandalaki/Housing Senses
		Soung Soo Shin/Sustainable Interconnectivity

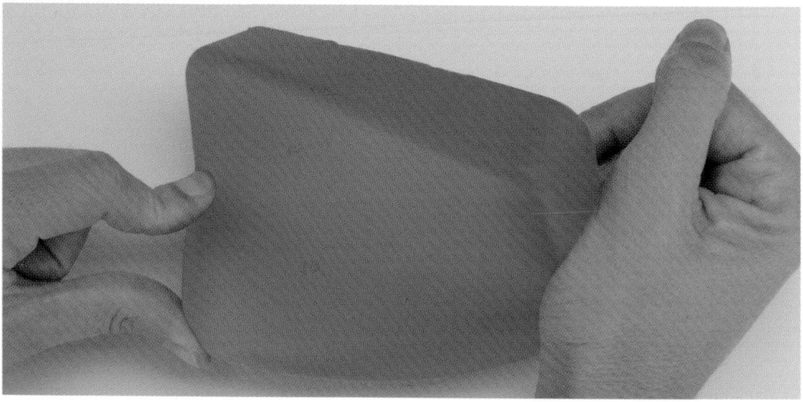

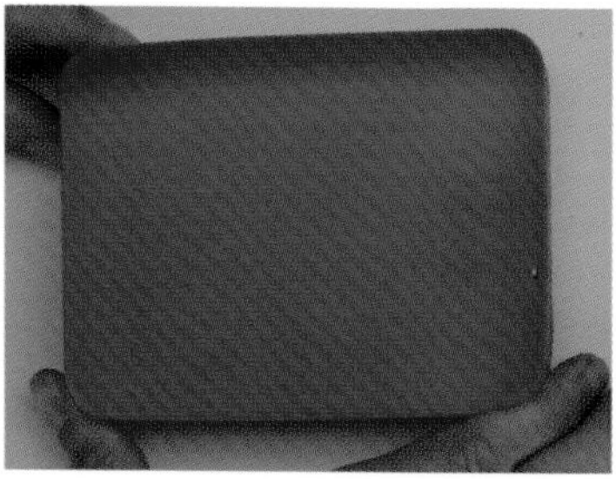

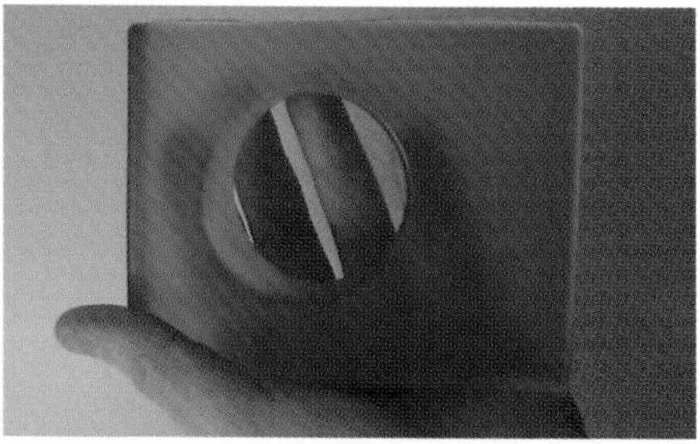

MATERIAL & TECHNOLOGY RESEARCH RESPONSIVE PERFORMANCE

Manufacturer
   Technogel® Italia SRL
   Via Bassanese Inferiore 32
   36050
   Pozzoleone (VI)
   Italy
   info@technogel.it
   www.technogel.it
   t: +39 0444463811
   f: +39 0444462837
Introduction year
   · not available
Properties
   · good pressure distribution
   · high shock absorption
   · shear force absorption
   · high elasticity
   · good recovery capability
   · non-irritating to the skin
   · breathable
   · light-stable
   · good shape memory
   · long working life
Current applications
   · interior design
   · furniture
   · medical and healthcare
     products
   · sport and leisure shoes
   · bathrooms
   · industrial components

Technogel is a product based on polyurethane. Due to the low degree of cross-linkage, Technogel is highly flexible, elastic and able to distribute pressure equally. Since plasticisers or other volatile components aren't used in its manufacture, it is very durable and retains its properties over an extended period of time.

Technogel is poured into moulds as liquid and can be laminated with decorative materials during manufacture, or bonded with standard PU glue.

It is chemically structured for use in many applications; such as in sport and leisure shoes, furniture and healthcare and medical products (cushioning for paraplegic, dystrophic and elderly patients).

VIEW CONTROL FILM

Manufacturer
  Glassfilm Enterprises inc
  PO BOX 2534
  Acton
  Massachussetts 01720
  USA
  jf@glassfilmenterprises.com
  www.lumistyfilm.com
  t: +44 9782639333
  f: +44 9782638996
Introduction year
  · not available
Properties
  · UV resistant
  · protection from shattering
    glass
  · changes from transparent
    to translucent
Current applications
  · interior design
  · shop-fronts
  · corporate architecture

Lumisty is a view control film that can be applied to glass surfaces, making the appearance of the glass change from transparent to translucent as your angle of view changes. In its translucent form it scatters transmitted light, and is virtually invisible, transmitting the same amount of light as in its transparent form. It reduces ultraviolet rays that cause fading and helps prevent the scattering of glass shards if a window is broken.

Lumisty is used for the most part in public architecture, to control the ambience and aesthetic of building designs. It is used widely in lounges, restaurants, hotels, museums, banks, offices and conference rooms as well as domestic architecture. Three version of Lumisty are available, each with different view control formats.

Lumisty was perhaps most famously used on the window of the shop Issey Miyake's Pleats Please boutique in New York.

TEMPUR
VISCO-ELASTIC MATERIAL

TEMPUR is a high-tech comfort material originally developed by NASA for the US Space Program, in order to improve seating comfort and g-force protection in spacecrafts. It is temperature sensitive and designed to mould to the body, yielding slowly under compression, and making no counter pressure until the load is distributed evenly over the entire area. When the load is removed, TEMPUR recovers slowly.

It can be produced to any softness and has unmatched durability. In a standard test, the thickness loss of TEMPUR after 80,000 compressions is less than five per cent, compared to approximately ten to 15 per cent for highly elastic polyurethane foam.

Due to small-scale production techniques, commercial applications were, for many years, limited to medical cushions and mattresses for pressure sore prevention. It is currently used on operating tables in hospitals, incubator mattresses, and in domestic bedrooms.

Manufacturer
Tempur UK Ltd
Tempur House
5 Caxton Trading Estate
Printing House Lane
Hayes
Middlesex
UB3 1BE
UK
info@tempur.co.uk
www.tempur.co.uk
t: +44 8000111083
f: +44 2085897094

Introduction year
· 1970 NASA development
· 1991 Available on the market

Properties
· shape memory material
· uniform distribution of pressure
· long durability

Current applications
· medical and healthcare products
· pillows and cushions
· mattresses
· beds

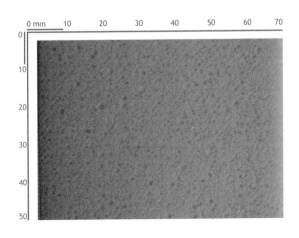

AQUACLEAN
SELF-CLEANING GLASS

Aquaclean is a glass which cleans itself by the action of water alone.

It consists of SGG PLANILUX clear glass to which a transparent coating of a hydrophilic mineral material has been applied.

When contact with the glass, water spreads out over the surface of this coating, causing a washing effect. It then quickly evaporates without leaving any marks. It is hydrophilic and water-repellent.

This remarkable advance makes SGG AQUACLEAN suitable for all sectors of the building industry, both for new buildings and for renovation, in applications where the glass is exposed to rain or water, in a vertical or sloping position: in private houses or blocks of flats (windows, doors, French doors, balconies, conservatories, rooflights) and non-residential buildings (glazed facades and curtain walls, overhead glazing, external shop windows, street furniture, industrial greenhouses).

Manufacturer
  Saint Gobain Glass
  Netherlands
  c/o Vetrotex Reinforcement GmbH
  Kaiserstrasse 100
  D - 52134 Herzogenrath
  Kohlscheid
  Germany
  www.saint-gobain-glass.com
  t: +31 318531311
  f: +31 318531305
Introduction year
  · not available
Properties
  · water-repellent (hydrophilic)
Eco-efficient
  · reducing maintenance cost
Current applications
  · indoor/outdoor
  · architecture
  · benefit for high-rise buildings facades that are hard to access and clean

## DISPLAY SYSTEM INTEGRATED ON TRANSPARENT GLAZING

MATERIAL & TECHNOLOGY RESEARCH RESPONSIVE PERFORMANCE

Manufacturer

Glas Platz GmbH & Co KG
Auf den Pühlen 5
D-51674 Wiehl-Bomig
Germany
info@glas-platz.de
www.glas-platz.de
glas-platz@mail.oberberg.de
t: +49 226178900
f: +49 2261789010

Introduction year

· **2000**

Properties

· **shatterproof**
· **contrast enhanced**
· **resistant to acid and lye**
· **resistant to UV radiation**
· **can be customised**

Eco-efficient

· **spatial, material and**
  energy efficiency

Current applications

· **interior design**
· **computer design**
· **media and display**

Case study applications

· **Jasmine Tsoi, Hybrid Living**

Operator glass is a manufacturing glass available in custom sizes. All types of glass have faceted edges to prevent injuries and are packed in safe dual-use packages. The product line covers various antiglare display and laminated safety glasses. Customised, silkscreen-printed glasses are also available.

Operator glass can be laminated for shatterproof types, coated for contrast enhancement and made with conductive tapes for an EMC shielded type. It is usually used in plasma screens, computer monitors, display systems and projection glazing.

operator glass® with digital touch-controller

GLASS SOUND
SOUND SYSTEM INTEGRATED WITH TRANSPARENT GLAZING

Glass Sound integrates hi-fi and loudspeaker systems with flat glass membrane technology. The use of a flat membrane made of glass, as opposed to conventional loudspeakers, guarantees more uniform volume distribution in space, and considerably improves audibility.

Any commercially available hi-fi system up to 50 watts can be attached as the amplifier. The devices are plain and unobtrusive, and not dangerous because of the low-voltage used. All of the components are entirely recyclable.

Manufacturer
  Glas Platz GmbH & Co KG
  Auf den Pühlen 5
  D-51674 Wiehl-Bomig
  Germany
  info@glas-platz.de
  www.glas-platz.de
  t: +49 (0)2261 78 90 0
  f: +49 (0)2261 78 90 10
Introduction year
  · 2000 no longer available
Properties
  · slim and transparent sound
    system
  · integrated hi-fi and sound
    emitting
Eco-efficient
  · slim and transparent sound
    system
  · integrated hi-fi and sound
    emitting
  · entirely recyclable
  · sound systems
Current applications
  · interior design
Case study applications
  · Jasmine Tsoi, Hybrid Living

MATERIAL & TECHNOLOGY RESEARCH RESPONSIVE PERFORMANCE

161

POWER GLASS

Power glass is made from a conductive, transparent track structure inside laminated glass with a wireless electrical energy supply. The signal transmission and power supply are carried invisibly via the transparent conductive coating. LEDs emit light from both sides of the glass, giving the impression of floating light spots, and can be configured to transmit light circles, lines, squares, grids, or even running text, either statically or dynamically switched, via an RS 232 interface in combination with a PC.

It can be used as a logo-facade with rope suspensions, or mounted directly in front of a windowpane. It is also available as insulating glass. The structure of the glass, patented worldwide, is based on a kind of 'transparent printed circuit board', similar to the plates in a television set. In contrast to conventional plates where power is applied to glass, the conductive coating is laid on a carrier glass. This metallic and electrically leading layer is so thin as to be imperceptible to the human eye. The reciprocally radiating emitting diodes are positioned on the carrier glass, and a second glass plate is fixed on the opponent side of the motherboard. Then the lamination is sealed and protected from outside.

Manufacturer
 Glas Platz GmbH & Co KG
 Auf den Pühlen 5
 D-51674 Wiehl-Bomig
 Germany
 info@glas-platz.de
 www.glas-platz.de
 t: +49 226178900
 f: +49 2261789010
Introduction year
 · 2000
Properties
 · LED diodes on transparent
   printed circuit board
 · laminated in glass or
   mounted in ropes
 · lighting from both
   sides while retaining
   transparency of panel
 · electrically insulated
 · lighting intensity and
   pattern variation can be
   customised
Eco-efficient
 · low energy consumption
 · low direct power supply
 · facade lighting makes it
   space-efficient
Current applications
 · building industry
 · media and design industries
 · lighting

LUMINEX
WOVEN OPTICAL FIBRES

Luminex is a non-reflective fabric that emits its own light and was developed in a collaboration between the italian company CEAN spa and the Swiss company STABIO Textile SA. The lumen fibres used in Luminex are special detectors of elementary particles used in scientific experiments on sub-nuclear physics, a field in which CAEN spa is prominent, producing of electronic equipment.

Using integrated electronics (microchips with greatly reduced dimensions and weight), Luminex not only gives exceptional luminous effects but is an intelligent material, able to process and respond to signals like heartbeat and body temperature and other environmental stimuli.

Luminex can be applied to many uses, such as clothing, interior design and furmishings for nightclubs and bars, and road signs.

Manufacturer
  Luminex
  Via dei Fossi 14-b
  59100 Prato (po)
  Italy
  info@luminex.it
  www.luminex.it
  t: +39 0574730283
  f: +39 0574730154
Introduction year
  · not available
Properties
  · highly customisable
  · electroluminescent
  · translucent
  · lightweight
Eco-efficient
  · lightweight
Current applications
  · interior design
  · safety systems
  · fashion
  · furnishings
  · stage sets

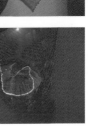

RE LIQUID CRYSTAL SHEET

Liquid crystal sheets are a substrate made from micron clear polyester in which liquid crystal is dispersed and encapsulated. They change colour from blue to red depending on their temperature, and can be used to illustrate these changes in classrooms. The sheets are printed on one side, first with the microencapsulated TLC (coated polyester sheet) coating, and then with a black backing ink.

The colour changes of the TLC coating are viewed through the clear, uncoated side of the sheet.

Standard sheets are available with or without, adhesive backing (pressure-sensitive adhesive) and the protective release-liner can be removed for easy adhesion to a variety of flat surfaces. Liquid crystal sheets could potentially be used in architecture, interior design and any application where there is a need to detect variations in temperature.

Manufacturer
  Liquid Crystal Resources Ltd
  Riverside Buildings
  Dock Road
  Connahs Quay
  Teeside
  Flintshire
  CHS 4DS
  UK
  sales@liquid-crystal.com
  www.lcr-uk.com
  t: +44 1244817107
  f: +44 1244818502
Introduction year
  · not available
Properties
  · changes colour
  · lightweight
Eco-efficient
  · lightweight
Current applications
  · interior design
  · coating
  · education (as a visual
    aid for explaining
    temperatures)

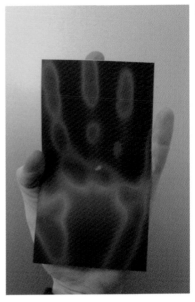

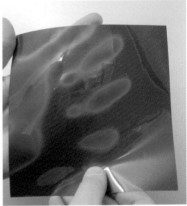

normal condition   heating   programmed condition

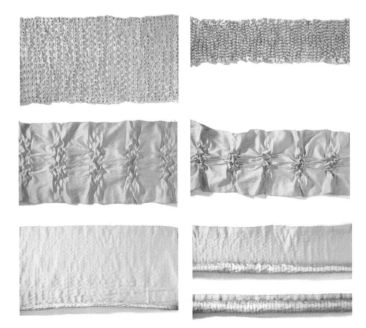

Manufacturer
Mariëlle Leenders
Koriandertsraat 63
5643 AP Eindhoven
The Netherlands
marielle_leenders@yahoo.com
www.marielleleenders.nl
t: +31 641853055
Introduction year
· 1998—concept
· 2000—prototypes
Properties
· very strong fabrics
· can be programmed to move
  at any temperature between
  -50 to +100 degrees centigrade
· super-elastic at
  programmed temperature
· can be formed in any shape
· lightweight
Eco-efficient
· lightweight
Current applications
· not yet on the market
Further applications
· clothing
· interior design
· car interiors
· home furnishings and
  appliances such as lamps,
  blinds and blankets

Shape memory textiles refer to fabrics that incorporate shape memory alloy (NiTi) wires. The wires are either woven into, or sewn onto the fabric, making the material susceptible to folding, rolling and shaping according to specifications.

Also referred to as moving textiles, because of their ability to respond to environmental aspects like heat, all prototypes are made with one-way memory metal. This means that they can be programmed at one temperature, or even at two temperatures.

With the one-way memory metal, the textile will have to be transformed into another shape to make it move again at the programmed temperature. It will change into the programmed shape at the programmed temperature limitlessly. This makes the shape memory textiles very strong, and they are also super-elastic at a programmed temperature.

Clothing made of moving textiles can be programmed to respond to the transition from wintry outdoors temperatures to heated indoor spaces. Sleeves can be made that automatically roll up and down, a jacket that opens and closes on its own, and a shirt that expands in both length and circumference. Other possibilities are blinds that descend when exposed to warm sunlight and roll back up when temperature drops. Although the material is not yet on the market, moving textiles could potentially be used for a variety of decorative and functional purposes.

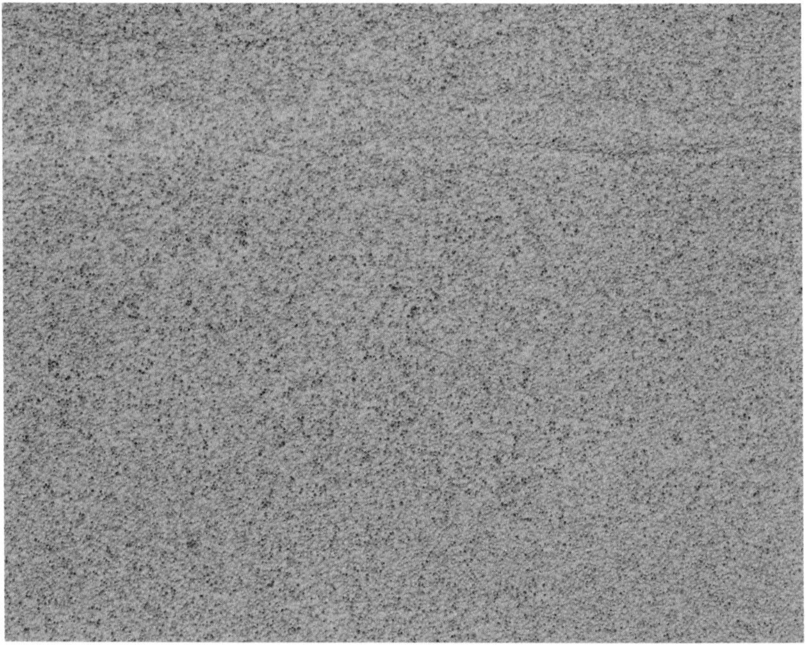

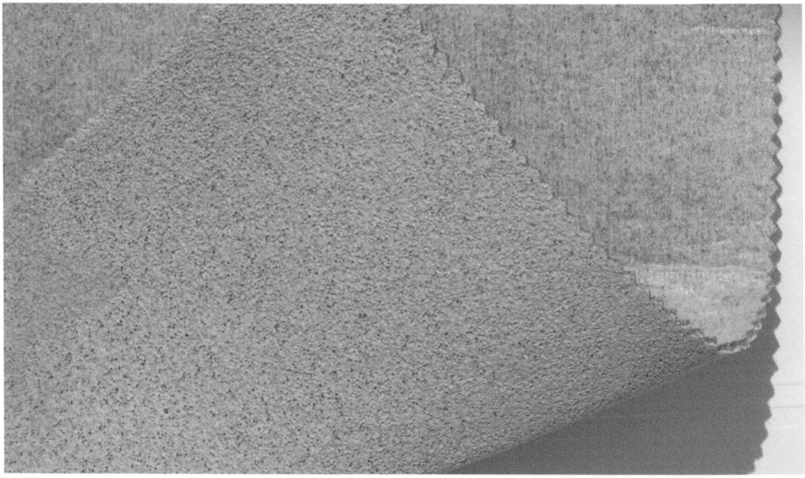

MATERIAL & TECHNOLOGY RESEARCH RESPONSIVE PERFORMANCE

Manufacturer
  Outlast Europe GmbH
  Ploucquetstrasse 11
  D-89522 Heidenheim
  Germany
  info@outlast-europe.com
  www.outlast.com
  t: + 497321272270
  f: + 49 7321272271
Introduction year
  · 1991
  · 1997, introduction to outdoor
    industries
Properties
  · translucency when changing
    from solid to liquid phase
  · temperature resistance,
    50-200 centigrade
  · non-combustible
  · durable elasticity
  · excellent mechanical properties
  · high dimensional stability
  · resistance to a variety
    of chemicals
Eco-efficient
  · improved thermal performance
  · low energy consumption
Current applications
  · indoor and outdoor architecture
  · sport and aerospace clothing
  · interior design
  · furniture
Case study applications
  · Maria Mandalaki,
    Housing Senses
  · Soung Soo Shin,
    Sustainable Interconnectivity

Outlast is a technology that incorporates phase changing materials (PCMs) into various industrial and consumer applications, usually textiles. PCMs change physical state in a narrowly defined temperature range by liquefying and solidifying and subsequently absorbing or releasing energy. Latent heat is the quantity of heat absorbed or released by a substance undergoing a change of state. There are more than five hundred natural and synthetic PCMs, such as paraffins, polymers, salt hydrates, metallics and salt eutectics. They differ from one another in their latent heat storage capacities and temperature ranges.

In architectural membranes, the PCM needs to be properly contained in order to prevent loss and migration while in the liquid state. Various methods of containment such as microencapsulation or polymer matrix encapsulation have proven successful. Compounds such as silicone rubber were also found to be an appropriate containment system. Membranes can be made by coating fibre glass fabric, PVC coated polyester fabric and silicone-coated fibre glass fabric by incorporating the PCM silicone rubber.

This technology has been used in architecture, especially in roof membrane structures, to improve their thermal performance. The PCM starts to absorb the heat provided by the solar radiation as soon as the membrane material's temperature exceeds a certain value. During This heat absorption, the temperature of the membrane material remains constant.

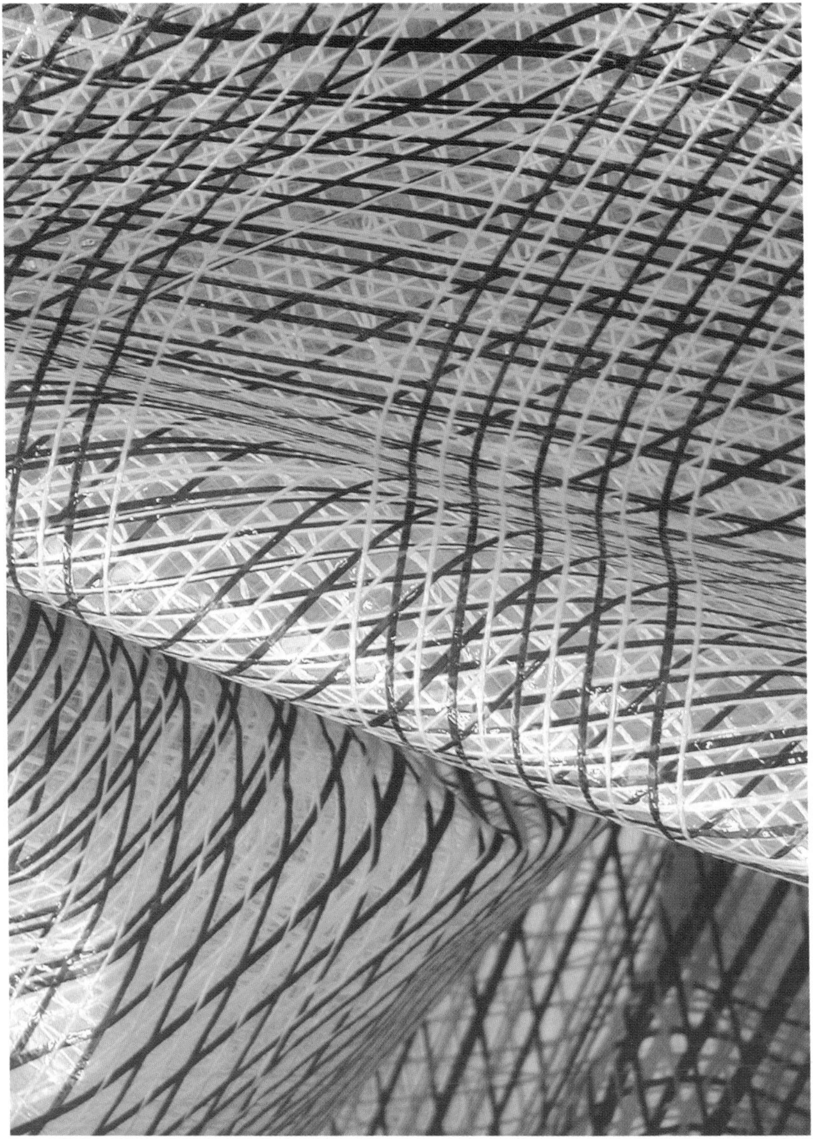

PROCESS TECHNIQUE

173

PROCESS TECHNIQUE

For the last two decades, new materials have been identified as a source of revolutionary technologies. These revolutionary technologies have been introduced with in highly specialised fields that, in very few cases, have started to be applied to architecture.

As previously mentioned, the exponential introduction of new materials during the final decades of the twentieth century has initiated change within the culture of materials. On the one hand, this phenomenon was followed by an obvious increase of potential applications, and on the other, by the loss of knowledge, information and control on the part of the end user—in our case, the designer.

At this point, it is necessary to clarify that technology refers either to the process through which the material, being more or less innovative, is produced, or to the process used to apply the material in an innovative process or use.

Hence, the first definition of technology is in the sphere of materials themselves, or more precisely, in the predefined sphere of designed materials. Thus, intervening in the technological process of material production signifies working on the manufacturing process that is developed ad hoc for a specific application. In other words, this is a made to measure material.

The second definition considers a technological approach with higher creativity levels. When discussing fields of application, one can bring up a wide range of possibilities for experimentation using an approach that is more related to design. This second definition of technology is the main focus of this chapter.

There is no doubt that in order to increase the possibility for the technological applications of a specific material, it is necessary to begin with a profound understanding of its ability. In other words, knowledge of every applicable technological process that concerns that material is required. This is the only possible way to discover new and more interesting applications that can be further investigated and validated. Regarding this last thought, technology that is considered 'third level' becomes radically important for the validating process.

Technologies grouped under the label 'rapid prototyping' represent, at the moment, an enormous challenge in architecture. This technology is able to very quickly test and validate the significance of applied intuition possibilities through the creation of a model that, in respect to various research parameters, is considered a prototype. Within the design process, however, this technology becomes an important tool for designing.

The opportunity of materialising a prototype using CAD (Computer Aided Design or Drafting) is a critical step towards facilitating the reduction of processing time and thus a decrease in production costs; The possibility of producing complex and easily controlled shapes, already tailored and adjusted at the drafting stage, contributes to more advanced design control.

These technologies generally use three dimensional modelling processes assembled through two dimensional simplification: horizontal sections of a complex form are organised by overlapping layers that are easily and quickly processed in CAD. It is important to note how precisely CAD software applications have influenced first research, and then application, by raising qualitative aspects and rationalisation of the process.

Considering other examples of 'technologies as tools' within the body of research, one must also note those that belong to the sphere of 'process with lost form', such as plaster moulding, investment casting, green sand casting, resin blinder moulding, and lost foam.

For example, the lost foam technique allows for several possibilities regarding the creation of a specific product in place of other more conventional mouldings, such as 'gravity casting process'. Advantages include the possibility of rapidly obtaining a single form out of a single block without using a core; reusing sand without any particular treatment; processing different metals; and that there are no limitations on object geometry normally imposed by the moulding and the core complexity. All of these techniques have the potential to easily achieve complex forms within a very short processing time.

New technological developments, along with new materials, are initiating a shift away from conventional technological approaches. This is understood as an improvement on previously known processes for optimising products, and leads has led to new experimental, innovative and less rigorous approaches. This can create new possibilities for expressing complex shapes.

Certain issues tackled within technological research are:
· the complexity of form
· the processing of difficult-to-handle materials
· the reduction of the component's weight
· the reduction of waste material
· the reduction of machine work and, consequently processing time
· the efficiency and subsequent economic advantages

It is apparent that technological research is responding to certain requirements, including the ability to generate complicated shapes; process materials that are difficult to process; gain efficiency and so cut production costs; reduce the component weight; and reduce processing time, the machine process and waste of materials.

The field of architecture is certainly not one of the major users of new experimental technologies. In general, a designer has no relevant economic support for this kind of research in comparison to fields that use different scientific models for the application of innovative technologies.

However, it is necessary to mention that, within the field of architecture, there are often technological aspects that are pure research, and where research into parameters is very relevant to the experimentation process. A few important examples are the research on materials by Herzog De Meroun, the considerable investigation by OMA for the Prada design project, and several research centres that are operating in the field of innovative materials. Materia, in Rotterdam, is an example of a research centre that mainly addresses application and design rather than materials themselves. Following this mandate, Materia is quickly advancing towards filling this gap by conducting important experiments in technology research.

There are eleven technological applications introduced in this chapter. Some of these applications were investigated by students who were researching the approach of the technology. In many cases, students used their research to establish a link, through the use of innovative materials, between the initial field of the application technologies and the field of architecture, always starting from a theoretical position that defined very clearly the objectives of the research.

PROCESS TECHNIQUE
PERFORMANCE/MATERIAL IDENTIFICATION

SHAPE PERFORMANCE	OPTICAL PERFORMANCE	SUSTAINABLE PERFORMANCE	INTEGRATED PERFORMANCE	RESPONSIVE PERFORMANCE

SHAPE PERFORMANCE	OPTICAL PERFORMANCE	SUSTAINABLE PERFORMANCE	INTEGRATED PERFORMANCE	RESPONSIVE PERFORMANCE
PARABEAM	CRINKLE GLASS	TENNAGE	ENKARDIN	AQUACLEAN
X -TEND		3D-VENDER	GLASS CYLINDERS	TECHNOGEL
PRESSLOAD	SHIMMER	FOAMGLASS	CUBEN FIBER	LUMISTY
WEB PLATES	PVC	POROUS CERAMICS	TRIAXAL FABRIC	LUMINEX
WOVEN WIRE MESH	3D RADIANT COLOR FILM	AEROGEL	DIAX-LSP	TEMPUR
STRUCTURAL PLATE	LEXAN	ALUSION AL.FOAM	CARBON-GLASS	RE LIQUID CRYSTAL SHEET
SUPERFORM ALUMINIUM	STARLIGHT	INSOLCORE	B-CLEAR GLASS	SHAPE MEMORY TEXTILE
FLEXIBLE HONEYCOMB		KAPILUX	SIBU MULTI-STYLE	GLASS SOUND
3D - TEX	REEMAY SPUNBONDED	ETFE MEMBRANE	TYFO FIBREWRAP	OPERATOR GLASS
TORHEX HONEYCOMB	YST	3M OPTICAL LIGHT	FIBRE REINFORCED	POWER GLASS
FORMETAL	MICA LAMINATES	CFAMC	CORIAN	OUTLAST
	PANELITE IGU			
	LITRACON			

· On the left page, the table shows a list of the relevant performance of each material
  under the five categories.
· On the right page, the table shows a column with a list of the selected process
  techniques and a column thatshows the student who used each process technique, and
  the name of their case study.

MATERIAL PROFILE	PROCESS TECHNIQUE	CASE STUDY APPLICATIONS
	SELECTIVE LASER SINTERING	Kiwoong Ko and Alexandros Vazakas/ Demand Versus Geometry
	STEREOLITOGRAPHY	Yoria Gabriel/Lost Form Andrea Fiecther/ How is Material Informing Architecture
	HYDROFORMING	
	LOST FOAM CASTING	Yoria Gabriel/Lost Form
	3DL TECHNOLOGY	
	5-6 AXIS MILLING MACHINERY	Yoria Gabriel/Lost Form
	SPACE FRAME	Noa Haim/Vertical Kibbutz
	WET LAY-UP	Andrea Fiecther/ How is Material Informing Architecture
	MONOCOQUE	Andrea Fiecther/How is Material Informing Pieterjan Vermoortel/Vertical City
	BOLIDECK SYSTEMS	Pieterjan Vermoortel/Vertical City
	TWISTED WINDOWS	Pieterjan Vermoortel/Vertical City

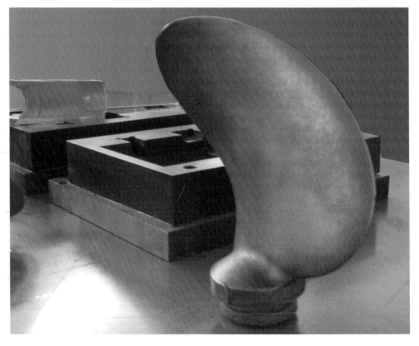

MATERIAL & TECHNOLOGY RESEARCH PROCESS TECHNIQUE

Manufacturer
  Centro Sviluppo Materiali SpA
  Via di Castel Romano, 100
  00128 Rome
  Italy
  info@c-s-m.it
  www.c-s-m.it
  t: +39 065055829
  f: +39 065055202
Introduction year
  · 1972
Properties
  · rapid prototyping
    techniques
Eco-efficient
  · reduced time to
    market, no scrap
Current applications
  · single prototype production
  · patterns for moulds
  · functional models for
    mechanics and industry
  · rapid tooling
Further applications
  · low number series
  · components design
Case study applications
  · Kiwoong Ko and
    Alexandros Vazakas,
    Demand Versus Geometry

Selective laser sintering (SLS) is a technique that uses the powder of several materials (thermoplastics, wax, metals, ceramics) to generate functional prototypes that have final properties very similar to the end product. In the process of selective laser sintering, a CO_2 laser beam is focused on a power bead. This focusing is obtained by means of actuated mirrors controlled by a computer.

A variety of thermoplastic materials such as nylon, glass-filled nylon, and polystyrene are available. Surface finishes and accuracy are not quite as good as with stereolithograhy, but material properties can be quite close to those of the intrinsic materials. For example, nylon powder is used to produce functional prototypes which have a strength of 90 per cent respect to the same obtained by conventional injection moulding. The best materials to use are thermoplastics, polymers and low to medium melting point metals.

The most productive material is polystyrene due to its low melting point which also minimises the shrinkage problems. Polystyrene models can also be used for casting, even if a wax infiltration pre-treatment is needed to avoid the slurry infiltration into the porosity. An epoxy infiltration is also possible in order to obtain higher strength and density without a significant impact on the production time, which is, in any case, less than with stereolithography.

Metallic powder sintering can be combined with Hot Isostatic Pressing (HIP) to obtain a higher final density and, consequently, improved mechanical properties, allowing the use of the prototype as a finished component.

STERIOLITHOGRAPHY
MANUFACTURING TECHNIQUE

Steriolithography (SLA) is a rapid prototyping (RP) technique based on the polymerisation of a liquid resin by means of UV light emitted from a laser source and focused on the polymer bath surface through mirrors. Four different technologies are involved in SLA: Laser, optic, polymer chemistry and software. The process consists of four main steps: First, a mathematical three dimensional model (CAD) of the component is needed. The native CAD is converted into a proper file format, called STL, for processing into the RP machine. Polymerisation then follows, with the model being built from the resin by a computer controlled procedure. After this comes post-treatment and completion of the polymerisation process, with all liquid parts included in the solidified model through a different process (the laser is used only to generate the model skins and other structural details). Finally, the supports are removed and the surface is cleaned and hand finished.

The materials used are high performance polymers. The most common are acrylic, with low viscosity, used for aesthetic models or anatomic parts and allowing low production times but lower precision; and epoxy, with high viscosity, used for high precision parts (functional prototypes). Other materials used include resin, for parts with elastomer like properties, and vinyl resins for investment casting applications. SLA can give good performances in terms of dimensional accuracy, allowing for the production of complex shapes and low thickness details with a good surface even before the final manual finishing. In the industrial field it is used for conceptual, functional and pre-release prototypes.

Manufacturer
  RP²
  Hagemuntweg 35
  4879 NM Etten-Leur
  The Netherlands
  rp2@rp2.nl
  www.rp2.nl
  t: +31 765089742
  f: +31 765089743
Introduction year
  · 1987
Properties
  · rapid prototyping
    techniques
Eco-efficient
  · reduced time to market
  · no scrap
Current applications
  · industry
  · medicine
Further applications
  · design
  · foundries and forges
Case study applications
  · Andrea Fiecther
    How is Material
    Informing Architecture?
  · Yorai Gabriel,
    Lost Form

3DL TECHNOLOGY
THREE-DIMENSIONAL LAMINATED SAILS

3DL technology is a laminate sail-making technology which closely resembles boat making: seamless sails of a maximum of 27 by 33 metres are made by carbon or kevlar fibres being sandwiched between two layers of mylar, an extraordinarily strong polyester film. Because the structural fibres are woven into a fabric, they can be aligned precisely along predicted load paths in the sail. First, an articulated mould assumes the designed shape. Mylar film is then draped over the mold and tensed. An armature suspended from a moving gantry overhead then applies structural fibre onto the surface of the film. The computerised armature 'draws' a pattern that precisely matches anticipated loads in the sail. Threads are applied under uniform tension and adhere to the surface of the film.

Once the yarns are laid, a second film is positioned on top of the sail, which is then covered with a large vacuum bag that compresses the laminate. The gantry head is then removed and replaced with a radiant heating element that cures the pressurised laminate. After curing, the sail is left on the mould to 'set' the shape. When the laminate has cured, corner reinforcements, bolt ropes, batten pockets and protective patches are applied by hand. The finished sail, produced in one continuous piece, is up to 30 per cent lighter than a conventional sail. Weight savings are achieved principally by a more efficient application of material in relation to stresses in the sail. The product can potentially be used for architecture, as it can produce a smooth compound curvature in all directions, amongst other qualities.

Manufacturer
North Sails
2379 Heybourne Rd
Minden, NV 89423 USA
T: +1 7757827744
F: +1 7757827747
bill@3dl.northsails.com
Contact: Bill Pearson
www.northsails.com

Introduction year
· 1992

Properties
· **excellent tensile strength/weight ratio**
· **high flexibility**
· **customisable**

Eco-efficient
· **lightweight**

Current applications
· **sails**

HYDROFORMING

Hydroforming is a forming technique based on high water pressure stamping material against a die. The initial material can be either a tube or a sheet, cut to defined dimensions and then closed into a die. Filling the die with water causes the material to deform and adopt the shape of the die surface, so obtaining the desired shape. With this technique it is possible to produce final shape components in a single stroke, instead of conventional stamping and assembly of sub-parts by riveting or welding.

It is possible to obtain lighter components (through flanges in assembly elimination) with better performance (greater stiffness and fatigue resistance) and aesthetic possibilities. Other operations, like piercing, can be integrated into the same process by further reducing the same manufacturing phases. Special operations, like forming with undercut (impossible with conventional punch and die stamping) are also possible by using special dies.

Hydroforming is a proven technology with cost and performance benefits fully demonstrated for tube-like components, and widely used in many car body details. Both steel and aluminium alloys can be formed, while other materials can be used too (Ti alloys), but their application is limited to very special cases. Hydroforming is performed by dedicated hydraulic presses, which are used to close the die and are equipped with a special high pressure unit for the water filling that is fully integrated with the press hydraulics. Current applications in the automotive industry include windshields, engine cradles, engine exhaust manifolds, body panels, truck axles, and motorcycle and bike frame components.

Manufacturer
    Centro Sviluppo Materiali SpA
    Via di Castel Romano 100
    00128 Rome
    Italy
    info.hydroforming@schuler.com
    www.c-s-m.it
    t: +39 065055829
    f: +39 065055202
Introduction year
    · 1970–1980
Properties
    · lightweight design
    · improved material formability
    · complex shapes manufacturing
Eco-efficient
    · lightweight applications for
      efficient full consumption
    · reduced manufacturing costs
Current applications
    · automotive industry
    · aeronautics industry
Further applications
    · motorcycles
    · interior design

Manufacturer
  Mercury Castings
  W6250-106 Pioneer Road
  PO Box 1939
  Fond du Lac
  Wisconsin 54936 1939
  USA
  castingsinfo@mercmarine.com
  www.mercurycastings.com
Introduction year
  · 1986
Properties
  · obtain rapidly a form
    in a unique block and
    without using a core
  · reuse sands without
    any particular treatment
  · process different metals
  · use endless casting
    geometry
Case study applications
  · Yorai Gabriel,
    Lost Form

Lost foam casting is created by first moulding desired shapes in polystyrene (foam).

These foam segments are then glued together to form a pattern when multiple pieces are needed due to the parts' complexity. The pattern is then glued to a sprue (multiple patterns glued to a sprue are called a cluster) and dipped into a ceramic slurry (which creates a semi-permeable coating).

The coated cluster is placed into a flask which is then filled with sand. While the flask is being filled, it is vibrated so that the sand will fill all the voids in the coated pattern and create compacted sand, which will support the cluster. Molten aluminum is then poured into a pouring cup (attached to the foam sprue) which will pyrolise (evaporate) the foam cluster and fill the space where the foam was. After the metal solidifies, the metal cluster is pulled from the flask and the coating is flashed off in the quench tank. The individual pieces are sawed from the cluster, thus creating complex castings.

Typical applications for foam parts include parts that would require many pieces, formed by other process, to be assembled. Lost foam casting allows complex internal features that are not possible in other casting technologies. Cylinder heads, engine blocks, manifolds, and other complex parts are potential candidates for this process. The parts will have good dimensional accuracy, will not require a sand core, and will have less gasket surfaces, as many of the pieces are cast together.

5–6 AXIS MILLING MACHINERY
CINCINNATI, 5 AXIS, 3-SPINDLE CNC GANTRY PROFILERS

5 and 6 axis milling machinery is a large group of industrial CNC machines made for performing complex geometries, carving, cutting and milling in different volumes. Offering greater geometrical capabilities than 3 axis or flat top machines (2 axis), the 5 and 6 axis machines are taking the place of older CNC machines as the next generation of automated manufacturing for complex parts varied from prototype mock-ups and moulds, with the ability to operate on a variety of materials from dense wood and plastics to aluminium and foams.

CNC products are based on digital representations making them a convenient tool for plotting geometrically complex three dimensional volumes. The technical specifications are as follows. Cincinnati 5-axis, 3-spindle CNC gantry profilers. Expanded Y-axis, 40 inches between centres, 15 feet wide x 60 feet long beds (identical machines). Capability of machining full bed width with a single spindle. 70 HP spindles, +30° spindle tilt, 40 to 7,000 RPM. 20-station tool changers (each spindle).

Capable of machining the full 13 inches bed width with a single spindle. Offering the capability to machine three parts simultaneously, with an approximate size of 4 x 60 inches: or a single part with a maximum size of 13 x 60 inches.

CNC machinery is often used in the aeronautical and ship building industry, for the production of aeroplane parts, surfboards and hulls for boats.

Manufacturer
Cincinnati Machine UK Limited
PO Box 505
Kingsbury Road
Birmingham
B24 0QU
UK
website@cincinmach.co.uk
www.cinmach.co.uk
t: +44 1213513821
f: +44 1213517891

Introduction year
· not available

Properties
· lowest work piece processing cost in comparison to other limited axis milling machinery
· complex geometries can be produced
· extremely accurate
· automated process
· ability to operate on large volumes

Eco-efficient
· cost-effective processing
· recyclable processed material
· indoor operation
· electric

Current applications
· used for cutting and milling of various materials from wood to aluminium

Case study applications
· Yorai Gabriel, Lost Form

MATERIAL & TECHNOLOGY RESEARCH PROCESS TECHNIQUE

Manufacturer
  Mero Systeme GmbH & Co KG
  Max-Mengeringhausen
  strasse 5
  D-97084 Wurzburg
  Germany
  info@mero.de
  www.mero.com
  t: +49 93166700
  f: +49 9316670409
Introduction year
  · 1930
Properties
  · maximising
    span length
  · no corrosion
  · flexible and
    yet infinite grid
Eco-efficient
  · lightweight
  · pre-assembling
Current applications
  · indoor/outdoor
  · architecture,
    particularly roofs
    and canopies
  · civil engineering,
    particularly bridges
Case study applications
  · Noa Haim,
    Vertical Kibbutz

A space frame is usually an open, three-dimensional framework of struts and braces which define a structure and distribute its weight evenly in all dimensions. This multi-axial load distribution serves to reduce the member forces and thus leads to lightweight and filigree structures. The system consists of members and nodes with a pin joint or bending resistant connections. The choice of the member length and their angles is linked to the loads which are to be carried. In plan view, they can establish a triangular grid or a quadrangular grid, while in section they can formulate single, double or triple layer.

As a product, space frames are delivered to the site as a pre-engineered kit, which is very simple and quick to assemble. Every structure piece can be easily lifted by a single worker, and even the unique space frames system requires only one bolt per joint. No special tools or skills are required. Space frame structures can be remotely pre-assembled to not interfere with other site activities, and are easily moveable to the final position required. Unless otherwise demanded, nodes are plated by electro-galvanisation while the nuts are plated by hot dipping or electro-galvanisation.

Due to their capacity to adopt almost any shape, and their light weightness of and large spanning, they are used for a variety of applications in the architectural and industrial fields. They can be used for all building envelopes, atriums, facades, canopies, special roofs such as the Globe Arena in Stockholm, and bridges. They are also viable in large scale storage spaces, due to the structure to space ratio they provide.

WET LAY-UP
FABRICATION PROCESS FOR FIBRE REINFORCES PLASTIC

For the process of wet lay-up; laminates use a mould to introduce the form, whereas the core of the sandwich composite introduces the form. This simple way of form introduction gives the material an unsurpassed formal freedom and allows a non-standardised pre-fabrication and non-standardised mass production.

Materials options include resins, such as epoxy, polyester, vinylester, phenolic; and any fibres, although heavy, thick fabrics can be hard to wet-out by hand. The fibres are in the form of woven, knitted, stitched or bonded fabrics. Cores such as foams, honeycomb and wood can also be used.

The main advantages of this process is that it can be widely used for many years, the principles are simple to teach, tooling is low cost if room-temperature core resins are used, wide choice of suppliers and material types available.

Unfortunately, there are disadvantages to using this method, which can produce varied results, as the resin mixing, laminate resin contents, and laminate quality are very dependent on the skills of the laminators. There are also health and safety considerations regarding using resins.

Manufacturer
SP Systems
St Cross Business Park
Newport
Isle of Wight
PO30 5WU
UK
katie.currie@gurit.com
www.spsystem.com
t: +44 236791114
f: +44 236799975

Introduction year
· not available

Properties
· lightweight
· cost-effective processing
· recycling not solved
· health and safety
  consideration of resins

Current applications
· indoor/outdoor
· marine
· transport
· design
· construction
· architecture

Case study applications
· Andrea Fiecther,
  How is Material
  Informing Architecture?

Introduction year
· 1930—first aluminium
  monocoque for airplanes
Properties
· excellent strength/
  weight ratio
· very thin for long spans
· equal distribution of forces
Eco-efficient
· lightweight
Current applications
· inside/outside
· boat construction
· airplane construction
· architecture
  and construction
Case study applications
· Pieterjan Vermoortel,
  Vertical City
· Andrea Fiecther,
  How is Material
  Informing Architecture?

The product is composed of three (monocoque) or two (semi-monocoque) layers of structural elements. The outside layers take two main kinds of force, shear and tension, while the middle layer takes the pressure. To do so, all layers should be connected directly to each other. The outside layers are preferably only one surface, consisting of a highly tension-resistant material like steel (heavy), high quality aluminium (expensive), or a composite with high strength fibres (glass fibre). The layers should also have a minimal surface shape, so as to maximise the force and minimise the pressure. A thinner and lighter structure will then be achieved.

The middle material should be thick enough to withstand the pressure and should not be a continuous surface, but more like a grid holding the outer skins in position. The material should preferably be the same as that used for the skin (normally aluminium or titanium), to ensure a seamless connection between the two. Until now, it has been very hard to connect different materials to each other unless they are mixed on totally different scales. First, the middle structure is fabricated and the surface shape is defined. After this, the outside layers are seamlessly connected to the structure preferably by welding as this creates one inseparable material.

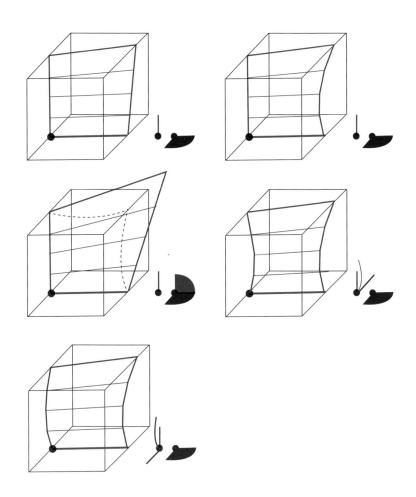

Manufacturer
Alcoa Architectuur Systemen
Daltonstraat 17
Postbus 391
3846 BX Harderwijk
The Netherlands
aasverkoop@alcoa.com
www.alcoa-
architectuursystemen.nl
t: +31 341464611
f: +31 341467350
Introduction year
· experimental
Properties
· possibility to have straight
  and easy-to-construct
  frame
Eco-efficient
· thermal insulation
· sound insulation
· cost-effective processing
  through repetition
  of the frame
Current applications
· indoor/outdoor
· architecture
  and construction
Case study applications
· Pieterjan Vermoortel,
  Vertical City

Twisted surface glass panels consist of two surfaces of hot deformed glass and a twisted frame. The novelty of this product lies in the fact that it uses a ruled surface for the geometry of the glass. Therefore, the frame can be easily mass-produced because it consists of straight elements, while the glass is double curved.

Before this geometrical was applied within the glass industry, you had the option to use double curved single layered glass panels without a frame (which results in low thermal and sound insulating) or to divide the double curved surface into faceted straight glass panels with a frame (which diminishes the optical effect). The main property of the panels is that by rigorously following the rule of ruled surfaces, you achieve straight edges on the glass panels. This means that you can make a frame consisting of straight elements, which is very cost-effective and possibly the only practical way of making a frame. The frame ensures that you can use double glass on its own or filled with an intermediary element. This results in better sound and thermal insulation and higher durability then normal used glass systems for double curved skins.

Twisted surface glass is still in prototype stage, and is undergoing, testing in a 150 metre tower designed by De architecten Cie, Vollers architecten at Arena south-east Amsterdam.

PROTOTYPE RESEARCH

DOMESTICATING TECHNOLOGY TRANSFER
Igor Kebel

High-rise developments and housing standardisations are notably one of the strongest, if not justifiably, the strongest, typological architectural achievements of the twentieth century. This is not without reason, and not without impressive consequences for the practice itself. Watching this state of emergence from the inside, it seems that the progress of knowledge production about the housing industry is proceeding only by degrees of refinement of previous operations in the past, thus mainly accumulating prior experience and trying to make it more concise. The experience is based on empirical knowledge, structures which are already given and known. So, why challenge well established practices?

This answer lies partially within the externalisation of the industry, which is in the process of merging differentiated production establishments. Then again, why not question the tower-like typology, which has never managed to fully supplement suburban dwelling habits: The typology that nature belongs to the horizontal, and that the artificial belongs to the vertical? One must acknowledge the fact that not just the population boom or evolutionary social and economical practices, but also technological inventions and material improvements, have substantially contributed to the establishment of specific housing conventions, which survived their intense development path from the prototypical to the stereotypical (typological) stage.

Throughout the entire history of domestic individual and collective spaces is the notion of materia strongly signifying all architectural actualisations. New inventions in industry often changed housing paradigms irreversibly; let us not forget, for instance, the origins of Domino. Can one think about the continuous flexibility of a modernistic floorplan without the predetermination of the structural grid? Is not the economical form of a prefab the one which was most instrumental to the modular ambition of shaping the new world? The history of inhabitable organisations is more engineered than designed—is an art of compromise.

Architectural research into the design techniques of the last two decades is thresholding another phenomenon of a particular typological achievement. It is as a result of the effect-driven research of form-finding organisations, which was never previously as successful, progressive and present as it is today. The dialectic of this particular research is facing suspension or succession of the given promise of the actualisation, of the materialisation. Where is the ambition to build, and to materialise these prototypes?

Furthermore, how do we move into a daily routine organisation without being reductive with recent design-driven-production? How do we learn from disciplines which are combining everyday convenience with advances in design? What should we understand from this new materiality, and what can it offer to its users in the end? Although these seem not to be entirely new questions at all, and even resemble even some unpopular past evocations, there is a clear challenge to practice. If there are questions for the new design model of the practice, then there has to be an intelligence to also surpass it. One should not confuse emerging technologies which are engineering and shaping our solidified surroundings with the emerging engineering of design tools: design tools are in the process of only delivering a local state of design stability, whereby production industries can deliver a global state of production design stability.

Daily design practice is inevitably moving into the circular, perhaps even spiral, model, where specialists from other disciplines are entering the design team at an ever earlier stage, without being considered only plug-in collaborators as an after thought and any architectural practitioner with the ambition to build is aware of. This involving more scientific, artistic and technocratic disciplines is not new, but the state space of their participation perhaps may be. And yet, where should we place these omnipresent propagations of new material and technological myths, how do we appropriate the knowledge of the emerging techné? What realisation is it going to take now, what are all the virtualities of the near future of and dwelling geometries?

DESIGN MODEL INTELLIGENCE
Igor Kebel

Hundreds of scientists, mathematicians, engineers and illustrators, amongst many others were registering their patents for the ideal shape of a paper clip. The Norwegian Johan Vaaler is usually, and falsely, called the inventor of the paper clip, as he registrered his patent in 1901, for the design sheet for, what we recognise still today, as the Gem clip. However, William Middlebrook patented a machine in 1899 that would make wire paper clips. There could be many shapes of clip that can hold a pile of papers just about as well as, if not better than, a Gem, but the ability to manufacture the clips reliably and in large quantities is what can make or break a company.

This analogy of performance driven design intelligence, is based on knowledge transfer, and on the production of knowledge. The research work of the Domesticating Technology Transfers studio involves investigating the dwelling potential and emerging technological transfers for mixed housing solutions in Madrid on various scales; from reinvention of structural forms to reconsiderations of economical and programmatic forms. The studio also searches for the relational sustainability of new understandings about geometrical ecologies. Some explicit material transfers, which were largely ignored or not yet used for the domestic tower-like organisations are also considered. The relationships that may radically affect building typologies are between new production technologies, emerging programmes and typologies and are linked with recent technological developments in connection with ongoing social changes.

The studio is, questioning, among other things the potential of technology transfers and the application of new technologies to our every-day experience of the housing industry—one of the most critical subjects in Europe today. As European economies shift towards services and the traditional family structure collapses, the demand for residential units is doubling around large cities. The convergence between these technical, topological, and typological issues was the subject of this advanced research group, which worked in collaboration with the Department of Experimental Housing of Madrid Local Government, Empresa Municipal de Vivienda y Suelo.

How should we understand the restrictive norms of current housing standards and make known market possibilities into an integral set of new organisational topologies? How are we to liberate them into the matrix of design opportunities? What are the parameters of material performance, structural novelties, and the inhabitation norms of everyday dwelling spaces? How are we to create their relational dependencies?

All contributors are ultimately testing their prototype performance at the given location in Madrid. Researching different streams of transfers, either technological or material, as well as but also relational and immaterial, it is about defining rigorous parametric conclusions which are measurable in terms of a building's geometry and the performance of the materials. The research question here is not only how to make a project buildable, but foremost how to make it inhabitable. Hence this collective study on technology and the domestic sphere.

How can materials inform specific architecture? How can an operational architectural form be informed with the dynamics of technological transfer?

High-rise ecologies, structural housing geometry, customisation strategies and industry transfers are clustered families within this collective effort. Varying in the starting point of their research, the finished design of each prototype is inevitably captured into dialectic negotiations between matter-form and container-content.

Thoughts about high-rise ecologies cannot be detached from the interrelationship of material organisms and housing environments. It would be too reductive to understand these feasibility studies purely numerically. Why not design in accordance with the natural light, why are we only theorising and not practicing such an important design feature of our daily environments? Why can't we start orchestrating the political notion of a 'green house' (beyond energy consumption) into a multilayered and relational design decision-making matrix, including all disciplinary intelligence which is producing intrinsic geometrical formations? Is there a way to transfer low-rise rural communal models of living-together into urban high-rise organisations? Can we actually transfer organisational otherness into the housing industry?

Structural housing geometry should be seen as the study of properties of given housing elements that remain unvaried under specific transformation. The history of tower like solutions crystalised widely acceptable solutions. Recent corporate solutions are clear about risk-free structural postulations which are governed by a financial and organisational marriage, based on risk eliminations, and the vertical space today is a huge prefab, with a face-lifting enclosure, called facade. So, what do we do with the extremes of the horizontal and the vertical? Is the diagonal or the spiral really a complete organisational oxymoron for vertical space? What about vertical continuity and staged experiences for new organisational encounters? And how do we inhabit the slope?

Current policies of advanced economies are largely deploying the notion of tailored individuality, even on the level of mass consumption and product placements. We know that customisation strategies are not new. But once again, how can we borrow these principles for common and habitual use? Do we have to become business consultants or to rigorously 'consult' our organisational geometries with new workstyles and lifestyles beyond the marketing appropriation?

Last but not least, we are surrounded by industry transfers; recent diligence in the deployment of industrial solutions from other industries can be systematically studied for useful purpose within the housing sector. Here, the notion of architectural digitalisation plays a significant role. For some time now, our daily goods have been produced and served behind invisible process of automation and seamless ventures between the creators and the producers. The in-forming process of matter and form is looping without the postponements and translation of meanings. Should we not reconsider this position?

STUDIO PROJECT BRIEF

Type

A columnless, high-rise organisation; a mixed programme, dominated by housings units/cells. We shall question the term 'high-rise' in terms of verticality and horizontality, as it is expected that emerging technologies will eventually be able to question, and possibly supplement, this strain of gravitational radicalism in contemporary architectural practice.

The following research will question the design process in terms of matter, technology and industrial process, without focusing exclusively on this methodological externalisation. How is matter informing architectural organisation and how can we domesticate these transfers? Which new future organisations can we disseminate?

Programming and Capacity

The total area of floor space needs to be at least 8,000 metres squared and not more than 10,000 metres squared. At least 70 per cent of the total building area must be domestic apartments and the other 30 per cent must embrace new ways of creating multi-functional spaces or 'mixed programmes. The mixed programme is dedicated to 'time-share' spaces, which could include rental office cubicles for business starters, multipurpose presentation/meeting rooms, recreational services and facilities (saunas, fitness centres, swimming pools) reception lobbies, community centres, event spaces and parking facilities (0.7 cars per housing unit) on the site.

The housing units must include varying room sizes with varying spatial distribution from single person units to traditional family set-ups. All norms of accessibility (i.e. for the disabled) and security (private property, communal spaces, public exchange) must also be taken into consideration.

Location

The demarcation area for the project is within the bracket of 21 × 21 metres. The height is limited to a range of 20 to 30 levels, although there is no specific height limit. The proposal would have to involve the concept of adaptive flexibility; how can we instrumentalise the organisation with the principle of adaptability to any location? Can we think about the proposal topologically, so that the organisation can change its own orientation, accessibility, landscaping and connectivity with the local environmental conditions to any (other) urban circumstances?

Organisation

The materialisation of the incorporeal is also what we will call the 'critical' geometry, through which we can locate a dialogue between the extremes of programmatic, social, financial, technological and location forms. An extrapolation of emerging parameters would lend weight to the integrity of previously opposed elements. Secondly, the repetition of elements with their differentiation of events and programmatic behaviour could be called the organisational phase. Thirdly, synchronisation (of integral elements within the organisation) would be a final phase in the application of the critical geometry.

The activation of such prototypes within the critical geometry is often called for when a hybridisation of programme, structure and economics into a continuous variable is required. Thematic definition of an organisation throughout its scale-less homogeneity is another quality yielding out of the process. The build-up of atmospheres, modalities and moods with the geometry of multiplicities and custom-made device-orientated variables is thus another inevitable consequence of this method.

In other words, 'critical geometry' has nothing to do with the critique of any geometry, since not a single 'type' of geometry possesses any ideological ambition in its purest sense. The 'critical' here means more an emergent, adaptive and filtered geometry that embraces the daily experience of users, programmes, cultural politics, structures and economics into the geometrical set of relational properties without prior determinations.

The traditional, European family house of the nineteenth century was a hierarchy of rooms, into which corridors were incorporated relatively late. Yet there was room for a fireplace, which was supplemented only in the 1960s with a television. The central nucleus of social and public importance changed with the organisation of the house. 50 years later, there should be time to rethink the notion of a television within domestic environments; furthermore, the silent revolution (so-called 'information sprawl') is entering our secluded spaces and also spreading to more sophisticated realms. How to think reflexively and instrumentalise these adverse circumstances is another important research (design) criterion of this studio.

Typology versus Topology (Domino Redesigned)

The first association one has with the word 'typology' is a notion of predetermination, the application of this word within the housing industry implies that there is a more or less fixed market demand, and that there is likewise already some known solution for that demand. The central question, however, remains the same: under what circumstances does a prototype become a monotype, before it is turned into a stereotype? These three distinguished phases are not always completed and only few products/solutions are spanned within all of them. Most of the time, prototypes remain within their respective incubation phase. Monotypes eventually succeed in their materialisation, yet it is only a set of economical standards, the market behaviour and other dynamics that define the transition into stereotype (typology, to bring the discourse back into the architectural industry).

Such was the case with the establishment of the Domino prototype, in which economical pressures after big catastrophes (world war) collided with the invention of the fabrication techniques of reinforced concrete. Further formal reductionism changed structural constellations into the form of a grid; the 'free-forming' floor plan became standardised along with the lengths and weights of materials.

Beyond pure rhetoric, where all dominos are nowadays posited, how are they actualised, what are they controlling and with what are we activating them?

Borrowed Technologies

To continue the story about the notion of a 'type' and to build up a segue to the notion of 'technology', let us rethink the function of a fireplace, which was still widely used at least until the nineteenth century as the main heating device for most of Europe. For this reason, the position of fire or heat within the living organisation established an anthropomorphic status. The functional heating device determined the central (and hence hierarchical) space of a house.

It was not until the 1960s that the fireplace was supplemented with a television (and before that only marginally with a radio). The organisation of the house remained the same, regardless of the fact that the television was used for the consumption of different matter (data intrusion and reception) than the fireplace (heating). If we forget about the social reasons and background for this sort of stereotype, we suddenly realise that, even within the last 50 years, the typology of our houses did not transgress at all.

And if we disregard the impact of the silent (informational) revolution that is questioning the postulation of any 'fireplace-like' living typology, we should not neglect the latest efforts of engineers and scientists who brought us to the frontier of bioengineering. There must be space for architectural interventions even before this ultimate stage of technological progress.

New adaptive materials, rapid production techniques and new realms of economics established a ground for the research into prototype novelties.

Let us detect them first.

SUSTAINABILTY

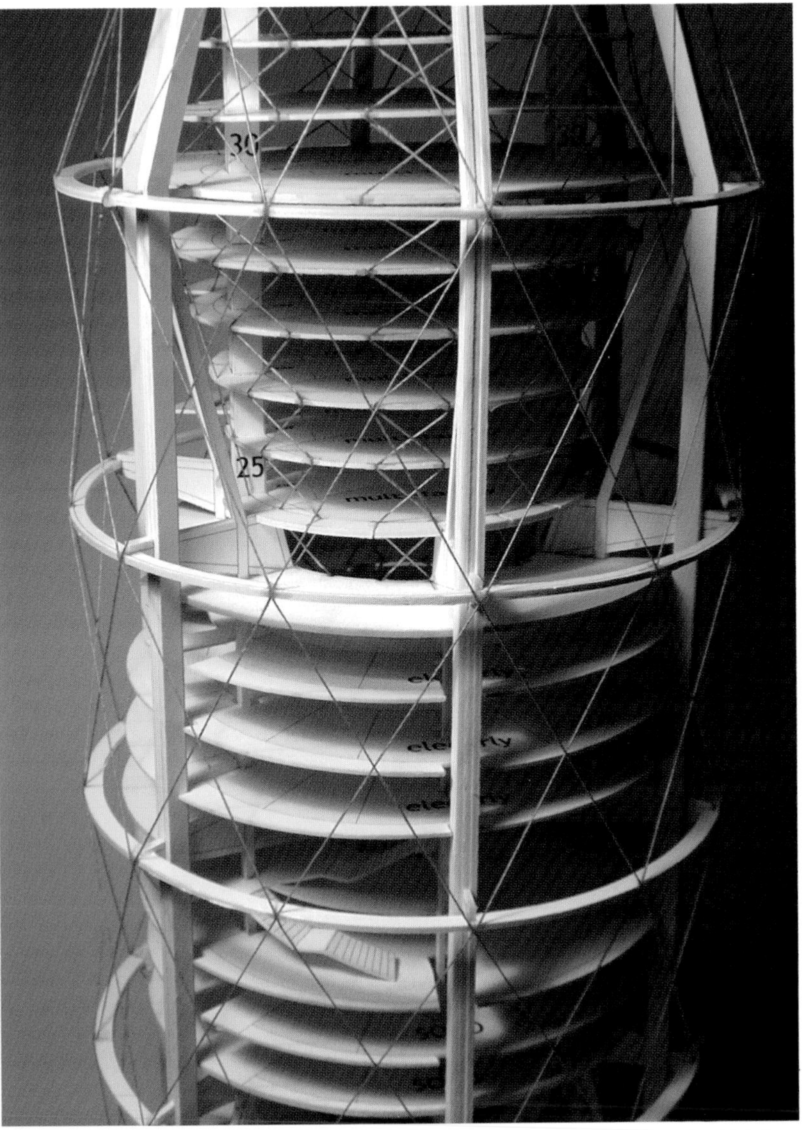
30
25

Hypothesis

What is the synthetic way to turn fragmented approaches of sustainability (economic, environmental and social approaches) into interconnected relations that could give us a geometric solution? This may only be possible if we consider overall parametric relations, such as energy, resources, and pollution on the basis of their respective architectural performance and geometric form, and optimise them into a prototype that is adaptive to the ever-changing environment.

Summary

Three fragmented approaches of sustainability have emerged in architecture; economic, environmental and social. The problem is not their agenda but their lack of connectivity. Due to this non-connectivity, the requirements of one of these criteria often contradicts those of another. For example, a less research-orientated economic approach sometimes results in lightweight but more pollutant-generating material. An architectural product is not a simple one and has a long life cycle; one should consider life-long assessment that spans a material's selection and construction, through building operation and maintenance, finally to waste treatment or recycling. Therefore, not only a synthetic, but also a long-term based approach has been developed in this thesis, by dealing with priorities and establishing their proper relations.

To do this, two crucial topics have been mainly investigated; selection and construction of materials based on recyclability, and building operation and maintenance. In the former consideration, the energy, resource consumption and CO_2 emission per required mass have been assessed to establish which materials are not only economically, but also environmentally, sound, with an emphasis on recycling.

New construction possibilities have been proposed to maximise the potential of the chosen material on the basis of this analysis. In the case of building operation and maintenance, the environmental approach has been developed to create economic sustainability by maximum use of natural resources, and to generate social interaction, which leads to social sustainability.

Methodology

In brief, the current approach has several problems. First, it is characterised by a weak connection between many different approaches. Secondly, it resembles a traditional manual in that it is rigid and delimiting. Thirdly, it is too additional and too reductive.

Against these related problems, the chosen methodology is exactly opposite in character. It is a synthetic solution that connects one approach to the other. It arrives from performance-based decisions and transformations into architectural geometry. More differentiated geometries which interact with various environmental situations have been employed.

In brief, the current sustainable approach has several problems, such as:

1 Weak connection between different approaches
2 Too 'manualistic'/no relation with architectural geometry and performance
3 Too additional, too reductive/weak interaction to ever-changing environmental performance

Against these current problems, my hypothesis and agenda is exactly the opposite:

1 Synthetic solution which connects one approach to the other
2 Drive up performance-based decision and transform it into architectural geometry
3 More differentiated geometry which interacts to various environmental situations

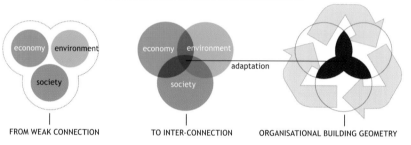

FROM WEAK CONNECTION   TO INTER-CONNECTION   ORGANISATIONAL BUILDING GEOMETRY

BREAKDOWN SUSTAINABILITY ISSUE INTO RESEARCH SUBJECTS

Among various subjects, three crucial topics will be researched through synthetic approach:

1 Material selection   2 Heating and cooling   3 Lift or vertical circulation organisation

Global impact of building industry

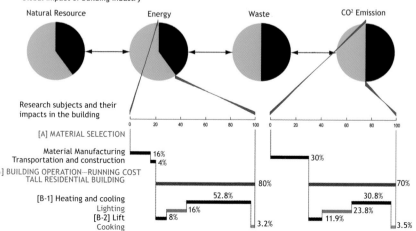

Natural Resource   Energy   Waste CO_2 Emission

Research subjects and their
impacts in the building

[A] MATERIAL SELECTION

Material Manufacturing — 16%
Transportation and construction — 4%   30%

] BUILDING OPERATION—RUNNING COST
TALL RESIDENTIAL BUILDING   80%   70%

[B-1] Heating and cooling   52.8%   30.8%
Lighting   16%   23.8%
[B-2] Lift   8%   11.9%
Cooking   3.2%   3.5%

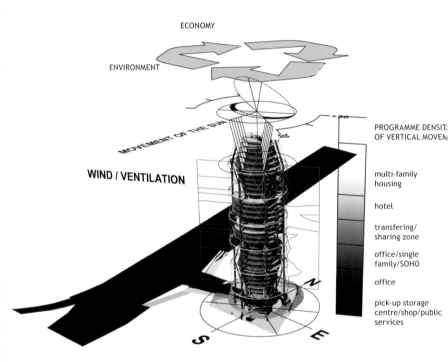

ECONOMY

ENVIRONMENT

MOVEMENT OF THE SUN

WIND / VENTILATION

S N E

PROGRAMME DENSIT
OF VERTICAL MOVEM

multi-family
housing

hotel

transfering/
sharing zone

office/single
family/SOHO

office

pick-up storage
centre/shop/public
services

In the selection of materials more than anything else, performance-based analysis has been carried out to find those that are sustainable in terms of low energy consumption and CO_2 emissions. To perform this analysis, not the per mass accounting like M/kg but the accounting per mass required for a particular structural function, it is best to refer to the terminologies of other disciplines such as material science, especially the concept of mass index.

And optimal architectural geometry has been employed with the sustainable materials that have been selected from the analysis by considering their individual properties.

In the research into building operation and maintenance, a synthetic methodology and solution which combines considerations of typical heat loss and solar gain has been employed in order to maximise the potential of heating and cooling operations. And this synthetic analysis leads to a more differentiated geometric solution which is able to more efficiently interact with ever-changing environmental conditions.

Finally, possible connections between an economic point of view and social interaction have been driven through prototypical hybrid programme organisations in the lift operation or vertical circulation topic.

ANALYSIS: ENERGY CONSUMPTION FOR CONSTRUCTION

research: less energy consumption-function: tensile strut and column/constrain: strength

				MANUFACTURING (m²)			TRANSPORTING FOR THE CONSTRUCTION				(TEC²)
Type	Material Option	Density	Failure Strength	Energy Content	Mass Index ρ / σ_f	Energy Index $\rho \cdot q$ / σ_f	transportation energy costs	Transportation distance	Mass Index	Energy Index	Total Energy Index
		(kg/m3)	(Mpa)	(MJ/kg)	(kg)	(MJ/kg)	MJ/(kg x km)	(km)	(kg)	(MJ/kg)	(MJ/kg)
Metal	Steel	7,850	328	32	23.9	766	0.005	160	24	19	785
	Aluminum	2,700	270	191	10.0	1,910	0.005	160	10	8	1,918
	Titanium alloy	4,480	845	1,000	5.3	5,302	0.005	160	5	4	5,306
Ceramic	Ceramic fiber - Aluminum oxide	3,960	2,950	20	1.3	27	0.005	160	1	1	28
Polymer	Carbon fiber	1,750	4,000	120	0.4	53	0.005	160	0	0	53
	PVC	1,380	50	59	27.6	1,628	0.005	160	28	22	1,650
Composite	Epoxy-Kevlar Composite	1,325	460	500	2.9	1,440	0.005	160	3	2	1,442
	Carbon Fiber Reinforced Plastic	1,400	250	460	5.6	2,576	0.005	160	6	4	2,580
	concrete	2,300	24	1.3	95.8	125	0.005	160	96	77	202

				MANUFACTURING (m²)			TRANSPORTING FOR THE CONSTRUCTION				(TEC²)
Type	Material Option	Density	Failure Strength	Energy Content	Mass Index ρ / σ_f	Energy Index $\rho \cdot q$ / σ_f	transportation energy costs	Transportation distance	Mass Index	Energy Index	Total Energy Index
		(kg/m3)	(Mpa)	(MJ/kg)	(kg)	(MJ/kg)	MJ/(kg x km)	(km)	(kg)	(MJ/kg)	(MJ/kg)
Metal	Recycled Steel	7,850	328	10	23.9	242	0.005	160	24	19	261
	Recycled Aluminum	2,700	270	8	10.0	81	0.005	160	10	8	89
	concrete	2,300	24	1.3	95.8	125	0.005	160	96	77	202

DATA MAINLY FROM
www.matweb.com

DATA MAINLY FROM
AIA: American Institute of Architects

DATA FROM
DEPA: Danish Environmental Protection Agency

ANALYSIS: CO² EMISSION FOR CONSTRUCTION

research: less CO² emission-function: tensile strut and column/constraint: strength

				MANUFACTURING (m²)			TRANSPORTING FOR THE CONSTRUCTION				(CE²)
Type	Material Option	Density	Failure Strength	CO2 emission	Mass Index ρ / σ_f	Emission Index $\rho \cdot q$ / σ_f	transportation CO2	distance	Mass Index	Emission Index	Total Emission Index
		(kg/m3)	(Mpa)	(kg CO2/ton)	(kg)	(kg CO2)	(kg CO2/tonkm)	(km)	(kg)	(kg CO2)	
Metal	Steel	7,850	328	2,800	23.9	67	0.278	160	23.9	1	68
	Aluminum	2,700	270	26,000	10.0	260	0.278	160	10.0	0.4	260
	Titanium alloy	4,480	845		5.3				5.3		
Ceramic	Ceramic fiber - Aluminum oxide	3,960	2,950		1.3				1.3		
Polymer	Carbon fiber	1,750	4,000	15,000	0.4	7	0.278	160	0.4	0.02	7
	PVC	1,380	50	2,240	27.6	62	0.278	160	27.6	1	63
Composite	Epoxy-Kevlar Composite	1,325	460		2.9				2.9		
	Carbon Fiber Reinforced Plastic	1,400	250	30,000	5.6	168	0.278	160	5.6	0.2	168
	concrete	2,300	24	160.0	95.8	15	0.278	160	95.8	4	20

				MANUFACTURING (m²)			TRANSPORTING FOR THE CONSTRUCTION				(CE²)
Type	Material Option	Density	Failure Strength	CO2 emission	Mass Index ρ / σ_f	Emission Index $\rho \cdot q$ / σ_f	transportation CO2	distance	Mass Index	Emission Index	Total Emission Index
		(kg/m3)	(Mpa)	(kg CO2/ton)	(kg)	(kg CO2)	(kg CO2/tonkm)	(km)	(kg)	(kg CO2)	
Metal	Recycled Steel	7,850	328	1,200	23.9	29	0.278	160	23.9	1	30
	Recycled Aluminum	2,700	270	1,500	10.0	15	0.278	160	10.0	0.4	15
	concrete	2,300	24	160	95.8	15	0.278	160	95.8	4	20

DATA MAINLY FROM
www.matweb.com

DATA MAINLY FROM
Gielen, IW, NIBE

DATA FROM
Van Witsen (1991)

STRENGTH
Aluminium has high ratio of strength/weight, so it need less mass for the strength.
It consumes less energy and produces less CO_2 than steel because of less requiring mass and high recyclability.

WEAKNESS
Steel is three times as stiff as aluminum. How can we make aluminum as stiff as steel?
Aluminum is also vulnerable to fatigue. How we can control the fatigue crack?

TABLE: Material properties | STRONG POINT | | | WEAK POINT |

Metal	Weight	Strength	Strength/ Weight	Life expectancy	Stiffness	Resistance to Fatigue
Titanium	1.00	1.00	1.00	Unlimited	1.00	Strong
Aluminum	0.57	0.29	0.51	2 years	0.60	Weak
Steel	1.67	0.59	0.35	1 year	1.72	Strong

life expectancy is the time for corrosion to penetrate gauge plate exposed to seawater on one side

STRENGTH is the maximum stress that a material can endure.
STRAIN is how much the material flexes under a given stress.
FATIGUE is a failure: a crack that forms when a material is repeatedly stressed above its fatigue limit.
STIFFNESS [modulus of elasticity] is the resistance of an elastic body to deflection by an applied force—
the value of stress devided by strain.

SOURCE: UNCHS 1991a

PROPOSAL: SOLUTION FOR THE WEAKNESS OF ALUMINIUM

STIFFNESS PROBLEM/SOLUTION
To make an aluminium tube as stiff and strong as a steel tube of the same diameter, we have to use three times as much aluminium. But it ends up being as heavy as steel.

But according to Ashby's index, the table below shows that, with the exception of tensional case, aluminium also needs less mass for the same performance of stiffness—1. We could use aluminium for the column or beam not for tensional element.

Funtions and Constraints	Stiffness			Stiffness	
	M (Material Index)	m' (Mass Index)		M (Material Index)	m' (Mass Index)
Tie (tensile strut) stiffness, length specified; section area free	$\dfrac{E}{\rho}$	$\dfrac{\rho}{E}$	Aluminum Steel	26 27	0.0038 0.0037
Beam (loaded in bending) stiffness, length, shape specified; section area free	$\dfrac{E^{1/2}}{\rho}$	$\dfrac{\rho}{E^{1/2}}$	Aluminum Steel	3.1 1.9	0.323 0.526
Column (compression strut, failure by elastic buckling) buckling load, length, shape specified; section area free	$\dfrac{E^{1/2}}{\rho}$	$\dfrac{\rho}{E^{1/2}}$	Aluminum Steel	3.1 1.9	0.323 0.526

	E = Young's modulus [MPa]	ρ = density [kg/m3]
Aluminum	70,000	2,700
Steel	210,000	7,800

Also, as the bending stiffness of a tube increasses by something like the fourth power of its diameter, we can make a stiff aluminium tube by making it bigger—2.

PROPOSAL: ALUMINIUM MATRIX COMPOSITE [AMC]/SOLUTION FOR FATIGUE

FATIGUE PROBLEM/SOLUTION

If we combine aluminium with fibre materials such as carbon fibre, ceramic fibres, then it will dramatically reduce fatigue problems. Fibres are independent of each other and therefore fatigue cracks cannot travel well.

This new composite material [Aluminium Matrix Composite] also increase stiffness and strength, while keeping lightweight density.

source: 3M Typical Properties Data Sheet/MatWeb

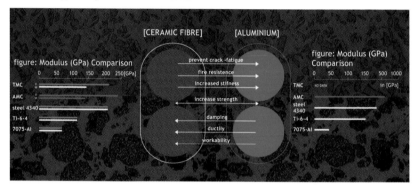

ANALYSIS: PROBLEM OF LIGHTWEIGHT MATERIAL

Low capacity to store heat energy:

As a result, in the lightweight structures, it is almost impossible to store heat energy during the day and release it during the night.

It means in terms of material production and construction, lightweight material like aluminium is energy efficient, but in terms of building operation, it may not be.

So, how can we increase the capacity of storing heat while keeping selected lightweight materials such as aluminium and fibres

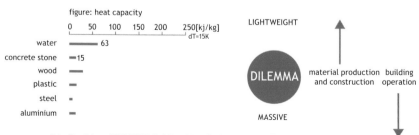

source: Data Sheet from RUBITHERM GmbH and Apache Point Observatory

Thanks to Phase Change Materials, such as paraffin, we can increase the capacity of storing heat dramatically.

As these materials use latent heat which is much more than sensible heat, and its melting temperature is around 24 centigrade.

Consequently, latent heat paraffins/waxes offer four to five times higher heat capacity than water at a moderate temperature.

Despite the heat input, the temperature of the material stays at a relatively constant level, even though phase change is taking place.

the heat storage medium is simply troweled onto the surface with the plaster

encapsulating plastic layer

PCM floor heating system: thermal bank and pipe integrated deck plate

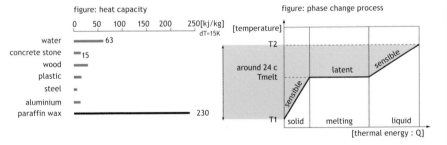

figure: heat capacity

figure: phase change process

source: Data Sheet from RUBITHERM GmbH and Apache Point Observatory

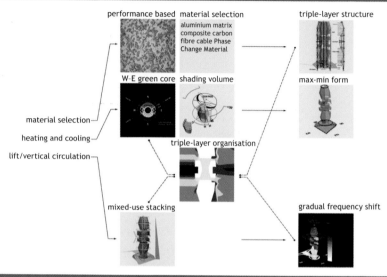

performance based   material selection
aluminium matrix composite carbon fibre cable Phase Change Material

triple-layer structure

W-E green core   shading volume

max-min form

material selection

heating and cooling

lift/vertical circulation

triple-layer organisation

mixed-use stacking

gradual frequency shift

PROTOTYPICAL PROPOSAL: MAX–MIN FORM

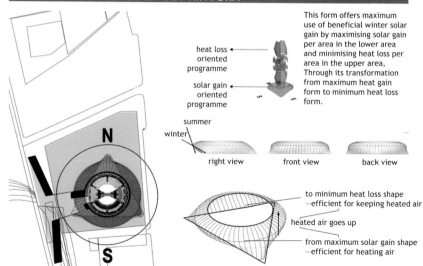

heat loss oriented programme

solar gain oriented programme

This form offers maximum use of beneficial winter solar gain by maximising solar gain per area in the lower area and minimising heat loss per area in the upper area, Through its transformation from maximum heat gain form to minimum heat loss form.

summer
winter

right view   front view   back view

N

S

to minimum heat loss shape —efficient for keeping heated air

heated air goes up

from maximum solar gain shape —efficient for heating air

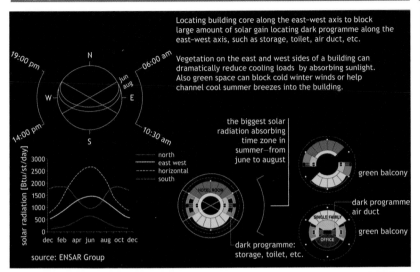

Locating building core along the east–west axis to block large amount of solar gain locating dark programme along the east–west axis, such as storage, toilet, air duct, etc.

Vegetation on the east and west sides of a building can dramatically reduce cooling loads by absorbing sunlight. Also green space can block cold winter winds or help channel cool summer breezes into the building.

the biggest solar radiation absorbing time zone in summer—from june to august

green balcony

dark programme air duct

green balcony

dark programme: storage, toilet, etc.

19:00 pm · 06:00 am · 14:00 pm · 10:30 am

jun aug

N · W · E · S

solar radiation [Btu/st/day]

3000 · 2500 · 2000 · 1500 · 1000 · 500 · 0

dec feb apr jun aug oct dec

.... north
——— east west
– – – horizontal
········ south

source: ENSAR Group

RESEARCH: RELATION BETWEEN FORM AND DYNAMIC ENERGY FLOW

If we consider dynamic energy flow, the typical minimum heat loss oriented apporach should be modified.

First, the glazing type should be changed to specific conditions and orientations; does not always lower U-value means better performance.

Second, typical energy saving shapes like circles can be differentiated into various options according to total energy flow and specific programmes.

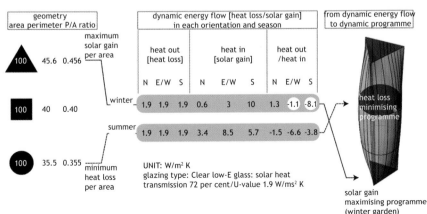

geometry area perimeter P/A ratio			dynamic energy flow [heat loss/solar gain] in each orientation and season									from dynamic energy flow to dynamic programme
			heat out [heat loss]			heat in [solar gain]			heat out /heat in			
		maximum solar gain per area	N	E/W	S	N	E/W	S	N	E/W	S	
100	45.6	0.456										
100	40	0.40	winter 1.9	1.9	1.9	0.6	3	10	1.3	-1.1	-8.1	
			summer 1.9	1.9	1.9	3.4	8.5	5.7	-1.5	-6.6	-3.8	
100	35.5	0.355 minimum heat loss per area										

heat loss minimising programme

UNIT: W/m² K
glazing type: Clear low-E glass: solar heat transmission 72 per cent/U-value 1.9 W/ms² K

solar gain maximising programme (winter garden)

PROTOTYPICAL PROPOSAL: MATERIAL SELECTION

Recyclability is very important in material selection because it has a strong relation with resource saving and waste reduction. Taking recyclability into consideration, aluminum is a very good option, as it takes only five per cent as much energy to be recycled as to be extracted.

As a result, aluminum needs less energy and gives off less CO_2 emissions than other materials where recyclability is concerned.

In the case of tensile structure, carbon fibre is the least energy consuming and CO_2 emitting material among selected materials.

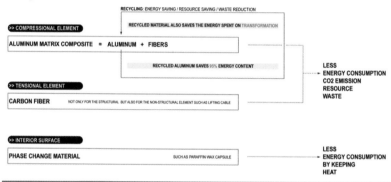

RECYCLING: ENERGY SAVING / RESOURCE SAVING / WASTE REDUCTION

>> COMPRESSIONAL ELEMENT

RECYCLED MATERIAL ALSO SAVES THE ENERGY SPENT ON TRANSFORMATION

ALUMINUM MATRIX COMPOSITE = ALUMINUM + FIBERS

RECYCLED ALUMINUM SAVES 95% ENERGY CONTENT

>> TENSIONAL ELEMENT

CARBON FIBER NOT ONLY FOR THE STRUCTURAL BUT ALSO FOR THE NON-STRUCTURAL ELEMENT SUCH AS LIFTING CABLE

LESS
ENERGY CONSUMPTION
CO2 EMISSION
RESOURCE
WASTE

>> INTERIOR SURFACE

PHASE CHANGE MATERIAL SUCH AS PARAFFIN WAX CAPSULE

LESS
ENERGY CONSUMPTION
BY KEEPING
HEAT

PROTOTYPICAL PROPOSAL: TRIPLE LAYER STRUCTURE

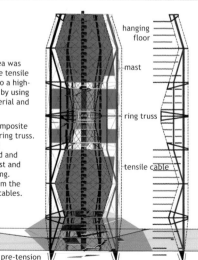

hanging floor

mast

ring truss

tensile cable

The initial idea was to incorporate tensile structures into a high-rise building, by using selected material and components.

1. A tubular aluminium matrix composite mast would be set up to hold ring truss.
2. Two layers of tensile synthetic fibre cables would be installed and pre-tensioned to keep the mast and truss from twisting and buckling.
3. Floors would be suspended from the upper ring truss by the inner cables.

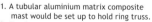

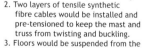

pre-tension

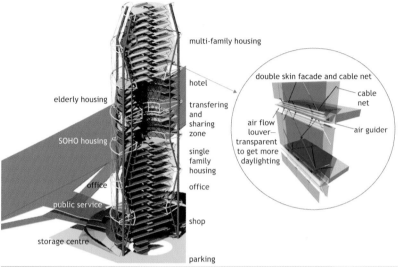

multi-family housing

hotel

transfering
and
sharing
zone

single
family
housing

office

shop

parking

elderly housing

SOHO housing

office

public service

storage centre

double skin facade and cable net

cable
net

air flow
louver—
transparent
to get more
daylighting

air guider

PROTOTYPICAL PROPOSAL: TRIPLE LAYER STRUCTURE

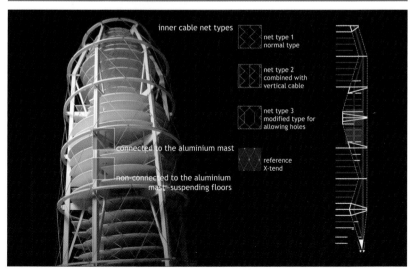

inner cable net types

net type 1
normal type

net type 2
combined with
vertical cable

net type 3
modified type for
allowing holes

reference
X-tend

connected to the aluminium mast

non-connected to the aluminium
mast- suspending floors

PROTOTYPICAL PROPOSAL: SHADING VOLUME

Carving out direct sunlight-reaching volume according to 'sun pass', to prevent direct solar gain and to make shading of building's own geometry driven from sun pass.

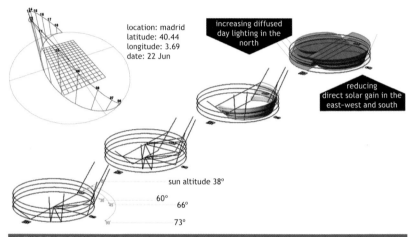

location: madrid
latitude: 40.44
longitude: 3.69
date: 22 Jun

increasing diffused day lighting in the north

reducing direct solar gain in the east-west and south

sun altitude 38°
60°
66°
73°

ADAPTATION OF PROTOTYPES

combinational proposal: heating and cooling and vertical circulation organisation

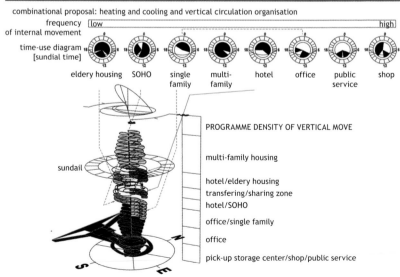

frequency of internal movement
low — high

time-use diagram [sundial time]

eldery housing | SOHO | single family | multi-family | hotel | office | public service | shop

PROGRAMME DENSITY OF VERTICAL MOVE

multi-family housing

hotel/eldery housing
transfering/sharing zone
hotel/SOHO

office/single family

office

pick-up storage center/shop/public service

sundail

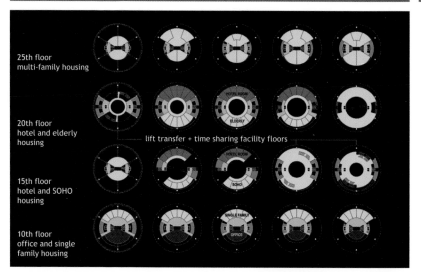

25th floor
multi-family housing

20th floor
hotel and elderly
housing

lift transfer + time sharing facility floors

15th floor
hotel and SOHO
housing

10th floor
office and single
family housing

PROTOTYPICAL PROPOSAL: TRIPLE LAYER ORGANISATION

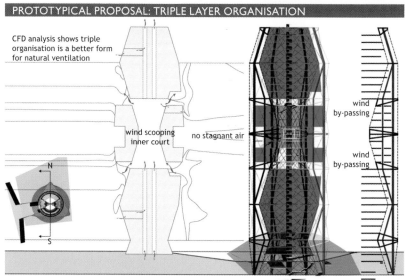

CFD analysis shows triple
organisation is a better form
for natural ventilation

wind scooping
inner court

no stagnant air

wind
by-passing

wind
by-passing

PRESSURE

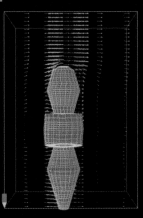

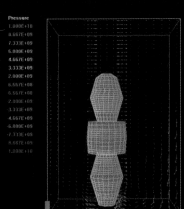

VELOCITY

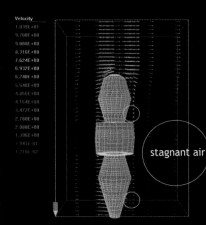

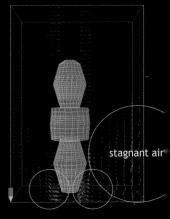

Pressure

5.424E+01
2.575E+01
-2.738E+00
-3.123E+01
-5.972E+01
-8.821E+01
-1.167E+02
-1.452E+02
-1.737E+02
-2.022E+02
-2.307E+02
-2.592E+02
-2.876E+02
-3.161E+02
-3.446E+02
-3.731E+02

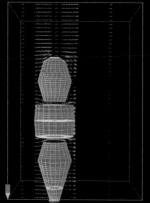

Pressure

3.314E+01
2.293E+01
1.273E+01
2.522E+00
-7.683E+00
-1.789E+01
2.809E+01
-3.830E+01
-4.850E+01
-5.871E+01
-6.891E+01
-7.912E+01
-8.932E+01
-9.953E+01
-1.097E+02
-1.199E+02

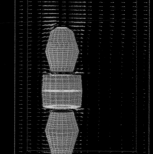

Velocity

1.810E+01
1.690E+01
1.570E+01
1.450E+01
1.330E+01
1.210E+01
1.090E+01
9.696E+00
8.496E+00
7.295E+00
6.094E+00
4.894E+00
3.693E+00
2.492E+00
1.291E+00
9.082E-02

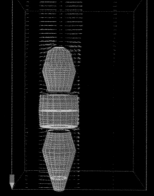

Velocity

1.521E+01
1.420E+01
1.319E+01
1.217E+01
1.116E+01
1.015E+01
9.138E+00
8.125E+00
7.113E+00
6.100E+00
5.088E+00
4.075E+00
3.063E+00
2.050E+00
1.038E+00
2.551E-02

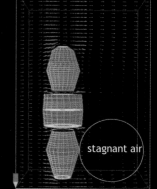

stagnant air

BASIC DIAGRAM: MATERIAL SELECTION AND RECYCLABILITY

Among various parameters, recyclability is very important as it has a crucial impact on other parameters such as the amount of waste and resources. In this analysis, the energy content and CO_2 emission of several materials will be calculated, taking recycled cases into consideration.

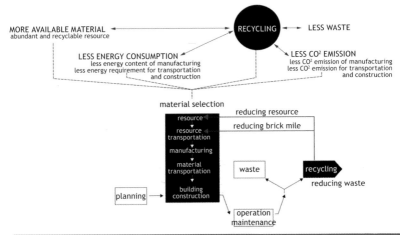

ANALYSIS: STRUCTURAL PERFORMANCE BASED ANALYSIS

How to assess Energy Content and CO_2 emission per required mass for certain structural performance

As we can know the value of following variables per unit mass from manufacturing to recycling

First, we should collect all the values.
Second, we should drive up required mass for particular structural performance.

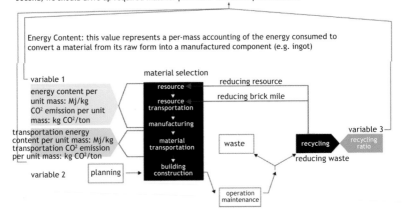

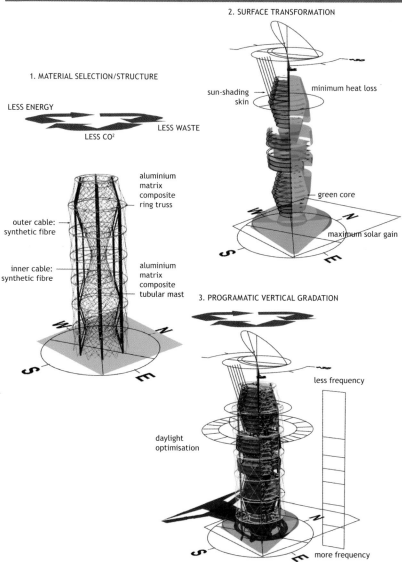

2. SURFACE TRANSFORMATION

1. MATERIAL SELECTION/STRUCTURE

LESS ENERGY

LESS WASTE

LESS CO$_2$

sun-shading skin

minimum heat loss

aluminium matrix composite ring truss

outer cable: synthetic fibre

inner cable: synthetic fibre

aluminium matrix composite tubular mast

green core

maximum solar gain

3. PROGRAMATIC VERTICAL GRADATION

less frequency

daylight optimisation

more frequency

Results

Through the aforementioned hypothetical agenda and methodology, we achieved the following results.

In the selection of material, analysis showed that even though aluminium needs huge amounts of energy to be manufactured, it could be the least energy-consuming and CO_2 emitting material among selected materials, if we simultaneously consider mass requirements, energy spent on transportation, and recycling ratios.

A possible solution to the fatigue problem of aluminium would be to make a composite material with fibres which would not only avoid this problem, but also increase stiffness and strength while maintaining a lightweight density.

In the case of tensional components, another interesting outcome is that some synthetic fibres consume very little energy and have low CO_2 emissions, as often only a very small mass is needed for certain structural applications.

For the interior surface material, phase changing materials like paraffin wax can keep more heat than water at a moderate temperature by using latent heat during its phase changing. It therefore compensates for its lack of a lightweight structure in comparison with materials like aluminium and carbon fibre. The proposed material selection proves energy efficient, not only in terms of manufacturing and construction, but also in terms of building operation.

In light of these outcomes, the optimal architectural geometry has been established by maximising the potential of the properties of selected materials. First, the wider-circumference aluminium tube or mast was introduced to make aluminium stiff, and tensile cables were installed to minimise energy content in the material's manufacture and construction. Floors are to be suspended from ring trusses through inner carbon fibre cables to remove columns.

When it comes to heating and cooling strategy, the synthetic relation between actual solar gain behaviour and architectural geometry has been investigated according to each orientation and time, through the dynamic energy flow concept, by a simultaneous consideration of heat loss and solar gain (this value is heat-loss minus solar gain, in other words, heat out-heat in). With this synthetic value, firstly, it has been found that superior U-value glazing does not always achieve better overall energy performance, and that the best option changes according to specific orientation. Secondly, the interrelation between this overall dynamic energy performance and particular architectural forms has been driven out. For example, if we want to make solar gain maximising programmes like winter garden, triangular shapes will be better than circular shapes because a triangle is the maximum solar gain per area form among minimum length polygons.

When it comes to a lift or vertical circulation strategy, arranging different 'programmes' or levels in a more dynamic order, to prioritise those which are busiest for the lower floors and those visited less frequently at the top, can reduce not only the volume of the elevators but also their frequency. As a

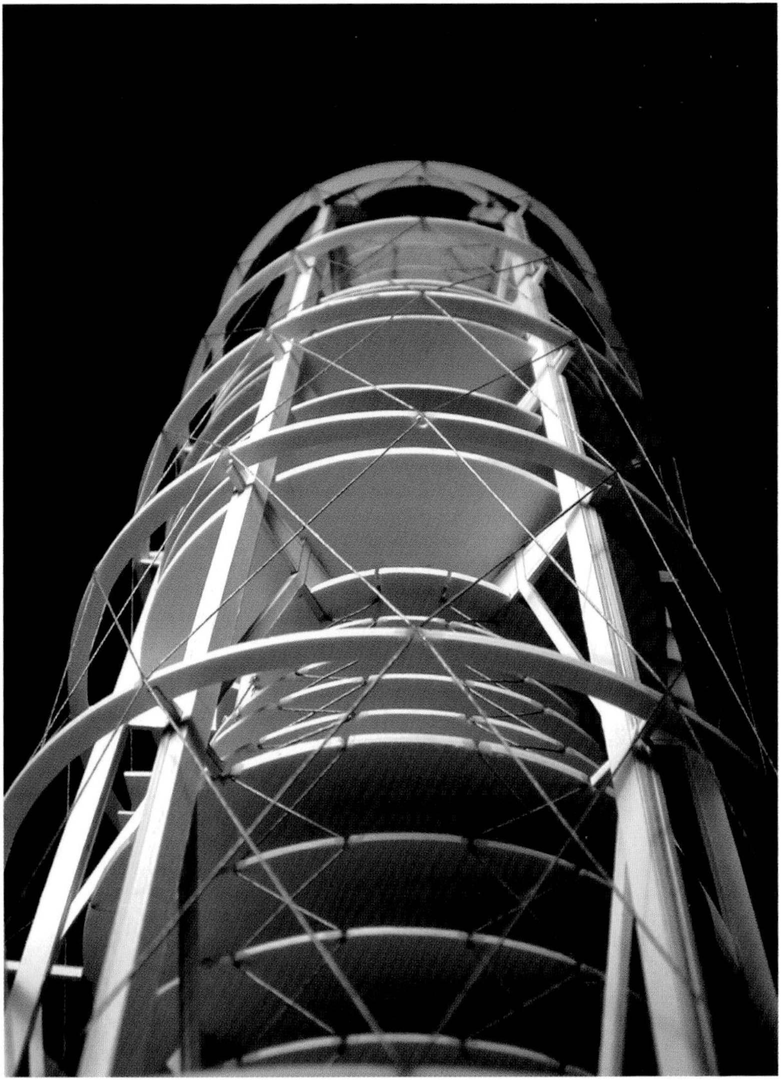

consequence, it shows that the potential of social interactions like sharing can be combined with economic considerations, like energy efficiency through hybrid programme organisation.

Conclusion

It has been shown from the research that the most important factor in the consideration of sustainability is not the energy-efficient development of technology, or any naïve 'green' approach, but a true understanding of environment and a synthetic method or thinking that maximises performance without sacrificing the over and below. It shows that only a synthetic approach can trigger sustainable development by discovering new possibilities in its own system and proper relations among them.

In particular, within every topic, the following have been established through this synthetic approach. First, in material selection, different properties and materials have been merged into better performing material (metal versus fibre). Secondly, in the heating and cooling strategy, more efficient synthetic solutions have been formed from the different approaches (heat loss orientated versus solar gain orientated). Thirdly, it was shown that the coexistence of different programmes can be more sustainable through the analysis and use of energy efficient lift organisation.

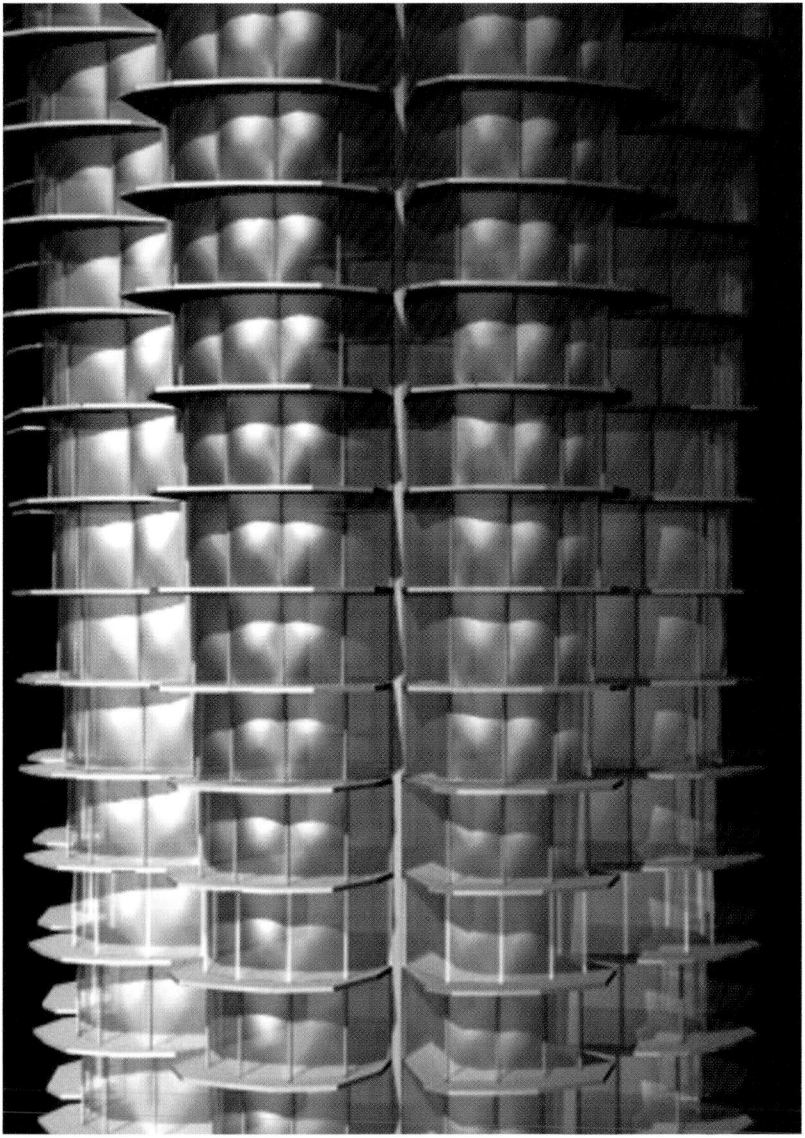

HOUSING SENSES design by daylight
Maria Mandalaki

Hypothesis

This project argues that the design of domestic space should take into
consideration the natural conditions that influence daily activities. The main
question is how best can we benefit from daylight and create interior living
conditions for different types of users and different activities? Can daylight-control
create, not simply comfortable living conditions, but also bring different moods
and atmospheres to the domestic space?

Can we create a daylight design manual?

Summary

What this thesis is trying to prove is that we can adapt our daily life to the
movement of the sun without moving our house. This kind of architectural design
of the domestic space can be informed by daylight. The aim is to filter external
daylight conditions and distribute light in the space according to the activities of
the users and their specific requirements.

This can be achieved via two interfaces, the geometrical and the material. Rules
have been created for the working of this system. In terms of geometry, in order
to take the most advantage of light distribution inside the space we have to create
the most possible variations of angles of incidence of sun vectors to the facade
surfaces of the building in order to have the maximum differentiations of daylight
entering the space.

The following concerns have been addressed: comparing spaces with different
geometrical shapes in order to define the relation of light distributions in these
spaces; focusing on the relation of light distribution to the borders of a space
and defining the soft and the hard relation; introducing the soft relation of light
with space—and this is the basic parameter for the design of a high-rise domestic
building.

In terms of materials, focus has been brought to the performance of fabrics in relation to the filtration of light. Fabrics have a variety of properties that influence light distribution. There are four main characteristics that influence daylight performance: transparency, reflectance, weave (solid, mesh fabrics) and colour. We can create different degrees of daylight filtration according to the properties above in relation to the characteristics of the orientation of the sun vector. We can therefore create different atmospheres of light and mutate the character of light that exists at any specific time of day. It is the above-mentioned material factors that determined the organisation of the high-rise building.

From the beginning, the housing unit has been perceived as a landscape of senses, determined by the activities within. The main question is how to organise activities in sequence with these senses: vision, olfaction, hearing, tactility and the ways they are triggered during the day.

Focus on the sense of vision has been a priority, since it plays the most important role in perceptual psychology, human beings absorbing 80 per cent of all the information that they receive via the eyes. Consideration of the distribution of daylight in the domestic space is one of the parameters that controls the sense of vision.

Case Study

All the investigations into the luminance and performance of fabrics are being performed in Madrid. That means that examining specific light conditions and how they are influenced by different fabrics. The conclusions drawn are based on specific degrees of longitude and weather conditions.

Methodology

The aim is to create an organisational diagram informed by the daylight parameters that will supply, in the first place, a specific geometry, and in the second, materials that are capable of producing a specific character of light.

According to James J Gibson, in the book *The Ecological Approach of Visual Perception,* there are two main characteristics of daylight: its direction, and the depletion of illumination. I will examine the influence of these characteristics on space: the distribution and the luminance that express the character of the light.

These characteristics will be measured using a software package called Relux and the methodology used is dictated and informed by the parameters of this software.

In the following diagrams, unit shells will examined with completely transparent or completely opaque walls (thin black line of the border or thick black line of the border) for 8 February, which is considered to be to be the darkest day of the year, and for three different times per day—the morning, mid-day and the afternoon. The same structure will be adopted in this research into light distribution and luminance in the unit shells.

The daylight design manual will be established by the conclusions of the research steps following. The methodology of the research of daylight reaction with space is organised in three parts and can be summarised in the following synopsis:

First Part—Sky Conditions
Examination of the different performance (distribution and illumination) of light for different conditions of clear and overcast sky.

For an overcast sky, the distribution of the light does not change during the day only its intensity changes—illuminance is changing. For a clear sky, the distribution and intensity changes during the day. How can we mutate overcast sky conditions while we have a clear sky? These conditions are suitable for public programmes that need stable light.

The chamfered shape is the most efficient in terms of distribution. Overall it performs the best—also in terms of illuminance.

Second Part—Geometry
Examining the different geometries of units in plan according to the number and orientation of openings and the possible structural elements of the construction.

Structural Elements
The influence of structural elements in the distribution of light. Comparison of rectangular, polygonal and elliptical units. We can conclude the following: the structural elements do critically influence light conditions, especially when they are orientated west or east.

Shape of Unit

Examining different closed units and evaluating the results of luminance and light distribution during the day. Going from a rectangular to an elliptical shape, the light changes in terms of distribution and intensity. We can see that in the elliptical shape the distribution of light is more unstable, with a lot of shadows created by the structural elements. To minimise the structural elements, the more chamfered the shape the better, with the illuminance in terms of degree and in terms of distribution. By means of a curved shape, we are maximising the amount of opening within the angle of total reflection.

For the rectangular shape, there are less differences during the day in terms of distribution and less shadow. But the distribution of the light is in an abtuse angle with the border of the unit. This we will call the hard relation of light with space.

In comparison the same topological entities and the different performance of light, the circle has the best performance in terms of giving the most illuminance and the most efficiently lighted surface with less glazing surface. The more circular the shape, the more soft the relation of the distribution of the light with the border of the structure. I will call this soft relation.

Orientation of Openings

With openings located in the south, we can gain the most of illuminance.

Evaluation of different orientated glazings and the variable performance of daylight in the interior space according to the orientation and the number of the glazings has been considered. The most illuminance appears in glazing in the south facade.

We have also looked at different interior conditions of light according to the orientation of the openings. We can see the possibility of different non-domestic programmes according the different orientations. The least amount of differences in terms of distribution of the light during the day were in the glazing in the north and east facade. We can conclude that these orientated openings are suitable for public programmes that need stable light. The most efficiently lighted surface is in the south-east glazing.

The distribution of housing activities in a unit will depend on the different orientation of openings.

Number of Openings

The limits of opening and closing surfaces needed according to specific programmes have been evaluated. Comparing the same amount of openings in different orientations, there was not much difference in terms of distribution for east and west openings, but there was difference in terms of activation during the day.

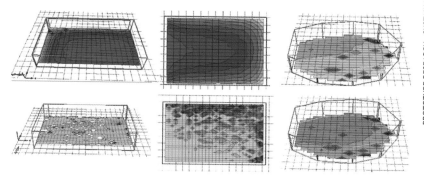

Rectangle South-West Opening   Rectangle South-West Opening   Chamfered West Opening

GEOMETRY—SHAPE OF UNTS

February 08:00   February 12:00   February 17:00

ll av = 413   ll av = 2590   ll av = 637

ll av = 388   ll av = 1730   ll av = 852

ll av = 202   ll av = 1250   ll av = 766

ll av = 210   ll av = 1440   ll av = 900

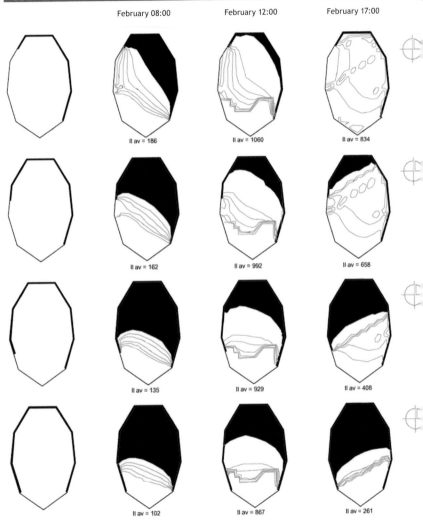

February 08:00   February 12:00   February 17:00

ll av = 186   ll av = 1060   ll av = 834

ll av = 162   ll av = 992   ll av = 658

ll av = 135   ll av = 929   ll av = 408

ll av = 102   ll av = 867   ll av = 261

The limits of opening and closing surfaces needed according to a specific programme. Comparing the same amount of openings in different orientations there is little difference in terms of distribution for east and west openings, but difference in terms of activation during the day.

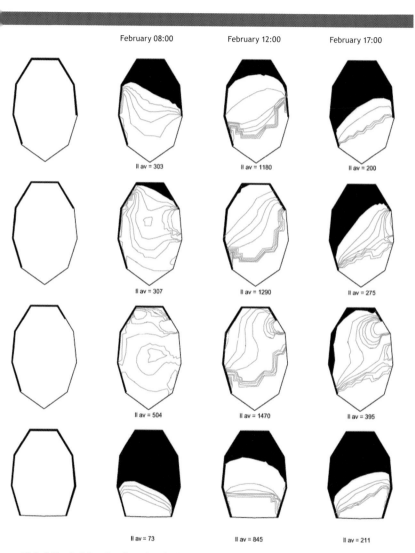

February 08:00   February 12:00   February 17:00

ll av = 303   ll av = 1180   ll av = 200

ll av = 307   ll av = 1290   ll av = 275

ll av = 504   ll av = 1470   ll av = 395

ll av = 73   ll av = 845   ll av = 211

All daylight calculations have been done for 8 February, the darkest day of the year in Madrid.
Software used for the daylight calculations: Relux.
ll av=average luminance for the specific time.

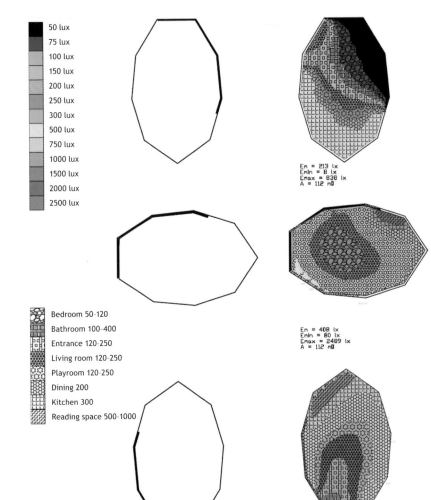

50 lux	
75 lux	
100 lux	
150 lux	
200 lux	
250 lux	
300 lux	
500 lux	
750 lux	
1000 lux	
1500 lux	
2000 lux	
2500 lux	

Bedroom 50-120
Bathroom 100-400
Entrance 120-250
Living room 120-250
Playroom 120-250
Dining 200
Kitchen 300
Reading space 500-1000

Em = 213 lx
Emin = 8 lx
Emax = 838 lx
A = 112 m0

Em = 408 lx
Emin = 80 lx
Emax = 2489 lx
A = 112 m0

Em = 368 lx
Emin = 15 lx
Emax = 1068 lx
A = 112 m0

```
Em  = 1216 lx
Emin = 0 lx
Emax = 4774 lx
A = 112 m0
```

```
Em  = 868 lx
Emin = 69 lx
Emax = 1480 lx
A = 112 m0
```

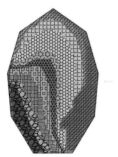

```
Em  = 1869 lx
Emin = 55 lx
Emax = 5027 lx
A = 112 m0
```

```
Em  = 869 lx
Emin = 22 lx
Emax = 4664 lx
A = 112 m0
```

```
Em  = 303 lx
Emin = 17 lx
Emax = 1745 lx
A = 112 m0
```

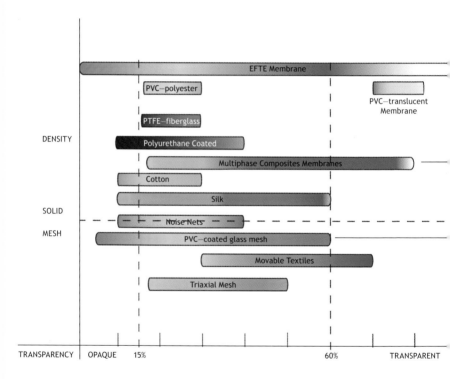

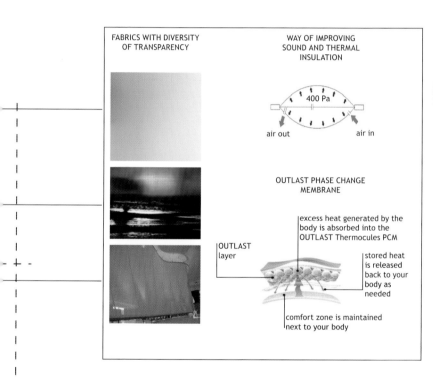

FABRICS WITH DIVERSITY
OF TRANSPARENCY

WAY OF IMPROVING
SOUND AND THERMAL
INSULATION

400 Pa

air out   air in

OUTLAST PHASE CHANGE
MEMBRANE

OUTLAST
layer

excess heat generated by the
body is absorbed into the
OUTLAST Thermocules PCM

stored heat
is released
back to your
body as
needed

comfort zone is maintained
next to your body

DISTANCE FROM THE FACADE

ANGLE OF LOOKING

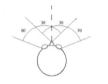

DISTANCE FROM SURROUNDINGS

DISTANCE OF PERCEPTION

	something exists	1/2-1 km
	perceive the sex (male/female)	100 m
	what is doing	70 m
	style and details and have lecture	30 m
	style and details and have lecture	1-1 1/2 m

DAYLIGHT PROPERTIES

direction of sunvector

weakening of illumination

properties of materials
light transmission
reflectivity
colours

MULTI PHASE COMPOSITES MEMBRANES

		SHADOW	VIEW TO OUTSIDE	RELATION TO DISTANCE
TRANSPARENCY 6%				
19%				
20%				

MESH PVC COATED FABRICS

SHADOW

VIEW TO OUTSIDE

RELATION TO DISTANCE

TRANSPARENCY 30%

21%

9%

SOLID PVC COATED FABRICS

SHADOW

VIEW TO OUTSIDE

RELATION TO DISTANCE

TRANSPARENCY 19%

13%/(WHITE)

13%/(COLOURED)

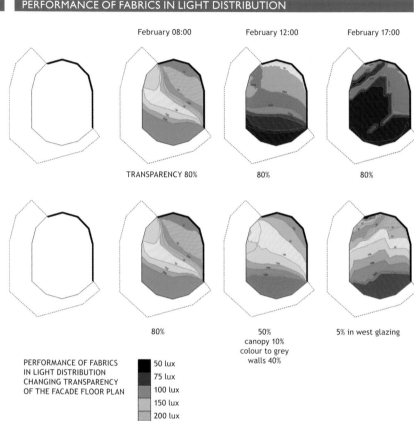

February 08:00   February 12:00   February 17:00

TRANSPARENCY 80%   80%   80%

80%   50%
canopy 10%
colour to grey
walls 40%   5% in west glazing

PERFORMANCE OF FABRICS
IN LIGHT DISTRIBUTION
CHANGING TRANSPARENCY
OF THE FACADE FLOOR PLAN

	50 lux
	75 lux
	100 lux
	150 lux
	200 lux
	250 lux
	300 lux
	500 lux
	750 lux
	1000 lux
	1500 lux
	2000 lux
	2500 lux
	3000 lux
	5000 lux
	10000 lux

ELEMENT	PROPERTY
window	transp 80%-10%
walls	diffus 50%
floor	diffus 30%
ceiling	diffus 70%
canopy	diffus 80%-10%

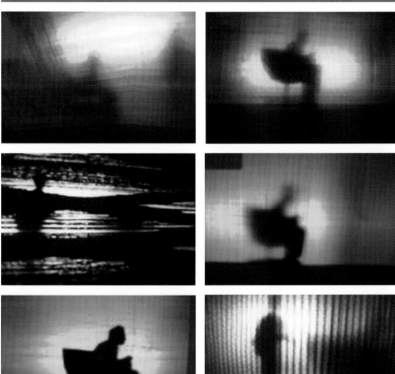

DAYLIGHTING DIAGRAM

Distribution of light in the 110 metre square units exposed in different orientations for three different times of day.
The different proportion of width and depth are informed by the daylight level of each unit.
All the units can have the same condition of light in different orientations.

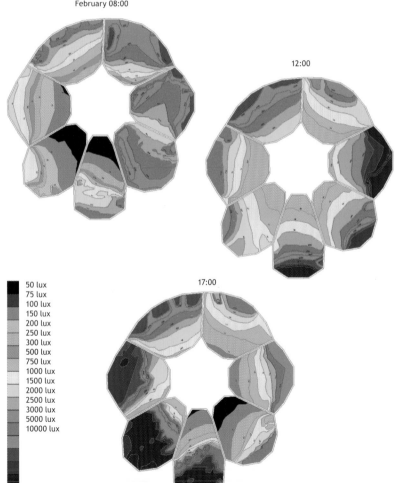

February 08:00

12:00

17:00

50 lux
75 lux
100 lux
150 lux
200 lux
250 lux
300 lux
500 lux
750 lux
1000 lux
1500 lux
2000 lux
2500 lux
3000 lux
5000 lux
10000 lux

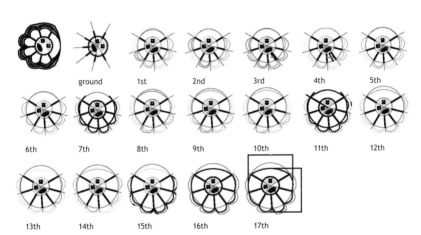

ground | 1st | 2nd | 3rd | 4th | 5th

6th | 7th | 8th | 9th | 10th | 11th | 12th

13th | 14th | 15th | 16th | 17th

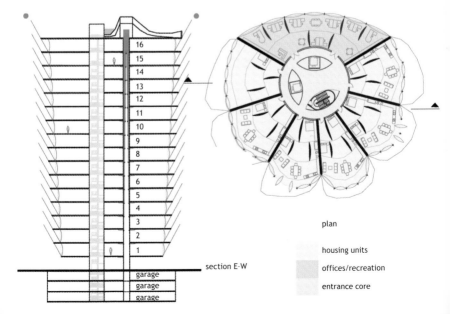

section E-W

plan

housing units

offices/recreation

entrance core

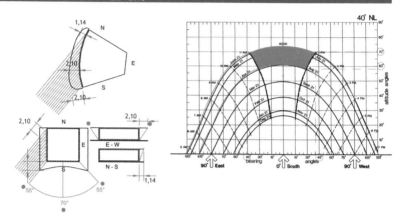

PROTOTYPE—UNIT SHELL

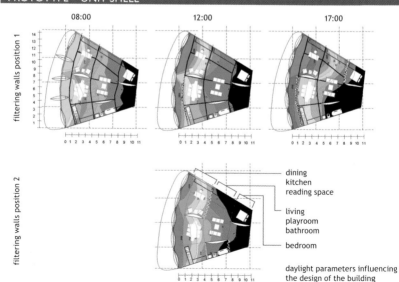

dining
kitchen
reading space

living
playroom
bathroom

bedroom

daylight parameters influencing
the design of the building

Conclusions

Point one: the soft and hard relation of the light with the border.
Focus is on the soft relation of the light with the border of the space because in this way the activities can be distributed in a parallel or vertical way with the light graduation. This enables the homogenous filtration of the light by the filtering walls. So the activities and the filtering walls are in a smooth relation and they are informed by the light direction.

Prototype

We will try to perform the above results in a high-rise building that is dealing with the problem of light control and its distribution in all the surfaces of the space. The housing units can be distributed in all the orientations and adapt their shape according to this orientation for best performance according to light illuminance and distribution.

Here, we will try to accommodate all the programme requirements of a high-rise building comprising offices, a recreation area for sports activities, meeting rooms that will take up 30 per cent of the whole building. The required number of units will be 70 per cent of the whole. The percentage and the required square metres for each unit are taken from the existing distribution of housing units in Madrid, defined as following: 27 per cent of 60 m^2, 32 per cent of 75 m^2, 22 per cent of 90 m^2 and 19 per cent of 110 m^2.

As described above there are two relations of distribution of light and the border of the space: the soft and the hard. we are interested in the soft relation of the light with the border of the space and will investigate this performance within the domestic space. This can be achieved better for circular shapes. The case study of the circle and the improvements that can be done for the best performance in relation to the internal distribution of the activities will be taken further.

The vertical relation of the units influences their geometry and the possibility of their transformation in order to arrive at the required result. The vertical connectivity of the structural elements is the constraint for the transformation of this geometry. The requirement of shading in the north, west and east facade is the second constraint of the vertical positioning of the units. So the higher the position of the unit, the bigger in square metres. The horizontal distribution is basically informed by the daylight diagram and the aim is to achieve the same level of light in all the orientations according to their required proportions.

The size and number of units is informed by the sizes and numbers of housing units in Madrid. The housing units are exposed in the maximum angle of sun movement. The structure is dividing the units in different proportions.

The interior organisation of the division of activities is creating different light distribution and depends on the geometrical relation with the border of the space facade and on the properties of their material. The south-facing border is used as the light source and position for the interior transparent and translucent partitions in order to filter this incoming light and create the low light character of the private spaces of the housing unit.

There is a different requirement of light illumination for all the programmes of the building. And there is a big difference between the domestic programme and public programme. The domestic programme requires diversity of light and the public programme requires stable light in terms of time and in terms of spatial distribution. I propose the positioning of the public programme in the north-facing edge and light filtered with solid materials in order to keep the light stable with no diversity inside.

The central core of the high-rise building is mainly illuminated by light pipes with translucent reflecting Lycra fabric. In order to achieve efficient luminance for the public entrance, five light pipes are needed.

Conclusions

Point two: the introduction of fabrics as new material that can be used for housing building. This is basically achieved by improving the thermal and sound insulation of the membrane by introducing air foil cushions. Air is the best means of insulation and we can take the most advantage of it inside transparent and translucent membranes by keeping the properties of the fabric itself in relation to the light transmission.

Point three: Gradient Versus Continuity
We are proposing a new way of organising the housing units that is based on the gradient and direction of light distribution in the space—proposing the 'monospace', the continuous space as a prototype for living. In this way, the housing unit is becoming the field of establishment of the end user that is following the light performance exactly as people use to inhabit the landscape according to the view and to the sun position.

We are proposing a system of controlling the distribution of daylight with the vertical and parallel partitioning placed towards the sun vector. The vertical has to act as a filter and the parallel as the reflector and distributor. The positioning of these systems is established by the programme requirements of the housing unit and the required light illuminance for each activity. The vertical one is the stable partitioning system and its aim is to reflect and distribute daylight into the housing units. In this way, the space is a continuous field of intensities.

Point four: Flexibility Versus Customisation
The material and the degree of filtration are customised by the end user according to the type of lifestyle that they want—a bright house, a dark house, a calm house, an isolated house, etc.. Different atmospheres are created by the filtration of light from the fabrics.

GEOMETRY

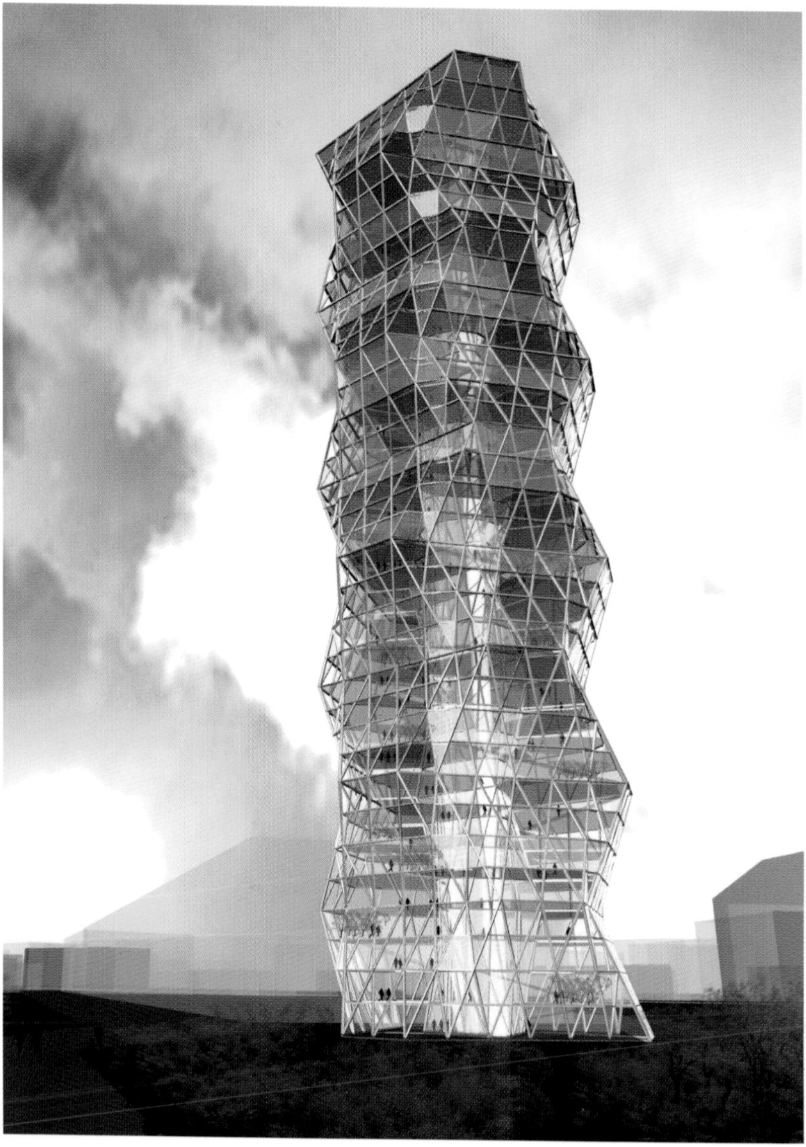

living prototype for emerging urban nomadism
Jasmine Tsoi

Hypothesis

How can we provide an integrated living prototype that will cater to the diverse living patterns, programmatic and spatial demands of the emerging quotient of urban commuters in Madrid in the coming 50 years?

Research dealing with programmatic organisation with reference to tenant demographics, modification of existing domestic prototypes; functional contingency zoning, structural geometry and materiality is conducted and the idea of 'hybrid living' for urban nomadism is optimised by incorporating the conclusions of this research into a high-rise structure.

Summary

From a sociological point of view Madrid will no longer be dominated by a traditional fixed family set-up in the coming 50 years, and emerging modes of living. The new urban nomadism is comprised of urban commuters, such as business commuters, immigrants, the elderly, individual professionals, and tourists, who will necessitate a new accommodation prototype to fit with their transient habitation of the urban landscape.

The hypothesis is to propose an alternative living model for the emergence of this nomadic living style, namely, the breaking down of traditional living programmes and remixing them with daily necessity programmes, resulting in a subversive hybrid form on a fundamental level in terms of building, logistics and organisation.

Tenant Demographics

Nine specific target groups are sampled and pinpointed for tenant demographic research: fixed families, immigrants, sabbaticals, business commuters, frequent commuters, bachelors, 'Sohoers', freelancers and tourists. Their collective living pattern and basic spatial programmatic demands are analysed and adequate programme areas are assigned to various tenant types that represent a particular group of users in the building. More emphasis is put on the commuters who have transient stays in the premises.

Marketing Strategy

In order to cut a niche directly into the housing market, traditional prototypes are borrowed, the service apartment, catered hospitality accommodation and general mass housing, which are already serving certain portions of the target groups mentioned above. For instance, hotels are catering to business commuters and tourists, while service apartments are serving the 'sohoers', bachelors, etc..

Programme Chart

The programme is divided into three major categories:

living space
working space
leisure and public space

The programmes are comprised of different floor area percentages in different phases according to the spatial and programmatic requirements of the target group. The contingent relationship of these programmes will also determine their subsequent spatial distribution in the building.

Functional Contingency Planning

If the three prototypes remained as they are and operated as separate phasing development in normal conditions, they would lose the potential of sharing public facilities and spaces in the whole complex and the cross-border between diversity and vividness of community will be greatly restricted. Thus, the idea of 'hybrid living' is introduced to reorganise the spatial and programmatic configuration.

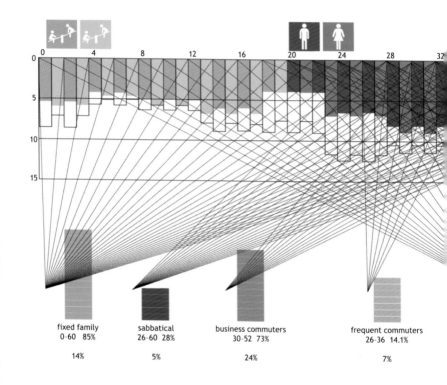

fixed family
0-60   85%

sabbatical
26-60   28%

business commuters
30-52   73%

frequent commuters
26-36   14.1%

14%

5%

24%

7%

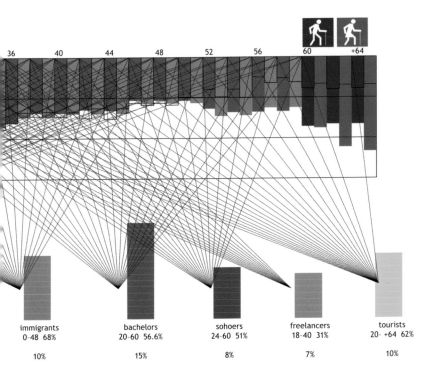

| 36 | 40 | 44 | 48 | 52 | 56 | 60 | +64 |

immigrants
0-48 68%

bachelors
20-60 56.6%

sohoers
24-60 51%

freelancers
18-40 31%

tourists
20- +64 62%

10%   15%   8%   7%   10%

LIVING   WORK   LEISURE

A-1 SERVICE APARTMENT	B-1 OFFICE RENTAL	C-1 CLUB

G-4
SOHO

G-3
URBAN
COMMUTER

BACHELOR
SUITE/FAMILY

GENERIC OFFICE SPACE

CONSIGNER SERVICE
GARDEN
CLUB CATERING
ATELIER
LIBRARY
SPA AND TREATMENT
BEAUTY PARLOR
CLINIC
NURSERY
KINDERGARTEN
SPORTSHALL
POOL
GYM

LONG-TERM STAY — CLUB

A-2 RENTAL	B-2 SERVICED OFFICE	C-2 PUBLIC PROGRAM

G-2
BUSINESS
COMMUTER

G-1
EXPATRIATE
COMMUTER

G-0
TOURIST

SINGLE
DOUBLE

OFFICE SPACE
MEETING ROOM
RECEPTION & SECRETARY
MAILBOX SERVICE
COMMUNICATION & PRINTING
AUTO RENTAL SERVICE
EXHIBITION
CONFERENCE
BALLROOM
PANTRY
STORAGE

CARPARK
SUPERMARKET
RESTAURANT
CAFE
SHOP
CINEMA/AUDITORIUM
DANCE CLUB

SHORT STAY — PUBLIC

CLUB		CLUB SKY GARDEN
OFFICE		CLUB RESTAURANT
OFFICE	CLUB	CLUB RESTAURANT
OFFICE	SUITE	CLUB CAFE
OFFICE	SUITE	ATELIER
OFFICE	SUITE	ATELIER
OFFICE	APARTMENT	ATELIER
OFFICE	APARTMENT	LIBRARY
OFFICE	APARTMENT	CONSIGNER SERVICE
OFFICE	APARTMENT	CAFE
OFFICE	APARTMENT	CAFE
OFFICE	APARTMENT	SPA & TREATMENT
OFFICE	APARTMENT	BEAUTY PARLOR
OFFICE	APARTMENT	CLINIC
OFFICE	APARTMENT	NURSERY
OFFICE	APARTMENT	PLAYGROUND
OFFICE	APARTMENT	KINDERGARTEN
OFFICE	APARTMENT	KINDERGARTEN
OFFICE	APARTMENT	SPORTS HALL
OFFICE	APARTMENT	POOL
OFFICE	APARTMENT	POOL
OFFICE	APARTMENT	GYM
REFUGEE	APARTMENT	REFUGEE
OFFICE	APARTMENT	DANCE CLUB
OFFICE	REFUGEE	DANCE CLUB
OFFICE	RENTAL	BAR
OFFICE	RENTAL	BAR
OFFICE	RENTAL	RESTAURANT
OFFICE	RENTAL	CAFE
OFFICE	RENTAL	EXHIBITION
OFFICE	RENTAL	EXHIBITION
OFFICE	RENTAL	EXHIBITION
OFFICE	RENTAL	CINEMA/AUDITORIUM
OFFICE	RENTAL	CINEMA
OFFICE	RENTAL	CINEMA
OFFICE	RENTAL	SHOP
OFFICE	RENTAL	SHOP
OFFICE	RENTAL	SHOP
PO BOX	RENTAL	SHOP
PO BOX	RENTAL	SHOP
RECEPTION	RENTAL	CAFE
RECEPTION	RENTAL	RESTAURANT
RESTAURANT	RENTAL	SUPERMARKET
SUPERMARKET	RENTAL	SUPERMARKET
SUPERMARKET		CARPARK
CARPARK	SUPERMARKET	
	CARPARK	
	CARPARK	

FLOOR PROGRAM
ROTATION

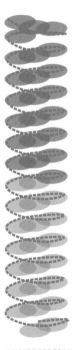

LEISURE PROGRAM
CONNECTED
CIRCULATION

From the building scale:

The living space and the two other programmes: cultural recreation and working are distributed vertically in each phase. The pattern is repeated vertically in the building.

In the adjacent phase, the same pattern reoccurred, but was shifted. This shifting pattern ensures the even distribution of programmes from various categories in the building, which implies equal access to similar functional space in the building, and at the same time the building is zoned with a repeated rhythm and functions as a mini-region in a repeated manner in the whole high-rise building.

From the local scale:

In each zone, the programmes are allocated according to the shift in order but also to the functional contingency logic so as to facilitate ease and efficiency of living for the tenants. The zone can accommodate changes within the target group, shifting of utilisation, etc..

Geometrical Translation

The triangulated relationship is translated as three vertex on plan, with rotation of 60 degrees as expression of programme shifting in programme chart, thus an even mix and distribution of programme could be achieved.

System

Ramp

Connecting of public leisure space in building, to facilitate inter-level circulation.

Core

Vertical core as rapid and efficient circulation and fire egress in high-rise building.

Leisure programme

As a continuous public space in building, connected by the continuous ramp: serves as a continuous greenery open space in the vertical city; enveloped by ETFE cushion, domesticating of greenhouse material in high-rise housing; leisure, cultural and catering programme scattering within the high-rise along the ramp.

ETFE

Application of greenhouse material for the greenery area along the ramp living space.

Provision of living space with its duration spanning from a couple of hours to years (service apartment, hotel and housing); with size spanning from individual cubicles to apartments.

Work and office rental
Incorporating working space in adjacency to residential programme and leisure programme, provision of easy access to working environment for urban commuters, with size spanning from office mail box, to individual cubicles to conference and exhibition centre.

Mix Slabs
Mix of three different spaces on each floor.

Structure
A combination of outer casing and inner core system, loads transfer from slabs to outer structure and inner core structures. Structural material steel tubes.

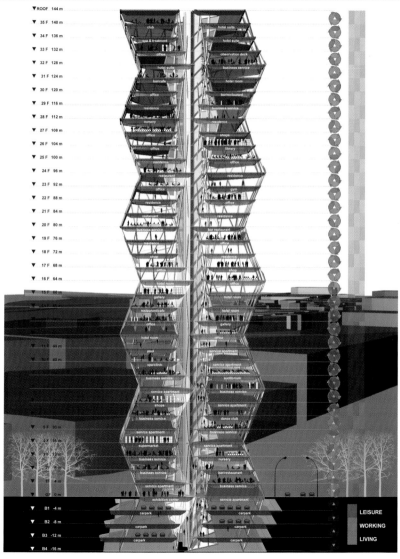

▼ROOF 144 m
▼ 35 F 140 m
▼ 34 F 136 m
▼ 33 F 132 m
▼ 32 F 128 m
▼ 31 F 124 m
▼ 30 F 120 m
▼ 29 F 116 m
▼ 28 F 112 m
▼ 27 F 108 m
▼ 26 F 104 m
▼ 25 F 100 m
▼ 24 F 96 m
▼ 23 F 92 m
▼ 22 F 88 m
▼ 21 F 84 m
▼ 20 F 80 m
▼ 19 F 76 m
▼ 18 F 72 m
▼ 17 F 68 m
▼ 16 F 64 m
▼ 15 F 60 m
▼ 11 F 44 m
▼ 10 F 40 m
▼ 5 F 20 m
▼ 4 F 16 m
▼ 12 m
▼ 4 m
▼ GF 0 m
▼ B1 -4 m
▼ B2 -8 m
▼ B3 -12 m
▼ B4 -16 m

LEISURE
WORKING
LIVING

Roof	Roof	Roof
hotel suite	club	business suite
hotel suite	spa and treatment	business service, office
hotel suite	obersvation deck	business service, office
hotel suite	gallery	office
hotel guest	bar/café	office
hotel guest	bar/restaurant	office
residence	elderly	office
residence	nursery	office
residence	shops	office
residence	library	studio
residence	restaurants	studio
residence	clinic/beauty parlor	studio
residence	gym	office
residence	sports hall	office
residence	restaurants	office
residence	bar/restaurant	office
residence	supermarket	office
residence	shop	office
hotel guest	shop	business service, office
hotel guest	shop	office
hotel guest	gallery	studio
hotel guest	restaurants/café	studio
hotel guest	exhibition and conference	office
hotel guest	ballroom	office
service apartment	pool	office
service apartment	spa/clinic	office
service apartment	auditorium	office
service apartment	cinema	office
service apartment	shops	office
service apartment	dance club	office
service apartment	gym	office
service apartment	supermarket	office
service apartment	nursery	business service, office
service apartment	bar/restaurant	business service, office
service apartment	library	business service, office
service apartment	exhibition centre	business service, office
carpark	carpark	carpark
carpark	carpark	carpark
carpark	carpark	carpark
carpark	carpark	carpark

1-Living	hotel guest room + service appartment + residential
2-Service	service + catering + cultural + recreation + hotel facilities
3-Office	office rental + business service

program	area	program	area	program	area
Roof	350	Roof	350	Roof	350
club	336	conference, business	336	hotel suite	336
business service,	330	hotel suite	330	spa and treatment	330
hotel suite	327	observation deck	327	business service	327
gallery	315	office	315	hotel guest	315
office	327	hotel guest	327	bar/café	327
hotel guest	330	bar/restaurant	330	office	330
elderly	336	office	336	residence	336
office	350	residence	350	nursery	350
residence	336	shops	336	office	336
library	330	studio	330	residence	330
studio	327	residence	327	restaurants	327
residence	315	clinic/beauty parlor	315	studio	315
gym	327	office	327	residence	327
office	330	residence	330	sports hall	330
residence	336	restaurants	336	office	336
bar/restaurants	350	office	350	residence	350
office	336	residence	336	supermarket	336
residence	330	shops	330	office	330
shops	327	business service	327	hotel guest room	327
office	315	hotel guest room	315	shops	315
hotel guest room	327	gallery	327	studio	327
restaurant/café	330	studio	330	hotel guest room	330
office	336	hotel guest room	336	exhibition and conf	336
hotel guest	350	ballroom	350	office	350
pool	336	office	336	service apartment	336
office	330	service apartment	330	spa/clinic	330
service apartment	327	auditorium	327	office	327
cinema	315	office	315	service apartment	315
office	327	service apartment	327	shops	327
service apartment	330	dance club	330	office	330
gym	336	office	336	service apartment	336
office	350	service apartment	350	supermarket	350
service apartment	336	nursery	336	business service	336
bar/restaurant	330	business service	330	service apartment	330
business service	327	service apartment	327	library	327
service apartment	315	exhibition centre	315	business service	315
carpark	327	carpark	327	carpark	327
carpark	330	carpark	330	carpark	330
carpark	336	carpark	336	carpark	336
carpark	350	carpark	350	carpark	350

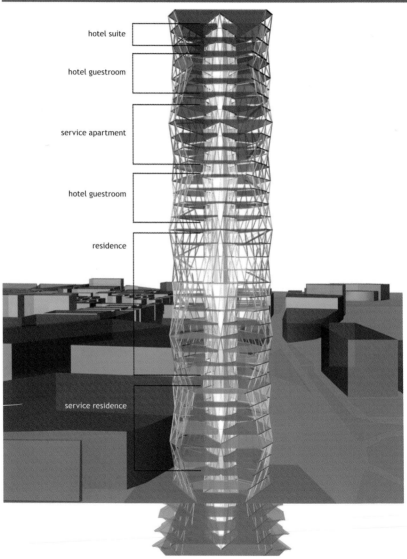

hotel suite

hotel guestroom

service apartment

hotel guestroom

residence

service residence

RAMP
connecting of public leisure space in the
building—facilitates interlevel circulation

CORE
vertical core as rapid and efficient
circulation and fire egress in high-rise
buildings

LEISURE PROGRAMME
as a continuous public space in the building,
connected by the continuous ramp;
serves as a continuous green open
space in the vertical city; envelope by
ETFE cushion, domesticating of
greenhouse material in high-rise housing—
leisure, cultural and catering programme
scattered throughout the high-rise

WORK AND OFFICE RENTAL
incorporating working space in
adjacency of residential programme and
leisure programme, provision of easy
access to work environment for urban
commuters, with size variable from office
mail box, to individual cubicles, to
conference and exhibition centre

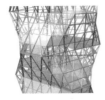

LIVING SPACE
provision of living space with its
duration spaning from couple of hours
to years (service apartment, hotel,
housing); with size spanning from
individual cubicles to apartments

MIX SLABS
mix of three different spaces on each floor

Office location inside
the building

Living location inside
the building

ETFE material
location

Slope/vertical
connection

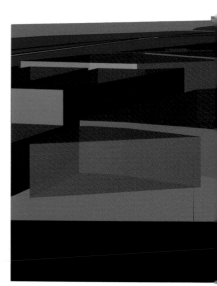

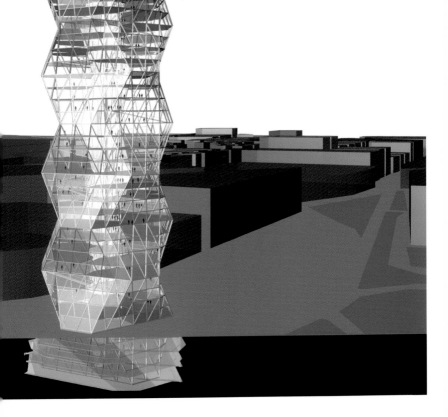

Served cell: Dwelling
Served cell: Dwelling
Served cell: Dwelling
Served cell: Dwelling
Served cell: Dwelling

INCLINED SPATIAL CONNECTORS inclined infrastructure
Jung Jae Lee

Why design an inclined housing infrastructure in Madrid?

Generally in structural terms, the main function of most of the vertical components in high-rise buildings is compression, but they are not flexible enough to withstand displacement by lateral forces like high wind load. Secondly, and regarding accessibility, there are vertical connections only through the core system; thirdly, regarding environmental concerns, there are various trials involved in making artificial vertical landscapes inside or outside high-rise buildings. What are the results if the building is inclined to solve these issues?

Summary

In the twenty-first century, high-density functions will be increasingly concentrated in cities. On the other hand, it is likely that there will be a similar increase in demands for co-existence with nature, based near greenery. With the ideal of creating an urban space that can maintain a good balance between these two environments, cities have grown up horizontally. In contrast to the horizontal expansion of cities, high-rise building (skyscraper) as a part of the urban infrastructure is a vertical sky city containing the same two environments as a horizontal city. The high-rise building is characterised by several different elements: a structural element with its high wind load, an accessible element with its vertical movement and connection, and an environmental element with artificial landscape either inside or out.

The oblique plane or structure constitutes the 'third spatial possibility', subverting the norms of known horizontal and vertical spaces. The oblique plane is considered here as the instigator of a tactile relationship between buildings and a body primarily activated by disequilibrium. In this sense, the oblique can open the way of the new connection between building and infrastructure.

Methodology

A rapid increase in population and immigration from other cities has meant that for several years there has been a lack of housing in the centre of Madrid. Immigrants illegally expanded their living spaces, adding housing in the court, and this has led to a lack of sunlight into their living spaces, significantly deteriorating their living conditions. This can be explained by the establishment of a dwelling cell without the additional access that connects the cell with the outside. This generates the 'interiorisation of the exterior hall' and therefore results in disappearance of the incoming sunlight. To solve this type of problem, I suggest that, as in the case of an ideal urban detached house, each housing unit should be a space with direct access to the outside.

In terms of accessibility, infrastructure is a mixture of incredibly diverse access to people, cars, and even urban information. The tunnel, compared to other infrastructure, is a structure with the sole function of transmittance from one end to the other. In addition to this, it is an exemplary infrastructure providing new access to places against natural obstacles like mountains and rivers. Infrastructure is an exoskeleton structure which combines the skin and the structure, unlike the modern architecture structure of an endoskeleton, where the skin and the structure are separated. The exoskeleton structure does not need another interior supporter; the vacant interior can function as a transit.

Infrastructure for transit includes overpasses, bridges, roads and tunnels. This infrastructure is an integration structure as an exoskeleton which operates as several combined layers in one, Each layer faithfully fulfils its function and at the same time, by vacating the interior space, it fulfils the most important function of transit. Going through a tunnel, tunnelling is the process by which a hole is made horizontally in the ground, with several layers, compared to a high-rise building process in a vertical direction. In terms of good accessibility of tunnelling structure, this layer system can be applied to high-rise building processes in a vertical direction.

In a structural sense, a tunnel is compressed on every side, for instance with earth load and water pressure. That is why a main principle of tunnel design is to pursue equilibrium and compatibility through interaction between the ground and the supports. As mentioned earlier, the tunnel structure is a combination of diverse access. To utilise this characteristic of the structure, the technology of the tunnel structure in the underground should be extracted and adjusted first, in order to be able to be applied to the high-rise building structure.

First, if the compression in the underground is removed, and secondly, if during the transfer to a living space, one of the upper dimensions is open for penetration of the sunlight. In order to fulfil these two conditions, an upper tension member holds both sides of the structure up to prevent a collapse of the structure due to the removed dimension.

There are two methods to support the structure in a safer way: triangular form and trapezoid form. The triangular form is the simplest and most stable structure which consists of two structural members and one tension. The trapezoid form, which consists of three structural members and one tension, is used to design car bodies, which minimis impact and deformation in the event of a car crash. A form of more than four structural members and one tension is important, since it causes an inward deformation within the structural members.

Along with, the structural issue, the issue of accessibility, and the environmental issue, wind load is a specific structural issue that has to be considered when designing a high-rise building. The farther it is from the ground level, the greater it becomes. Because of the wind load, the principle of the basic structure of a high-rise building is the same as the cantilever. In other words, rotating a high-rise building with lateral load by ninety degrees is exactly the cantilever structure.

Basically, we suggest the use of an inclined structure by applying the triangular and trapezoid form from the tunnelling structure to the cantilever structure. In this structure, load from above causes a widening of the structure as a whole.

However, the tension members in the triangular and trapezoid form will support the structure. Secondly, by also using the folding structure, the structure can be stabilised: when you hold a flat piece of paper, it bends, but a folded paper holds itself up. Thirdly, as you can see in a tower crane, the bending moment of itself can be reduced by adopting the bow structure. Fourth, in order to maintain the equilibrium of the inclined structure, it must be counterbalanced. And finally, to prevent distortion, there are shear wall, frame and cross methods in the bracing system. The belt wall or truss system used with the bracing system is employed together with the outrigger, to minimise the horizontal displacement of a high-rise building. As a result, we are convinced that a combination of these systems can basically support the inclined structure.

In an urban sense, there are two ways to improve accessibility. The first one is to build a path between two points and set up a programme according to the path, and the second one is to create a programme first and then set up a path that naturally follows the programme. When using the first method, the criterion to improve accessibility is the amount of surface that is connected to the road. Especially for commercial buildings, it is important to know the number of people the building attracts. From this point of view, if the same amount of surface is connected to the road, it would be advantageous to connect the lower level to the road than the higher level of the building.

Therefore, it is better to plan public buildings on the lower level and install a ramp or stair that is not sensitive to velocity, which will lead to a natural flux. And on the higher levels, a private programme is more appropriate, but it should be made more accessible with the help of an elevator. The interior of the structure on the low level usually consists of public programmes. Using the second way of urban networks, if you install a programme as an instigator on a high level in the middle of a residential area, accessibility can activate between low and high level. Therefore one should install dwelling cells on the higher levels.

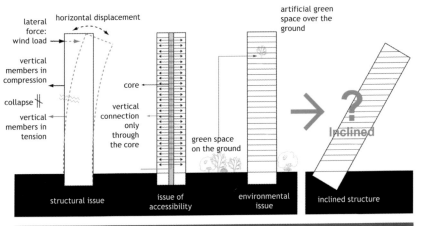

lateral force: wind load

horizontal displacement

vertical members in compression

collapse

vertical members in tension

core

vertical connection only through the core

artificial green space over the ground

green space on the ground

Inclined

structural issue

issue of accessibility

environmental issue

inclined structure

ENVIRONMENTAL ISSUES WITH AN ARTIFICIAL VERTICAL LANDSCAPE

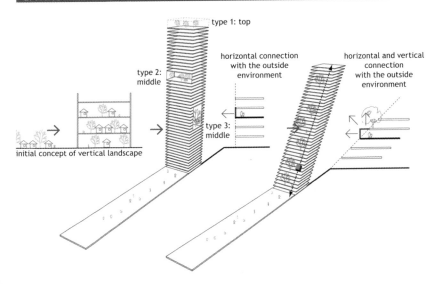

type 1: top

type 2: middle

horizontal connection with the outside environment

horizontal and vertical connection with the outside environment

type 3: middle

initial concept of vertical landscape

Oblique plane by Claude Perrault and Paul Virilio

The concept is derived from the book *Architecture Principle* by Paul Virilio and Claude Perrault published in 1966. They mention the concepts of the oblique ground and habitable circulation and angular plane that constitutes the 'third spatial possibility for architecture' subverting the norms of horizontal and vertical oriented space.

They comment "architecture will no longer be dominated by the visual, the facade, but will relate to the human body as a receptive totality".

The oblique plane works as not only passage but also surface with programmes.

The oblique plane alters the relationship of space and weight: gravity affects perception since "the individual will always be in a state of resistance —whether accelerating as going down or slowing down as climbing up, whereas when one walks on a horizontal plane, weight is nil".

The oblique plane, as third axis in the Euclidean system, offers the opportunity for habitable surface and circulation to become one continuous space.

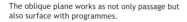
STRUCTURAL ISSUE WITH HIGH WIND LOADS IN HIGH-RISE BUILDING

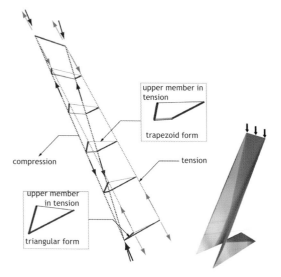

upper member in tension

trapezoid form

compression

tension

upper member in tension

triangular form

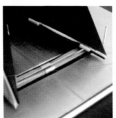

folding structure as form resistent structure

bow structure against bending moment

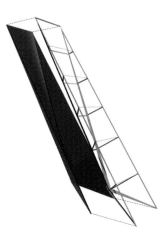

counterbalance to maintain equilibrium against

belt wall against shear force

plan

prototype of parking lot

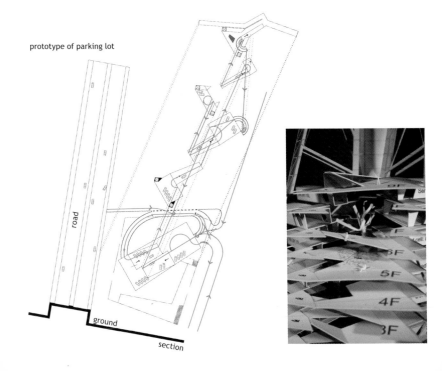

road

ground

section

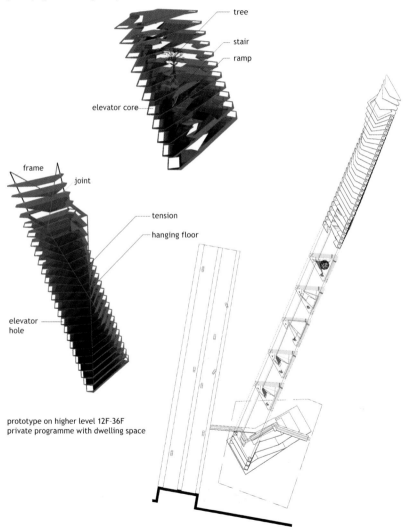

prototype on lower level 1F-11F
public programme with green space

tree

stair

ramp

elevator core

frame

joint

tension

hanging floor

elevator
hole

prototype on higher level 12F-36F
private programme with dwelling space

Networking type A on the lower level
accessibility (between road and building) activation
(semi-public or public programmes)

Networking type B on the higher level
activation (programme as an instigator) accessibility
(between lower and higher level)

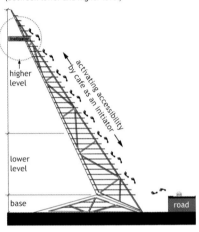

higher
level

lower
level

base

road

worse

accessibility to building from road

better

higher
level

lower
level

base

road

activating accessibility
by cafe as an initiator

instigator

BUFFER ZONE/NOISE PROTECTION FROM ROAD

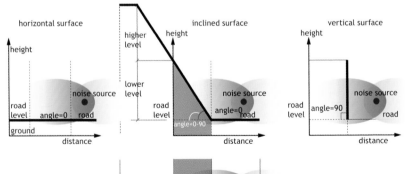

horizontal surface

height

road
level

angle=0   road

ground

distance

noise source

inclined surface

higher
level

height

lower
level

road
level

angle=0   road

angle=0-90

distance

noise source

vertical surface

height

road
level

angle=90

distance

noise source

road

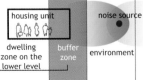

housing unit

noise source

public and semi-public programme
vertical and road connection
vertical landscape

dwelling
zone on the
lower level

buffer
zone

environment

programme zoning
by buffer zone

not only path but also surface with programmes

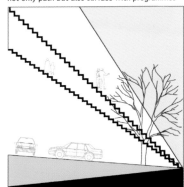

private stair:
max rise 220 mm
min going 225 mm
max pitch 42°

any other stair:
max rise 170 mm
min going 250 mm
max pitch 34°

Gradient of ramp 1:15
between 2 to 5M

Gradient of ramp 1:12
between 0 to 2M

Gradient of ramp 1:20
between 5 to 15M

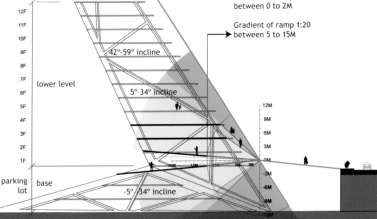

inclined elevator 59°

12F
11F
10F
9F
8F
7F   lower level
6F
5F
4F
3F
2F
1F

42°-59° incline

5°-34° incline

-5°-34° incline

12M
9M
6M
3M
0M
-3M
-6M
-8M
-12M

parking
lot   base

SERVED AND SERVING CELL PENETRATED INCLINED SURFACE

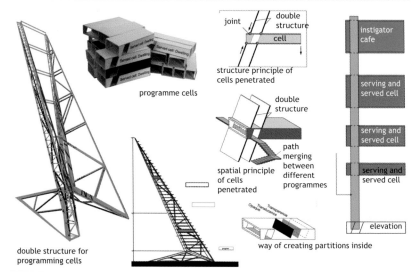

programme cells

joint · double structure
cell

structure principle of cells penetrated

double structure

path merging between different programmes

spatial principle of cells penetrated

double structure for programming cells

way of creating partitions inside

instigator cafe

serving and served cell

serving and served cell

serving and served cell

elevation

CO-EXISTENCE OF PROGRAMMES/SERVING AND SERVED CELLS

served cell for dwelling into green floor on the lower level

served cell for green space into dwelling floor on the higher level

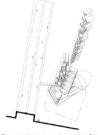

in-between space as a connector of floors with each cell

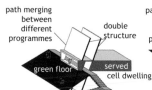

path merging between different programmes

double structure

green floor · served cell dwelling

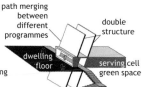

path merging between different programmes

double structure

dwelling floor · serving cell green space

in-between space as a connector of floors with each cell

Results

The second issue of accessibility around a high-rise building is the vertical connection. Generally, the core of a high-rise building is the main structure, the hole for most of installation, and the vertical connection linking each horizontal floor. There are four types within the core system, namely, centric, concentric, tube and double core, and the existing core system has a volume like the inside of a box which connects each floor. It is nonetheless uniform and not diverse.

The vertical connection of the core system in the form of a box is one-directional. Nevertheless, if the form of a box is changed to a surface and it is inclined, one can use the sides of a building, allowing the possibility of diverse access and connections. As with the Madrid housing problem, units with their own diverse access constitute a space according to the inclined surface. Ultimately, the question of how to merge infrastructure and a high-rise building concerns the relationship between the road and the housing unit. The inclined structure is a possible solution to this problem. There is a various velocity range within the question of access. The ramp and stair with a low speed constitute a surface and the inclined elevator corresponds to the high accessible speed.

As for the third, environmental issue, there is the vertical landscape. High-rise buildings in Korea, for example, are generally residential buildings, compared to high-rises as office buildings in other countries. One of the critical points of designing a high-rise building, is the vertical landscape on the inside, as sometimes inhabitants cannot open the windows on upper floors due to high winds. Architects have therefore tried to create artificial landscapes in the form of 'sky gardens'. After a long evolution, high-rise buildings now occasionally have an artificial landscape on the top or a middle floor, creating an imitation ground level by accumulating houses and their natural surroundings. Compared to an erect high-rise building that only has a horizontal connection with the outside environment, an inclined structure has both a horizontal and a vertical connection.

In designing a parking lot, a process with a natural element between a house and its garage will also be possible. This will enable the parking lot to become a friendly space that is coexistent with the dwelling space, as opposed to a separation between the two.

Conclusion

Material and structural change are dissolving the traditional boundaries between building and infrastructure. In our society, the city is not a single coherent entity but a diverse collection of hybrid buildings and complex cultural networks. The traditional conception of a high-rise building is being replaced with more adaptable, fluid and flexible environments, reflecting the pace at which our global society is evolving.

Everything on the ground is affected by gravity; therefore the individual structure must always be in a state of resistance in order to be stable, which is a limit to, or a possibility, of architecture, depending on how we use it. In this sense, inclined structures could be one of the instigators reflecting the current pace of the high-rise building, in order to create diverse connections between road and building, and low and high levels.

I conclude with the question: what, from the three issues (the structural, environmental and accessibility issues) do the existing high-rise buildings lack and how can one improve living environments with the help of these issues?

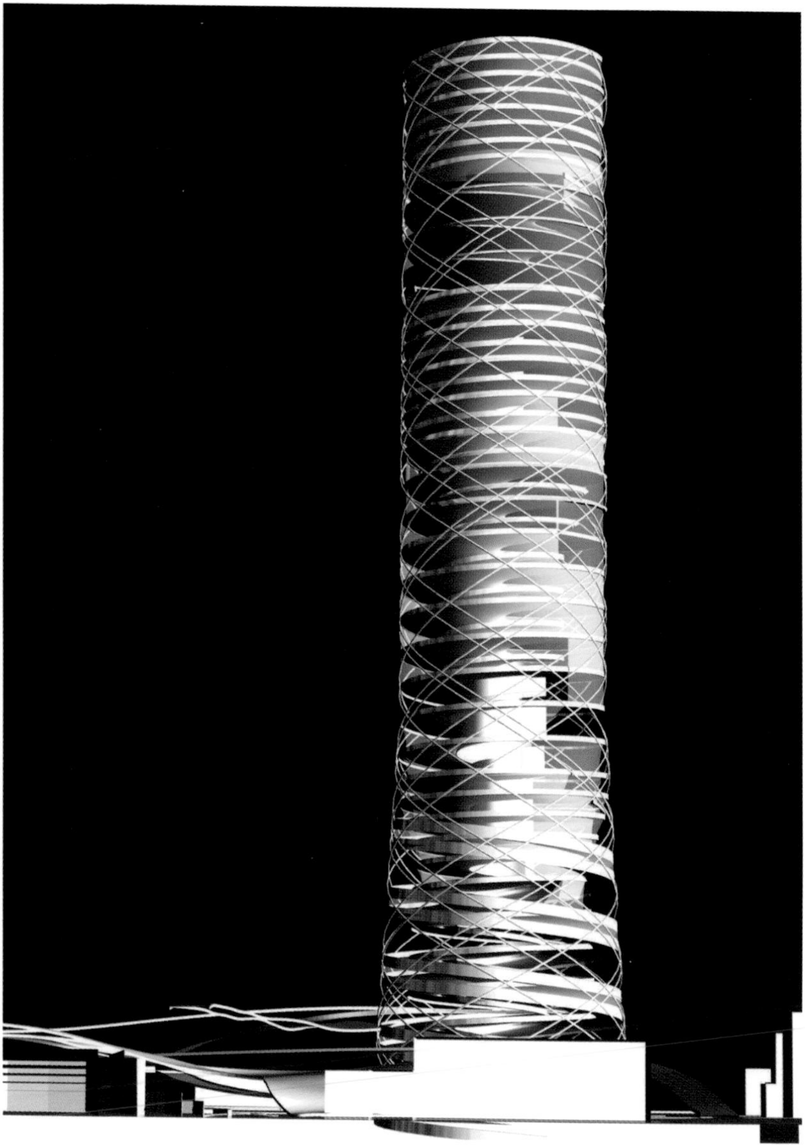

VERTICAL CITY inhabitable slope
Pieterjan Vermoortel

Hypothesis

How can one create a vertical city that treats the high-rise as an adaptive system? The subject of this research is a city regarded as a 'network city', wherein different routing and circulation possibilities exist that enable connections from one point to another. In the service of established programmatic interests, the prototype may call for a solution that includes a circulation system that also integrates programme and service.

This research deals with the effort to make spiralling organisations operational for the high-rise organisation, and hence is about the "city as a differentiated container with sameness".

Summary

In sociological terms, society has changed from a 'group-orientated' into an 'individualised' society. The former social system centred on the nuclear family unit and has now shifted into one in which groups are ordered according to their interests. Social contact and activity became based on one's interests and active participation in them. Difference is created by the way in which identical elements are put together in a different order.

It is believed that, in traditional terms, helix-like organisations are redundant for the high-rise; however, their inefficiency can be considered in light of its potential for including structural and social forms into the inseparable one. Whilst winding around a central pole and gradually receding according to the sloping speed, this organisational principle has the potential for seamless transitions between different programmes and target groups and converting its initial disadvantage into design opportunities.

In a similar fashion to the DNA helix, I tried to achieve continuous organisational difference by slight changes in the order of identical elements attached to each other by spiral circulation. This circulation is the binding element, accommodating programmatic changes and various spatial configurations along its vertical evolution, whilst keeping the same structural form and infra-structural independence.

How can we create a vertical city of inhabitable circulation?

The city proposed is regarded as a network city, wherein exists a multitude of possibilities to go from one point to an other according to your (or your groups') interests. This city would be a container of difference within sameness or a 'multi-generational, multi-programmed city'; the city as difference within a framework of similitude.

Summary

The idea of contemporary society as a network of varying social activities in which we shape our identity (or choose our own world) by participation in group activities designated by interest, is nicely illustrated by the DNA helix, in which We tried to achieve difference by slightly changing the order of identical elements attached to each other by the circulation. Circulation is the binding element.

Methodology

Parallel investigation structure (form)—slope programme
Because age is now perhaps the only possible way to speak of coherent social groups, analyse of user groups (which are nowadays still groups of common interests) by this classification system has been employed here. We investigated the daily schedules of people of different age groups in a search of pre-existing and possible new overlaps within them. Out of this research, we arrived at a list of activities (categorised by 'leisure', 'services and working' and 'living') that are shared or needed for several groups or not shared at all. Each category evolves

itself around the building from more public to private uses and is positioned in overlap with other categories according to mutual interests and needs. The programme is put to a different speed of circulation.

The next step was to decide how to set up the relation between these different activities: physical connectivity. We can divide this term further into three groups; sequential contact, constant contact and no contact. The physical connectivity within the programme is itself defined by the speed of the slope, and the interconnectivity between different programmes is defined by the distance between crossings of other programme slopes (that turn in the reverse direction). Since the accessibility rate of the programme increases with the increase of the angle of the slope we can call it a privacy indicator. For example, family housing has a slope of 35 degrees whereas shopping has a slope of three degrees. The distance between the crossings defines the height of the rate of possible programme intermingling. Each user group was divided into percentages of people using the alternated programme. The elevator in this research was considered to be the most private means of accessibility because it has a vertical slope and is thus used for making shortcuts between the different macro units (which are mainly defined by the user groups). From the point at which the elevator stops, we can start to gradient the different slopes.

Structural (formal) research

Is there, as in the building of DNA, similarly a simple combination of structural rules able to accommodate the difference in programme (and circulation according to the programme)? Is there, as in the DNA helix, a structure capable of generating all of the differences by very simple rules? The helix is the carrier and generator of different combinations of information. In this research, the spiral is the carrier and also the generator of the different programme. By the placement of reverse-turning spirals, we can create a structural cage. The spiral is also the generator of the programme and circulation.

Analysis of ruled surfaces

Like the DNA helix, ruled surfaces exist out of a generator and a generated. The surface is thus generated by moving a straight line along the generator (curve). The generator in my case, defined by the slope and the form of the programme, generates a surface consisting of straight lines. Here, the information determines the construction of the shape. The straight lines can be replaced by straight elements. Since the construction of buildings is still a very indeterminate business, straight building elements can easily be constructed.

Case study
Manufacturing: cooling tower, towers: formal freedom: Philips Pavilion.

The cooling towers show how a net in the form of the generated lines of the ruled surface can be held up to reinforce the minimal surface (a surface that has a minimum of bending moments). Afterwards, concrete is sprayed onto it. In other buildings the generated lines are replaced by steel bars to create a structural framework. There is the case of the Philips Pavilion, designed by Le Corbusier for the World Expo of 1958 in Brussels, in which generated lines are replaced by pre-cast concrete slabs, poured in situ. The generators are created from cold bended steel profiles that hold together the concrete slabs. The Philips Pavilion is the first example of a ruled surface that really explores the maximal formal freedom facilitated by ruled surfaces.

Ruled surface research: catalogue (matrix): (slope network) as parametric generator, programmatic analysis of the created forms, programmatic conclusion.

In the catalogue we tried to find the relationship between the surface generation and the programme. It consists of three parts: the change in the parameters of the generator of the ruled surface that creates different surfaces; the analysis of the created surface in terms of visual and physical connectivity; and no square metres needed to transform it into one flat surface (step), and which kind of programme it fits into best, according to communication area, divided space and shaft and surface. In the first attempt to really understand these forms, the slope and the shape were placed as constraints to the generator. The parameters of the ruled surface are the reverse or the same direction of rotation of each generator to another, difference in scale of the generators, planar shape of the generator and position of the generators to each other. The fact that these parameters are part of a gradual change is shown by some illustrations. The final shape is analysed in terms of the three above-mentioned categories.

The first question asked in the criteria of the analysis is whether or not the created shape consists of continuous surfaces. If yes, does it consist of one or more surfaces? And then we can answer the questions of physical connectivity, visual connectivity, and possible metres squared of flat surface (defined by the surface between different height lines). If it is one continuous surface, we can answer the next question of physical connectivity: what is the shape of the vector lines, being lines of constant slope: least to be followed for circulation, linear, circular, and elliptical? Are there disruptions? Where is the maximum density of vector lines reached (surface which is no longer walkable). In consideration of visual connectivity, we should ask if there is a void or split-level, or both. If we have two continuous surfaces, we should ask within the same categories (visual, physical, metres squared of flat surface) questions of the relationship between the two different surfaces. And is there visual connectivity between the two surfaces? If so, does it happen through split-level or void, or both? In terms of physical connectivity, does the surface split at one point into two surfaces?

We can use this list of questions to programme the answers as to which programme best fits this form, if any. For example, one small and one big circular spiral generator, rotated 180 degrees to each other, creates two continuous, but different in radius, circular surfaces that are not physically connected but split-level visually connected. This would ideally accommodate young people on the big surface and young peoples' offices on the smaller surface, because there is a visual relation between work and living, but accessibility is independent from both. This forms our conclusion on shape. Through this research, we came to the conclusion that only a point-symmetrical shape for the generator could create a non-rippled surface. So the circular and the elliptical spiral were the only usable generator forms. Another outcome already envisioned by the illustration is that we can gradually change the space from park to sports ground to theatre, or vice-versa. And we can change the spaces from elderly housing with a separate path for services to family housing with a separate path for offices, back to elderly housing with a separate path for shopping, to young peoples' housing with a separate path for flexi-time working, to shopping again. The use of reverse turning spirals creates a structural form consisting of triangles.

Structural implementation

Site implementation
Creation of different entry points: connection with the infrastructure of the environment. The connection with a lot of infrastructure is advantageous since this prototype is created for a high user rate.

For cars, we integrate the highway lanes into the parking facilities within the complex and reconnect it to the local environment. For pedestrians and cyclists, we integrate the nearby park (which also connects to the nearby train station) into the building.

Creation of multiple built prototypes mutually connected.

Since it would be absurd to make each of these prototypes separate from the outside environments, it makes sense to put more of these prototypes on the site, mutually connected. It also creates more mass for each user group, since each of the prototypes could hold more of the same programme.

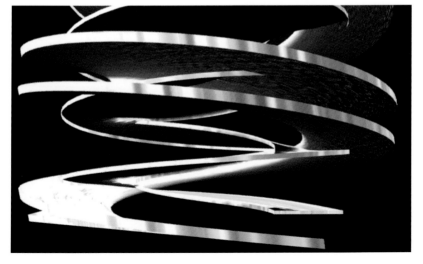

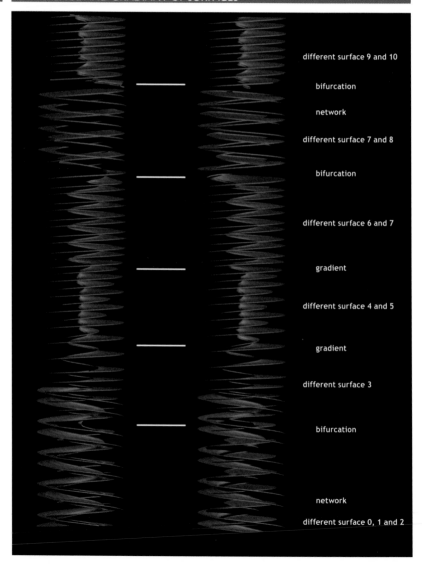

different surface 9 and 10

bifurcation

network

different surface 7 and 8

bifurcation

different surface 6 and 7

gradient

different surface 4 and 5

gradient

different surface 3

bifurcation

network

different surface 0, 1 and 2

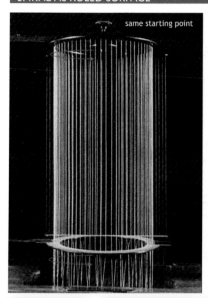
same starting point

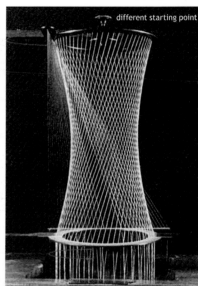
different starting point

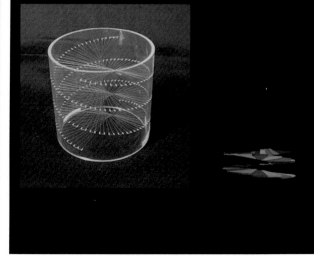

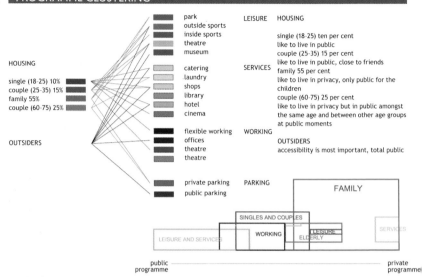

LEISURE
park
outside sports
inside sports
theatre
museum

SERVICES
catering
laundry
shops
library
hotel
cinema

WORKING
flexible working
offices
theatre
theatre

PARKING
private parking
public parking

HOUSING

single (18-25) ten per cent
like to live in public
couple (25-35) 15 per cent
like to live in public, close to friends
family 55 per cent
like to live in privacy, only public for the children
couple (60-75) 25 per cent
like to live in privacy but in public amongst the same age and between other age groups at public moments

OUTSIDERS
accessibility is most important, total public

HOUSING

single (18-25) 10%
couple (25-35) 15%
family 55%
couple (60-75) 25%

OUTSIDERS

FAMILY

SINGLES AND COUPLES

LEISURE AND SERVICES

WORKING

LEISURE
ELDERLY

SERVICES

public programme — private programme

THE SPEED OF CIRCULATION DEFINES THE PROGRAMME

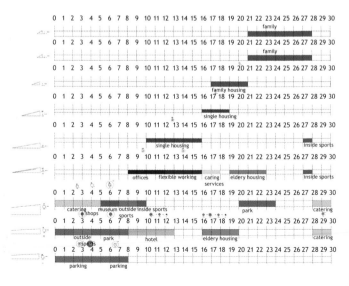

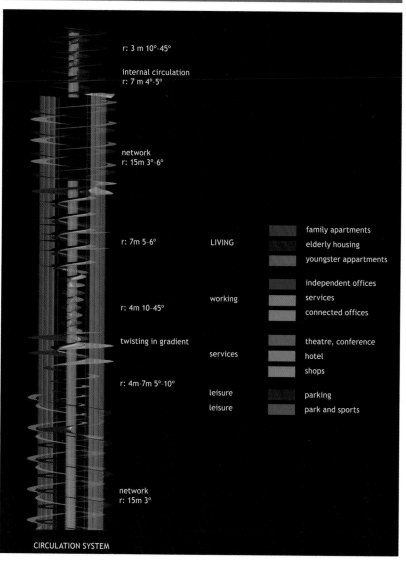

r: 3 m 10°-45°

internal circulation
r: 7 m 4°-5°

network
r: 15m 3°-6°

r: 7m 5-6°   LIVING   family apartments
                                             elderly housing
                                             youngster appartments

                             working   independent offices
r: 4m 10-45°   services
                                             connected offices

twisting in gradient   services   theatre, conference
                                             hotel
                                             shops
r: 4m-7m 5°-10°
                             leisure   parking
                             leisure   park and sports

network
r: 15m 3°

CIRCULATION SYSTEM

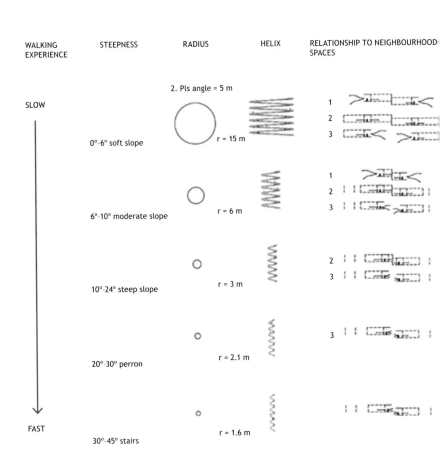

WALKING EXPERIENCE	STEEPNESS	RADIUS	HELIX	RELATIONSHIP TO NEIGHBOURHOOD SPACES
SLOW	0°-6° soft slope	2. Pls angle = 5 m / r = 15 m		1 / 2 / 3
	6°-10° moderate slope	r = 6 m		1 / 2 / 3
	10°-24° steep slope	r = 3 m		2 / 3
	20°-30° perron	r = 2.1 m		3
FAST	30°-45° stairs	r = 1.6 m		

DEPTH OF OUTER SPACES

according to the height
(daylight) and the function

ONE-SIDED light

houses: depth 7m/height 3m
offices: depth 12m/height 3m

No light

theatre
disco
cinema
parking

Indirect light

shopping complex
lobby of hotel
museum
internal circulation office
building

two or more sided light

panoramic restaurant

PROGRAMME

1 RECREATION
   outside sports, park
   musuem, library
2 SHOPPING COMPLEX

3 SHOPPING COMPLEX
   with central hall
   internal musuem,
   lobby of a hotel
1 restaurant health centre
   with panoramic views

2 AND 3 BIGGER OFFICE
COMPLEX entrance of services,
laundry, travel agent,restaurant
3 elderly home, school, disco
   communal centre, theatre

2 internal circulation office,
   fitness club
3 atelier, restaurant, bar
   entrance for more communal
   housing for singles, elderly

3 internal circulation atelier,
   restaurant, bar, circulation in
   office building, with separated
   offices, entrance for private
   housing

3 normal fire staircase when
   entrance is normally by
   elevator or private office
   spaces entrance of private
   houses internal circulation in
   house, office

COMBINATION

· fast speed can't
  be somewhere fast
  enough: private
  housing, offices

· intermediate speed:
  communal spaces,
  services, offices,
  semi-public living

· slow speed:
  looking around
  relaxed, shopping,
  park

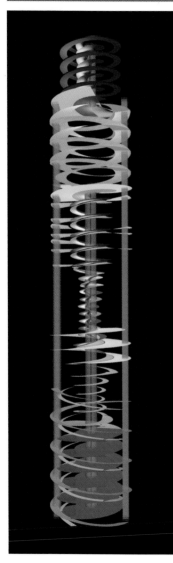

straight

no partitioning

twisting

straight

twisting in gradient

straight

twisting

PARTITIONING SYSTEM

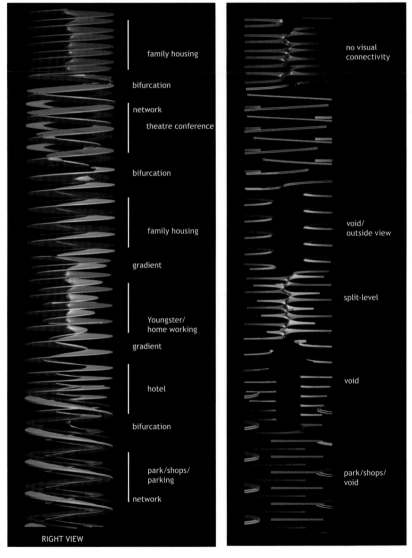

family housing

bifurcation

network

theatre conference

bifurcation

family housing

gradient

Youngster/
home working

gradient

hotel

bifurcation

park/shops/
parking

network

RIGHT VIEW

no visual
connectivity

void/
outside view

split-level

void

park/shops/
void

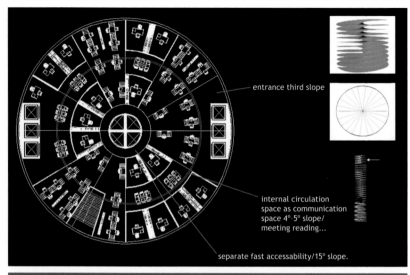

entrance third slope

internal circulation
space as communication
space 4°-5° slope/
meeting reading...

separate fast accessability/15° slope.

SHOPPING

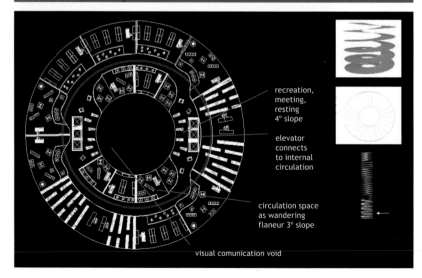

recreation,
meeting,
resting
4° slope

elevator
connects
to internal
circulation

circulation space
as wandering
flaneur 3° slope

visual comunication void

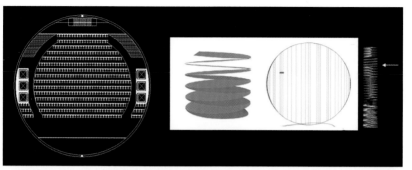

PARK AND KIOSKS

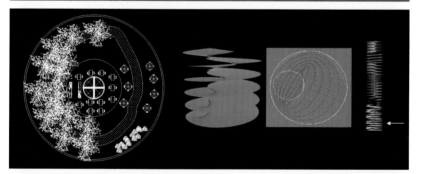

YOUNGSTER HOUSING/WORKING AT HOME BUT SEPARATE

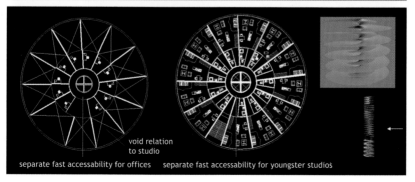

void relation
to studio

separate fast accessability for offices   separate fast accessability for youngster studios

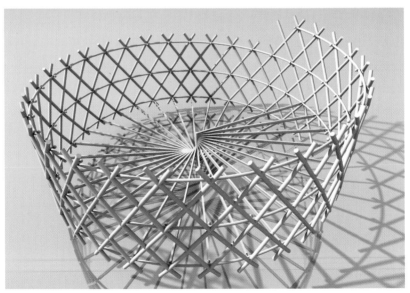

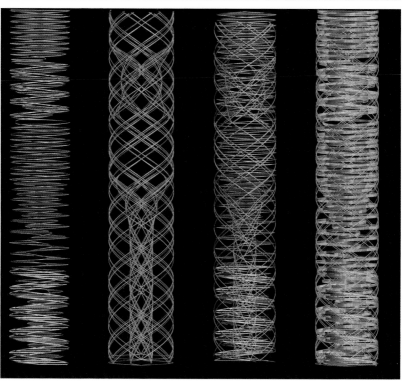

generated spiral
generated steps

primary structure

integrated structure

reality of the thickness
of the steps

Result

What I have done is tackle the traditional concept of a high-rise organisation. The high-rise typology is characterised by its stacked organisation with the elevator as the main means of accessibility. This typology has never been questioned because of the perceived efficiency of such a system. Indeed, the high-rise only came into existence after the invention of the elevator. The stacking and the position of the elevator as the main means of accessibility results in big lobbies that are incredibly public or in private entrances to the facilities. This is almost to the exclusion of in-between spaces and interrelated spaces. This ultimate division of every space has also meant the disappearance of conflicting spaces, or spaces that accommodate conflicts of interest.

In this sense, a new type of 'densification' should be able to restore relations between people. A new prototype based on circulation was developed for this purpose; a system that integrates programme, circulation and structure in one, to form a society of interest groups—a system that incorporates difference within itself, and not difference as separate entities but as variations of the same structural principle, the same circulation system, and the same programmatic infill. It is only through dealing with the perceived efficiency of the former high-rise system that we can hold up a more accurate mirror of present society. Only through exploring the borders of this system can we engender new forms of architecture. As in every human field, borders are opened through knowledge to create new possibilities.

Conclusion

The thesis becomes a combination of two elements: the programme informing the layout, and the way around the construction that informs the programme. On one hand, we have the surface that informs the programme; bounded to each other by a path of circulation that can either split into two paths or end, according to the gradient. And on the other hand, we have the creation of a network of different paths by pushing the different surfaces through each other, as a result of this programmatic analysis.

VERTICAL KIBBUTZ high-rise prototype throughout polyhedral space frames
Noa Haim

Hypothesis

How research into a cooperative rural organisation (in this case, a kibbutz) and the polyhedral space frame (unit based structure) can inform established conventions of a high-rise typology. Or in other words, can space frames be inhabited and how can they contribute to the notion of a social cooperative housing system?

Summary

The kibbutz is the most distinguished outcome of the Zionist movement of the last century. It is an organisational whole of a collective form of living, which arises out of periodical necessities to adopt Marxist social ideology.

The main organisation principles are the following:
1. Whole organisation; programme and age
2. Constant rotation; inhabitants are shifting in between housing units and professional occupation
3. Egalitarian society
4. Organically expanded
5. Unit based organisation

The first attempt of my research was to translate a horizontal organisation into a vertical one, while maintaining the differences in programmatic capacity, exposure, sequence, routing and permeability. The second phase was to coordinate the vertical organisation with a structural system which can accommodate the organisation capacity and maintain two of the organisation principles—these being unit based and organical growth.

Space frames are mainly used for building envelopes, facades, canopies, special roofs, and are barely used in the housing industry today. They are lightweight, prefabricated and can lead to an infinite grid. In order to increase the surface capacity (packing principle) tessellation techniques have been introduced which allow more daylight to enter the building.

The prototype proposes two elements in relation to high-rise typology. The first is from the structural point of view, a three-dimensional organism in opposition to the conventional one which is extruded bottom to top. The second is the different permeability model, which arises out of my kibbutz research, and translates the principle of an egalitarian society into a contemporary urban context.

The whole prototype represents a form which is the outcome of a reverted displacement processes. The first displacement is in the ideas and people who are shifting from the urban European context to rural Palestine/Israel at the beginning of the last century, and reversed in this prototype proposal from the Mediterranean rural environment back to the European urban one.

Methodology

The methodology is divided into three segments:
1. Kibbutz cases studies
2. Space frames and tessellation technique
3. Madrid scenario

Kibbutz case studies

Kibbutz—the Hebrew word is driven from the root KBZ which in English can refer to a group, and is also used to describe a particular type of collective rural settlement.

The first kibbutz was established in 1910 by a Zionist youth group from Poland. Today, there are 276 kibbutzim throughout Israel, inhabited by 102,000 people —which is 1.8 per cent of the Israeli population.

Three different Kibbutzim have been chosen as case studies:
Ketura—founded in 1973, accommodating 335 inhabitants
Reshafim—founded in 1948, accommodating 515 inhabitants
Bet Zera—founded in 1927, accommodating 730 inhabitants

The logic behind this selection was that each of them is of a different capacity scale and founded in a different period. All of them are located on the outskirts of Israel—Reshafim and Bet Zera in the north-east, and Ketura in the south-east.

The different foundings indicate organisational planning versus the non-planned. Bet Zera was founded as a commune and grew organically, while Ketura was planned specifically as a kibbutz, and Reshafim was founded as a kibbutz but not planned according to specific kibbutz master planning. All three case studies have been mapped according to different zones: housing, working, commune spaces and childrens facilities, accessibility and permeability (members versus non-members). The main public facilities have been measured (square metre per person) according to the number of users in each of the case studies.

In order to give a vertical representation to the kibbutz organisation (horizontal), a synthetic map which represents the different zoning and communication populations has been translated into a diagram which represents the quantities and qualities of the organisation parameters.

The case study conclusions are clustered into quantities and qualities. The quantities are the minimum/maximum square metre per person in the public facilities and the sequence of programmatic exposure to the user (housing, working, commune and children). The qualities are the organisation permeability in terms of members/non-members, which differ from other communes' vertical whole organisation typology.

Space frames and tessellation techniques

In order to translate the kibbutz' vertical representation into a building, a structural system had to be used which could accommodate the whole organisation, to allow for organic growth based on the repetition of the same unit. These three constraints lead to the choice of polyhedral space frame. What is a space frame structural technique? Usually it is an open three-dimensional framework of struts and braces (as employed in buildings and racing cars) which defines a structure and distributes its weight evenly in all dimensions. In algebraic topologies, the term polyhedron is defined as a space that can be built from such 'building blocks' as lines, segments, triangles, tetrahedrals, and their higher dimensional analogues by 'gluing them together' along their faces. More specifically, it can be defined as the underlying space of a simplified infinite complex—Munkres, 1993.

By using 400 centimetre long diagonals, a rigid mesh of octahedrals and tetrahedrals has been created. The outcome of this rigid mesh is a hexagonal pattern. In order to inhabit this mesh, we first need to find out which diagonals can be deleted in order to create vertical communication, variation of spaces and carry the inhabitable loads. The research adopted J François Gabriel's structural philosophy from the book *Beyond the Cube*. According to this source, two different structural meshes can be created; the skeleton and the perforated. The skeleton repeats the octahedral/tetrahedral organisation on a large scale and can carry heavy loads as inhabitable ones and vertical communication. The perforated is based on the speculation that out of seven hexagons (in floor plan) only one has to be structural and the location of the structural one is shifted on each floor. This mesh allows the spaces natural and tessellated variation.

Tessellation, or the tiling used in convex geometry, is a description for the covering of space by a family of sets which forms as a packing at the same time. The tessellation research has been done using 3-D Max software as a simulating programme. A hexagonal unit (2.8 metre radius) has been manipulated by the tessellation modifier which contains four parameters, and the operation can be done on a triangular or rectangular surface and can be operated when the direction of the face is oriented to the centre of the hexagon or to the edge of it. Two more parameters are the level of tension and iteration. By using the tessellation technique on the polyhedral frame, the surface interface is increased and allows more variation in the surface itself.

Madrid scenario

Madrid is the prototype case study, were this would be implemented virtually and its performance evaluated. Madrid as a case study could actually represent any other large scale European city, and the parameters which it constrains in the prototype are the variation in the dwelling size and the quantity relations between them.

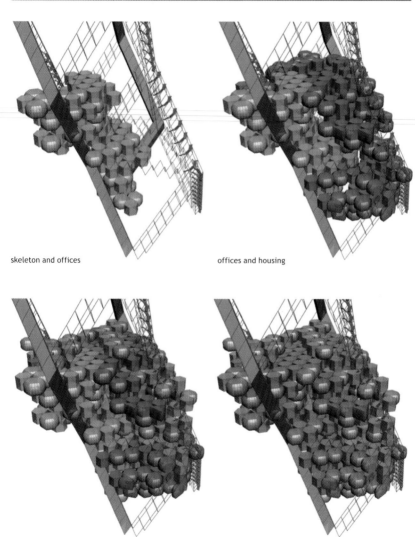

skeleton and offices

offices and housing

offices, housing and commercial facilities

the whole organisation

of the whole

organically expanded

Kibbutz organisation case studies

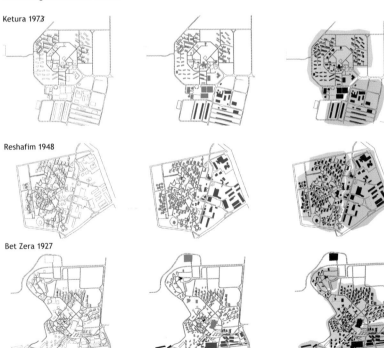

Ketura 1973

Reshafim 1948

Bet Zera 1927

organisation

zoning

permeability

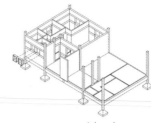

egalitarian society   constant rotation   unit based

member: 160
temporary: 35
child: 140
total: 335

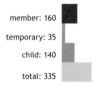

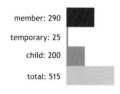

member: 290
temporary: 25
child: 200
total: 515

● living
● working
● sharing
● children

member: 320
temporary: 222
child: 152
total: 730

● members
● non-members

demography   planning versus non-planning

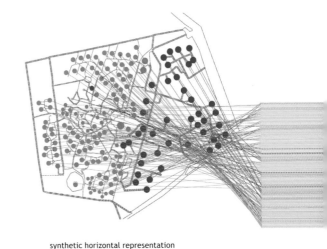

living

working

sharing

children

---- private pedestrian

—— public pedestrian

—— motor way

synthetic horizontal representation

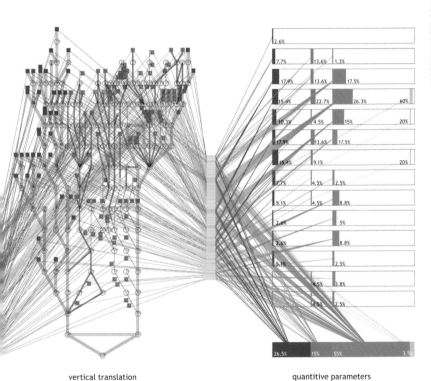

vertical translation

quantitive parameters

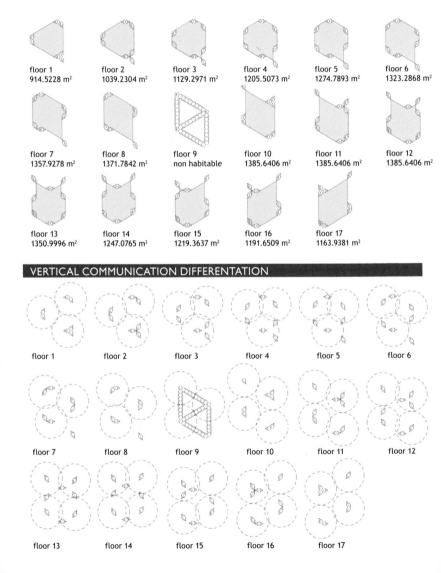

floor 1 — 914.5228 m²
floor 2 — 1039.2304 m²
floor 3 — 1129.2971 m²
floor 4 — 1205.5073 m²
floor 5 — 1274.7893 m²
floor 6 — 1323.2868 m²
floor 7 — 1357.9278 m²
floor 8 — 1371.7842 m²
floor 9 — non habitable
floor 10 — 1385.6406 m²
floor 11 — 1385.6406 m²
floor 12 — 1385.6406 m²
floor 13 — 1350.9996 m²
floor 14 — 1247.0765 m²
floor 15 — 1219.3637 m²
floor 16 — 1191.6509 m²
floor 17 — 1163.9381 m²

VERTICAL COMMUNICATION DIFFERENTATION

floor 1, floor 2, floor 3, floor 4, floor 5, floor 6, floor 7, floor 8, floor 9, floor 10, floor 11, floor 12, floor 13, floor 14, floor 15, floor 16, floor 17

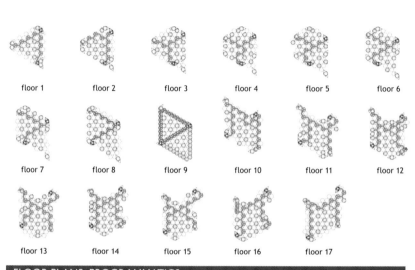

floor 1 floor 2 floor 3 floor 4 floor 5 floor 6

floor 7 floor 8 floor 9 floor 10 floor 11 floor 12

floor 13 floor 14 floor 15 floor 16 floor 17

FLOOR PLANS PROGRAMMATICS

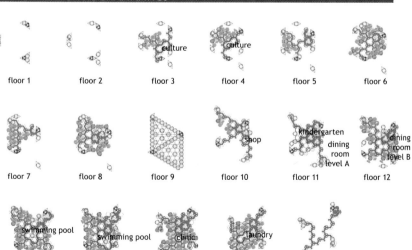

floor 1 floor 2 floor 3 floor 4 floor 5 floor 6

floor 7 floor 8 floor 9 floor 10 floor 11 floor 12

floor 13 floor 14 floor 15 floor 16 floor 17

Results

The results shaped the prototype's form and informed it programmatically and structurally, which leads into the typology. The results can be ordered under three main topics; the kibbutz organisation and its vertical translation, the space frame production technique as a three-dimensional organism, and how these carry vertical inhabitable loads, and the assemblage between them.

The kibbutz case study results can be divided into quantities and qualities. The quantities are the programmatic ecologies which are re-shaped according to the Madrid housing market. The qualities are the different vertical permeabilities (members versus non-members) in the model, which is an outcome of the egalitarian society organisation principle. The differentiation is in the mixture of usage all along the organism, contrary to the familiar high-rise typology where the users are distinguished along the core (bottom to top).

The space frame, can carry inhabitable loads in two different ways in relation to the different meshes mentioned previously—the skeleton and the perforated. If one is using the perforated mesh only, then the tubes need to become thicker in the bottom to middle floors, which means less inhabitable spaces in those segments. Meanwhile, the skeleton mesh can carry those loads while using lightweight tubes (not more than 20 cm diameter) along the organism. This is enabled by the special geometry which repeats itself in the small as in the big members. These results led the research to the development of an assemblage between the two meshes; while the skeleton is used for defining the 'outlines' and the vertical communication of the whole, the perforated is used to fill the 'outline' of the kibbutz organisation and the Madrid case study. When the infill is smaller than the outline voids are created. When the infill is bigger than the outline cantilevers are created in the first step. For the second, some of the programme shifts into the floor below or above, while maintaining the specific connections between programmes which are not located in the same floor but belong to the same one.

The skeleton mesh is a whole structural one so it is not tessellated. The perforated mesh can be tessellated when it is a facade, and the specific unit is not structural. In this way, the packing principal of the whole prototype becomes bigger and allows more daylight to enter, and gives more variety between the inhabitable spaces.

Conclusions

The research was trying to translate a horizontal non-planned rural organisation of a cooperative into the vertical, by using space frames and implementing them in an urban context. What is the novelty of this proposal? And how can it contribute to the notion of high-rise typology today?

The prototype proposes two new elements in relation to high-rise typology. The first is from the structural point of view—a three-dimensional organism in opposition to the conventional one which is extruded bottom to top. The second novelty is the different permeability model, which arises out of kibbutz research, and translates the egalitarian society principle into a contemporary urban context.

The whole prototype represents a form which is the outcome of reverted displacement processes. The first displacement is in the ideas and people who are shifting from an urban European context to rural Palestine/Israel at the beginning of the last century, and reversed in this prototype proposal from the Mediterranean rural environment back to the European urban one.

CUSTOMISATION STRATEGIES

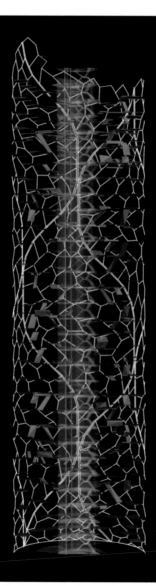

THE HOUSE FOR THE DIFFERENCE
potential housing for forthcoming generations
Eriko Watanabe

Hypothesis

Is it possible to imagine collective housing, not for the general public or the family, but for diverse individuals? Taking housing as the family habitat, to shift nature to the next stage, individualisation and the social encounter are taken into account. 'Honeycomb' material is employed as the skin, the structure, and in the individual cells.

Short summary

The main object here is to set up a housing prototype to meet the social demands of people whose identity no longer belongs to a defined 'standard'.

Verticality and the communality of the high-rise apartment are taken as the potential to provide the basis of a dynamic configuration. The high-rise is taken as the battle between the new and existing systems, the envelope being the new, and the core being the existing system in this project. The core system is a domino system, the representative of the high-rise typology of the twentieth century. The organic configuration of the new honeycomb material is borrowed and emphasised as an envelope as a perimeter tube structure, so that the skin might project the dynamic expression of the individual. The gap between the two systems is filled with four different layers in order to connect them in organically. The gaps among the four layers would function as a device to connect or disconnect them physically or psychologically.

Methodology (process) description

The issues here are not new or even directly related to the main theme of the project. The following description explains the conceptual process of the project. It is very important to remind oneself that we are dealing with the typology of an apartment.

An individual's identity depends on one's cultural background. As one transcends the framework of locality or nationality, as one is put in a superficial communication without common consensus, and transcends invisible codes, one faces giving up one's original identity. Possibly, one could arrive at new kinds of identity.

Taking the view that humans understand or judge their personality through the 'other', as the media becomes personalised, and the borders of personal territory become more diffuse, one doubles the number of the 'other'.

> There becomes no need to consider depths any more as people can do quite a lot of things with only superficial communication. On one hand, it seems that we are able to see everything in the world due to the smooth circulation of information. On the other hand, we see very few things because it is too smooth.... On one hand, we have become more and more dependent on invisible codes (information); on the other hand, we try and stay within visible (spectacle) things.

> Hiroko Azuma

The dissociation of the local and the global, the real and the virtual, complicates one's personality, by continually splitting it. One not only doubles the quotient of the 'other' but also increases the distance between oneself and the 'other'.

In the twentieth century, flexibility implies freedom within a fixed restriction. In architectural terms, it signifies a homogeneous space. Here, flexibility is an open space within a container. I believe that in the twenty-first century, flexibility should mean free relationships within the series of privileged spaces based on a minimum unit, regulation or system. 'Free relationships' implies that one doesn't need to be related to the other. Here, the basic unit is rather small, preliminarily defined, well-functioned, and loosely overlapped with others that have the same principles.

Family housing in the twentieth century was designed to accommodate a nuclear family. The arrangement of rooms—a living room with a television and a couch big enough to accommodate the whole family, a dining room with a table and as many chairs as family members, a master bedroom with a double bed for the parents, a kitchen, bedrooms with a desk and a bed for the children, and an extra room for visitors (if there was any space left)—are all based on the family fantasy. And on the media's encouraging people to hurry out and buy the ideal family housing. People sank half their salary into buying a space full of expectations.

Has the family changed?

On one hand, one would say no, as it is still the accepted ideal, but on the other hand, one must say yes: single parents, gene manipulation, gender mixture, gay society, generation Y (those born in the computer age), the decline in the number of children, child abuse, childless couples, etc.. The ideal image of the modern family, 'husband and wife' and 'parents and kids' closely tied together, is not a long lasting definition, rather, it's constantly changing in an unstable society. Yet, the image of the modern family looked so beautiful and fashionable that it became more powerful, more natural than reality. When society took precedence over the image, reality was neglected.

In some advanced countries, there are people born in the computer age who don't know how to communicate with people. They have been sitting in front of a screen and been educated through educational television programmes or the computer. They know how to behave, only based on generic rules or manuals. They know how to input information but don't know how to output it since they are not able to foresee how others would react to them. The importance of face-to-face communication should be refocused. Communication by mobile and the Internet are not perfect, as they lack the complexity of the expression of the human body and our emotions.

Globalisation generates diverse values, not on a nation-wide level, but on an individual level. This phenomenon diversifies the relationship between individuals. We are in a situation that has to allow for different kinds of values. What does it mean for us allow for diverse values? It means that we need to allow people difference, even if they do not share one's values.

> It is impossible to transmit one's sense of values to the others.
> One merely learns value from the surroundings. If the relativity of
> circumstance changed, the consequence would be totally different
> no matter how one tries to transmit one's value in the same manner.
> Hence, what we need is not the transmission of values but the
> reorganisation of mechanisms that maintain today's society.

Shinji Miyadai

As new individuals are connected on a private level (ie. private company, private interests, private friends,) privileged spaces would be the ones that allow any individual to use them—sharing information or function—without further expectation.

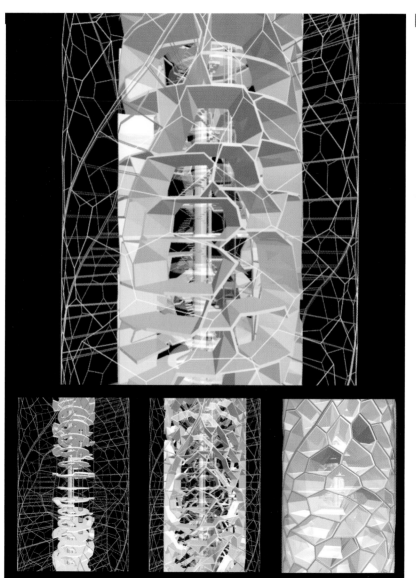

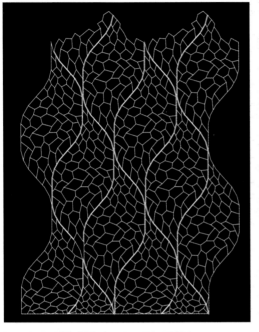

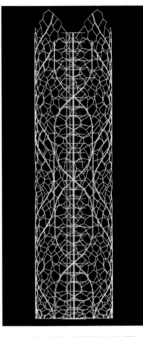

borrowing THE GEOMTETRY from THE NEW MATERIAL

SKIN=STRUCTURE=INDIVIDUAL UNITS

HONEYCOMB MATERIALS

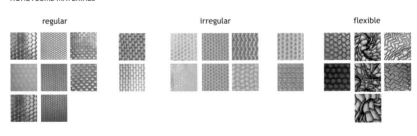

regular

irregular

flexible

PANELITE http://www.e-panelite.com / Nuovopovero http://www.nuovopovero.com

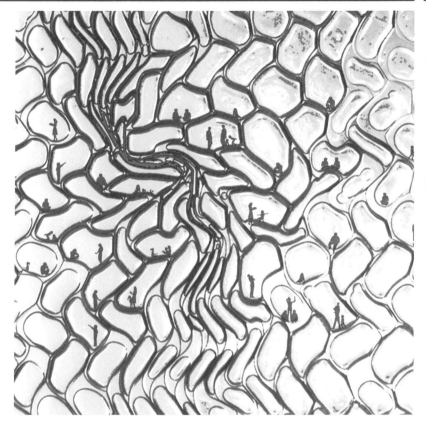

gravity   vertical loads

perimetry tube structure: vertical load take down

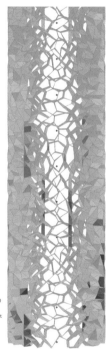

Scale: 1:348.3
Deformation magnification: 320.0
2-D Projected Stress,
Stresses are at MIDDLE of element

3.501 N/mm²
3.064 N/mm²
2.628 N/mm²
2.192 N/mm²
1.755 N/mm²
1.319 N/mm²
0.8827 N/mm²
0.4464 N/mm²
0.01011 N/mm²
-0.4262 N/mm²
-0.8625 N/mm²
-1.299 N/mm²
-1.735 N/mm²
-2.171 N/mm²
-2.608 N/mm²
-3.262 N/mm²
Case: A4: wind
Case: L4: wind

Scale: 1:348.3
Deformation magnification: 320.0
2-D Projected Stress,
Stresses are at MIDDLE of element

3.501 N/mm²
3.064 N/mm²
2.628 N/mm²
2.192 N/mm²
1.755 N/mm²
1.319 N/mm²
0.8827 N/mm²
0.4464 N/mm²
0.01011 N/mm²
-0.4262 N/mm²
-0.8625 N/mm²
-1.299 N/mm²
-1.735 N/mm²
-2.171 N/mm²
-2.608 N/mm²
-3.262 N/mm²
Case: A4: wind
Case: L4: wind

wind loads

bending

perimetry tube structure: horizontal stability

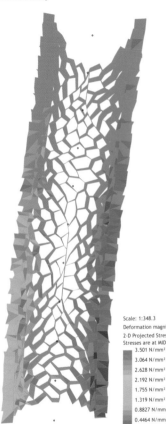

Scale: 1:348.3
Deformation magnification: 320.0
2-D Projected Stress,
Stresses are at MIDDLE of element

3.501 N/mm²
3.064 N/mm²
2.628 N/mm²
2.192 N/mm²
1.755 N/mm²
1.319 N/mm²
0.8827 N/mm²
0.4464 N/mm²
0.01011 N/mm²
-0.4262 N/mm²
-0.8625 N/mm²
-1.299 N/mm²
-1.735 N/mm²
-2.171 N/mm²
-2.608 N/mm²

-3.262 N/mm²
Case: A4: wind
Case: L4: wind

Scale: 1:348.3
Deformation magnification: 320.0
2-D Projected Stress,
Stresses are at MIDDLE of element

3.501 N/mm²
3.064 N/mm²
2.628 N/mm²
2.192 N/mm²
1.755 N/mm²
1.319 N/mm²
0.8827 N/mm²
0.4464 N/mm²
0.01011 N/mm²
-0.4262 N/mm²
-0.8625 N/mm²
-1.299 N/mm²
-1.735 N/mm²
-2.171 N/mm²
-2.608 N/mm²

-3.262 N/mm²
Case: A4: wind
Case: L4: wind

Scale: 1:348.3
Deformation magnification: 320.0
2-D Projected Stress,
Stresses are at MIDDLE of element

3.501 N/mm²
3.064 N/mm²
2.628 N/mm²
2.192 N/mm²
1.755 N/mm²
1.319 N/mm²
0.8827 N/mm²
0.4464 N/mm²
0.01011 N/mm²
-0.4262 N/mm²
-0.8625 N/mm²
-1.299 N/mm²
-1.735 N/mm²
-2.171 N/mm²
-2.608 N/mm²
-3.262 N/mm²

Case: A4: wind
Case: L4: wind

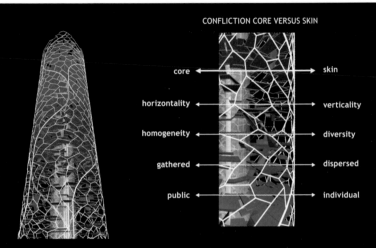

CONFLICTION CORE VERSUS SKIN

core	→ ←	skin
horizontality	→ ←	verticality
homogeneity	→ ←	diversity
gathered	→ ←	dispersed
public	→ ←	individual

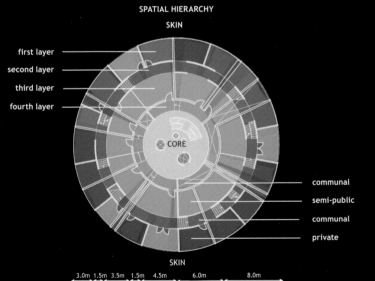

SPATIAL HIERARCHY

SKIN

first layer
second layer
third layer
fourth layer

CORE

communal
semi-public
communal
private

SKIN

3.0m 1.5m 3.5m 1.5m 4.5m 6.0m 8.0m

28.0m

POPULATION DISTRIBUTION

TOWER SECTION 1:250 SCALE

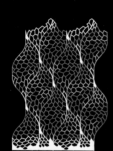

first layer

second layer

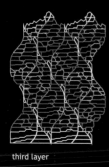

third layer

TARGET GROUP (1–4 numbers
per house)/Database: INE 2004
(population statistics in Madrid)

🚶	single	24.1%
👫	single + child	7.8%
👫	couple	19.6%
👪	couple + child	20.4%
👪	couple + children	18.3%

96000

super
market

entrance

carpark

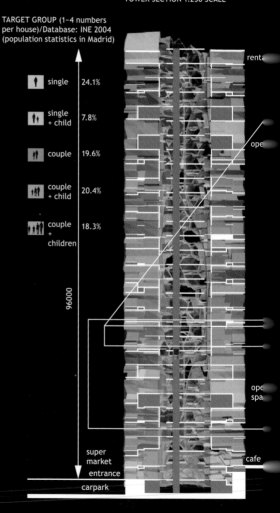

renta

ope

ope
spa

cafe

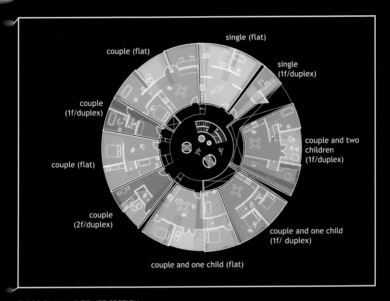

Single (flat)
couple (flat)
single (1f/duplex)
couple (1f/duplex)
couple and two children (1f/duplex)
couple (flat)
couple and one child (1f/ duplex)
couple (2f/duplex)
couple and one child (flat)

FLOOR PLAN AND TOWER SECTION

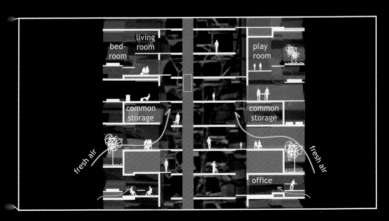

bed-room
living room
play room
common storage
common storage
fresh air
office
fresh air

Results

The idea of borrowing geometry from organic honeycomb material came from the consideration of the sociological phenomena relating to housing problems. The interesting aspect of today's honeycomb material is how it has become flexible—from the rigid, homogeneous material constructed from hexagonal cell configuration. It seems that the process of today's material developments and social trends can be seen as overlapping. Nevertheless, the difficulty here, as well as the benefit, is that it immediately starts to create unexpected difficulties and effects after a honeycomb geometry is installed as part of a building's skin.

The biggest problem is that flexible and organic honeycomb are not yet rigid enough. This is the structural reason for using the solid core, to prevent torsion. Yet, the intention to overlap organic honeycomb skin on a domino core is not only for structural purposes. It is also meant as the representation of a society full of contradictions.

There remain a lot of problems to be solved in this project. Since skin geometry doesn't have any consistent axis, it has to be made out of 4,120 different prefabricated concrete (panels just for the outer ring), which hold the individual cells in place. The critical point is not only the number of different panels but the difference between the gross area and the net area, which is substantial big for the apartments. Yet, it's also naive to look at these critical points as being only negative. Today's computer programmes are able to manufacture different panels relatively efficiently, and the gap between the floor panel and the structure wall can be used as storage, as well as ventilation or for the top lighting. By installing aluminum foam (manufactured by alusion) a natural atmosphere can be created by constantly transmitting external light. This apartment is for nomadic-like people who prefer to live in a compact, well-functioning and well-defined spaces—rather than a vast, blank space. The result is that the apartments keep their autonomy for each form of housing, while giving a distinguishable identity for each individual space. From the outside, nobody can recognise how each individual cell is connected to another, except for the occupants themselves. Here, family relations are put behind diverse individuality.

Conclusion

The discussion in architecture today mostly concerns unique buildings. If we look at the buildings which are at the core of contemporary discourse, the buildings which are most published by the professional press and exposed internationally, they are singular, individual buildings, with exceptional budgets, and buildings of deliberately spectacular form. As Jacques Herzog said; architects can only design *crème de la crème*. It seems that the generic matter of developer-driven architecture has completely escaped architectural ambition. But this is exactly what our urban condition consists of…

There seems almost no space left for architects to play a main role in the housing market. Nevertheless, there is the chance to precede this petrified. This project is a proposal, a possible suggestion of the future development of the apartment typology. To put together and to conflict two different unique systems in one frame (in this case, high-rise apartments) its intention. The layers inserted between the two systems are not just a structural solution to connect them organically and vertically. It also reveals a gap between architectural trends and social premises, and shows what a possible reaction to this might by.

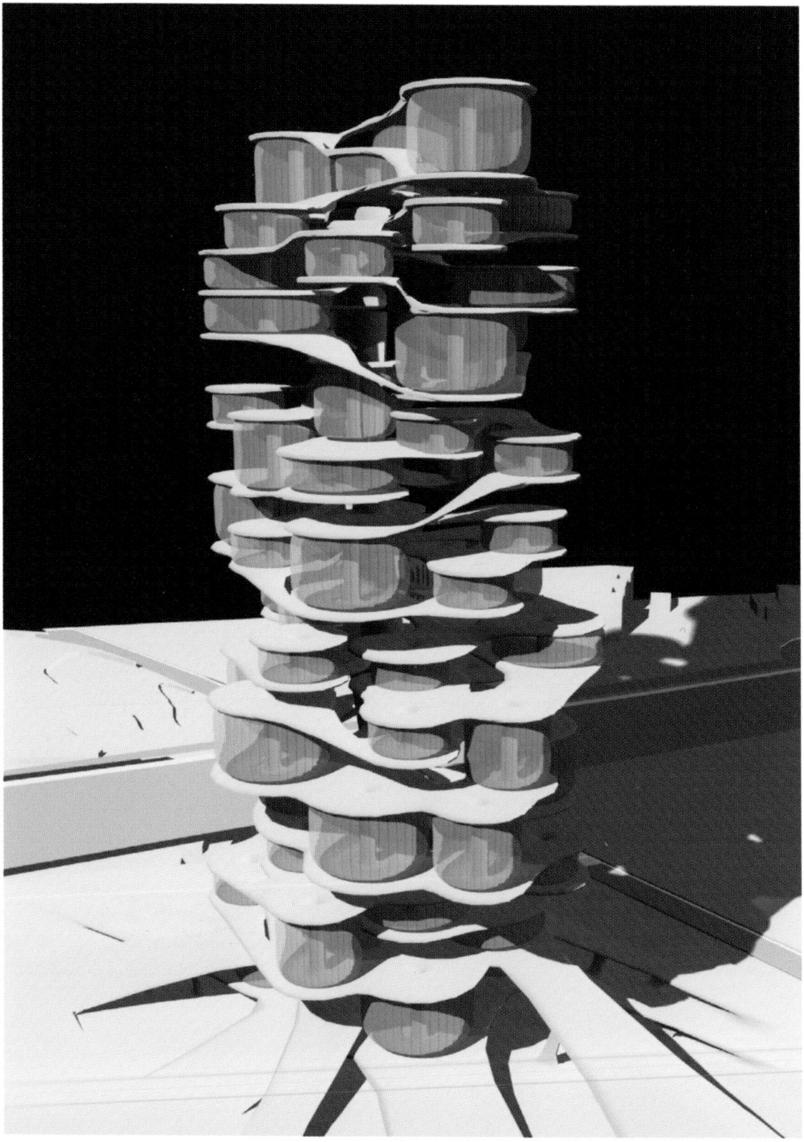

DEMAND VERSUS GEOMETRY
designing through 'local' relationships
Kiwoong Ko and Alexandros Vazakas

Hypothesis

Can we design a building organisation that arises more out of local relationships between its parts than out of overall (top down) design decisions? Is it possible not to design the end form of a building but to define it by defining a set of laws of interrelations?

Summary

We approached the subject by designing a parametric model, instead of an actual building. The ambition was that this model would combine the parameters of structure, circulation, programme, climatic and site conditions into one virtual building entity. It was also an ambition that this model would incorporate as parameters some of the individual needs and wishes of the end users. Finally, this model would be directly linked to a set of manufacturing processes, providing actual machining instructions for the production of each one of its parts.

Case Studies

1. Parametric design process
Surface Generator V 1.0 in Maya (Alias Wavefront) and Fragment Design in TopSolid (Missler Software)

A continuous exercise is structured to define an overall process of parametric design in architecture. This process has two main steps. Step 1 (Surface Generator V 1.0), creating a surface (which has a certain affordancy for human activity and can be proliferated and differentiated by the local condition of the geometrically-defined elements—three points in a space) and fragmentation of the surface by triangulation. Step 2, segment (component) design (TopSolid). Among three geometrically different conditions of segments, a typical case (with three adjacent faces) is designed to be manufactured through a 'machinic' process. The main purpose of this model is to use the structural property of the surface generated by Surface Generator as parameter to define the thickness of a segment which varies on each vertex of the triangle.

We perceive this process as a model to translate the conventional design process to the numeric design process within contemporary technology.

2. Concept of the platform in the car industry
Model for customisation—GM's 'Autonomy' prototype platform

This car floor platform allows, through a plug-in system, the adaptation of different skins and multiple interior configurations. Our focus in this study is on how to translate this model to the housing industry.

Among the many functionalities of the car floor/platform, we find that the following points can be translated and adapted to the housing industry. Infrastructural function—plugs connecting the service installations like kitchen, bathroom, etc., in different positions. Structural function—slits that secure the house skins into the platform. Installation supply—electrical, gas, water installations running through the platform supplying the house.

Methodology

The given brief asked for a high-rise housing building on a specific site in Madrid. As a result of local market research, we decided that we would use, besides housing, a public and semi-public programme consisting of a pedestrian street for commerce, four hanging semi-public gardens, one public garden on the ground floor, and some offices and sports facilities, mainly intended for use by the inhabitants. The programme is located according to height, in relation to the degree of publicness or privacy.

We developed a model for the building organisation that located all these programmes on the site, taking into consideration the following parameters:

    1. Programme connectivity
    2. Local distance (density) between the housing units
    3. Specific sun accessibility for each garden
    4. Building regulations (height and volume restriction)
    5. Noise level
    6. Building's location on the site
    7. Sizes of the individual units

1. Programme connectivity
We decided upon a specific connectivity between the public and semi-public programmes. The commercial/pedestrian street is directly connected to the gardens, and the sports and the business facilities.

2. Density
The housing units are clustered around the four hanging gardens.
In the model simulation, we used a script written by GZ based on "boids

theory", by Craig Raynolds, that simulates flock behaviour. The gardens are used as attractors and the individual units are located according to this specific mathematical model keeping a minimum and a maximum distance among themselves and between themselves and the garden.

3. Sun accessibility
Each garden has a specific character, due to the time period in which the sun is 'allowed' to directly access its surface. In the model, we use the specific sun vector for each garden as a repellant, so no housing unit can be placed on the sun path.

4. Building regulations (height and volume restriction)
We used an envelope of 30 metre diameter and a height restriction plane of tangent 2/3 in relation to the neighbouring streets.

5. Noise level
We placed on the site a changing colour particle grid that is affected by the noise generated by the adjacent highway and surrounding small industries, but also by the noise generated by our implemented programmes (like the garage) in a real time interactive simulation. In this way, we could eliminate cases where the housing units are located in an area with more than 70 decibels.

6. Location on the site
The building's entrance is represented by a point on the ground floor. This point is not fixed, as its position can vary on the plot, and along with it the pedestrian/commercial street, vehicle access, and, of course, the upper building itself.

7. Size of the individual units

To each 'house' point of the model we assigned a platform, the structural part of the individual unit, but also of the whole building.

We used four models of platforms with different sizes and proportions in order to cover different housing needs. In order to incorporate the structural and circulation parameter into the model, we had to use one instance of the simulation, test the structure and then go back to the model again. We merged all the platforms into one continuous surface that guarantees a smooth circulation between the individual units and the semi-public spaces. We used all the platform rooftops as semi-public spaces. Concerning the individual units, we developed a model that takes into consideration the following parameters:

1. Household composition

We made a chart of all the possible scenarios of co-existence between different groups within each housing unit. These are in-principle scenarios of sharing, of family housing or of both situations together between families, couples and single people.

2. Volumetric connectivity between spaces

Every house has a specific type of connectivity between different functional spaces, which is a translation of the lifestyle of different users. A secondary skin encloses the individual units and transforms these parameters into actual space through a continuous geometry. Partitions that contain supporting activities separate the space when desired, obtaining horizontal separation. Vertical separation is obtained through bifurcation of the continuous geometry of the frames.

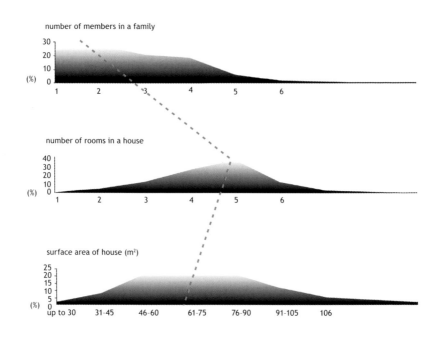

number of members in a family

number of rooms in a house

surface area of house (m²)

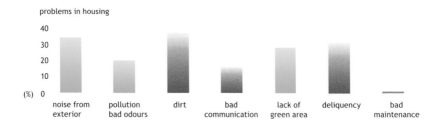

problems in housing

source: Instituto Nacional de Estatistica.Madrid.org

The programme is located according to height in relation with the degree of publicness or privacy

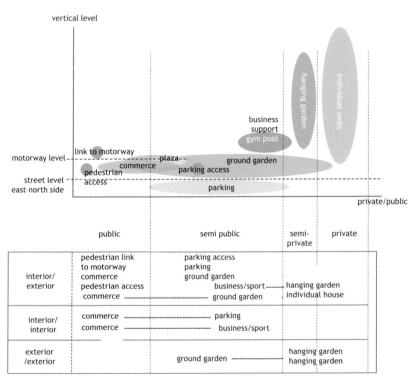

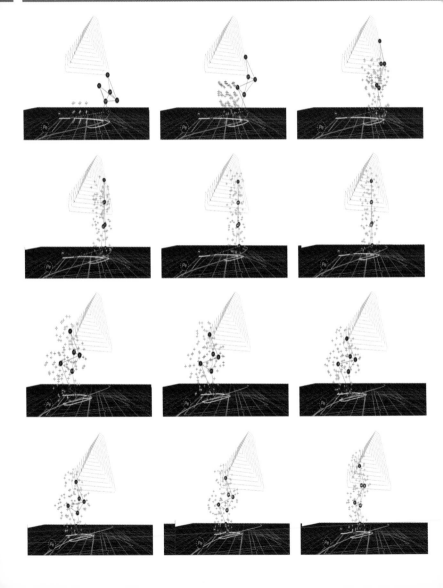

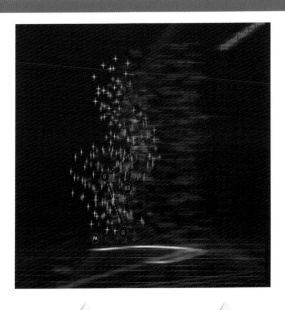

LM	pedestrian link to motorway
Pe	pedestrian access
C	commerce
PA	parking access
BS	business/sport
P	parking
GG	ground garden
G	hanging garden
H	individual house
sPu	semi-public
Pu	public
sPr	semi-private
Pr	private

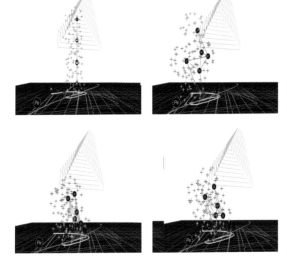

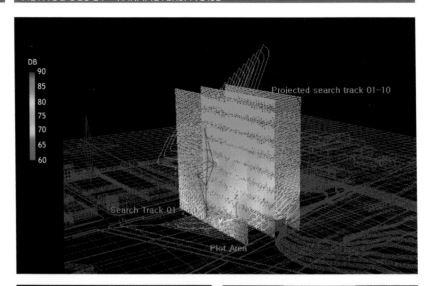

DB
90
85
80
75
70
65
60

Projected search track 01–10

Search Track 01

Plot Area

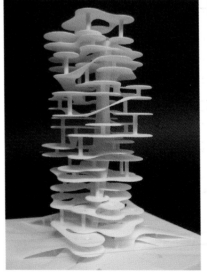

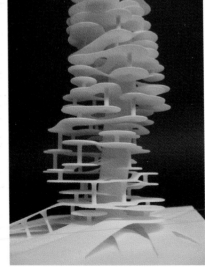

Concerning the individual units, we developed a model that takes into consideration the parameters of household composition and volumetric connectivity between spaces. We made a chart of all the possible scenarios of co-existence between different groups within each housing unit. These are in principle scenarios of sharing, of family housing or of both situations together between families, couples and single people.
Every house has a specific type of connectivity between different functional spaces, which is a translation of the lifestyle of different users.

household composition

individual unit: space connectivity matrix

4 separate spaces	3 separate spaces	3 separate spaces	4 separate spaces	2 separate spaces

	single person	B	bathroom
‖	couple	K	kitchen
ꜱ	couple and children	B	bedroom
ꜱ	single parent and children	L	living room
		D	dining room

individual unit: space connectivity device

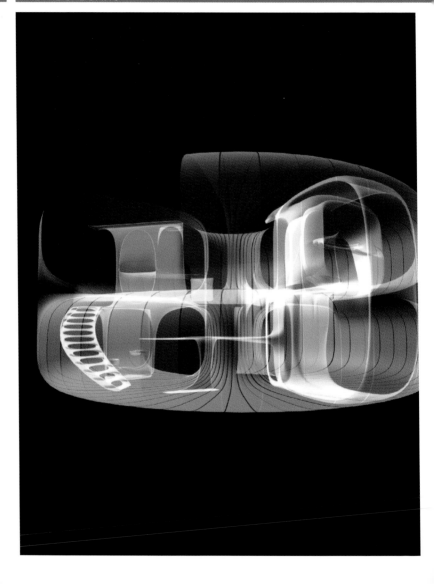

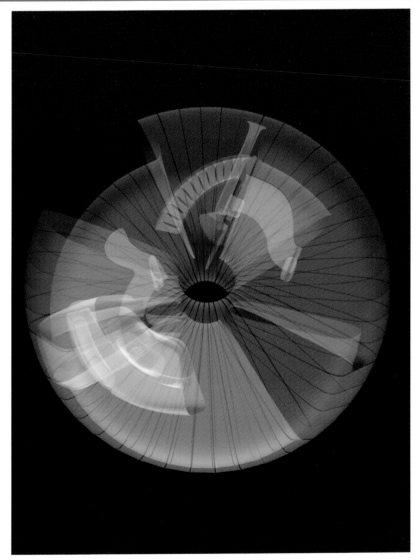

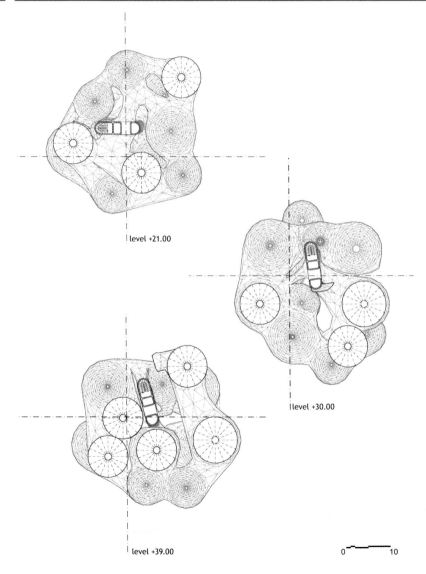

level +21.00

level +30.00

level +39.00

0   10

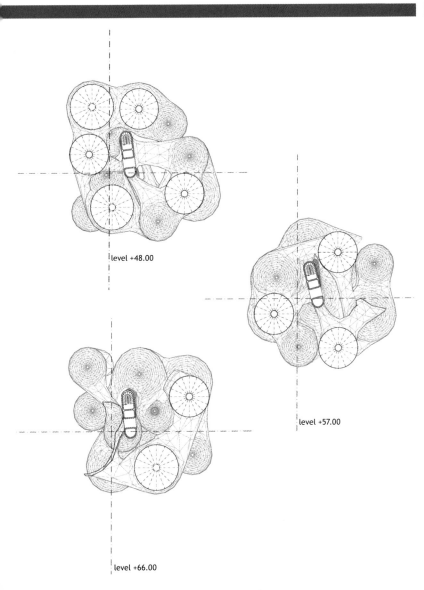

level +48.00

level +57.00

level +66.00

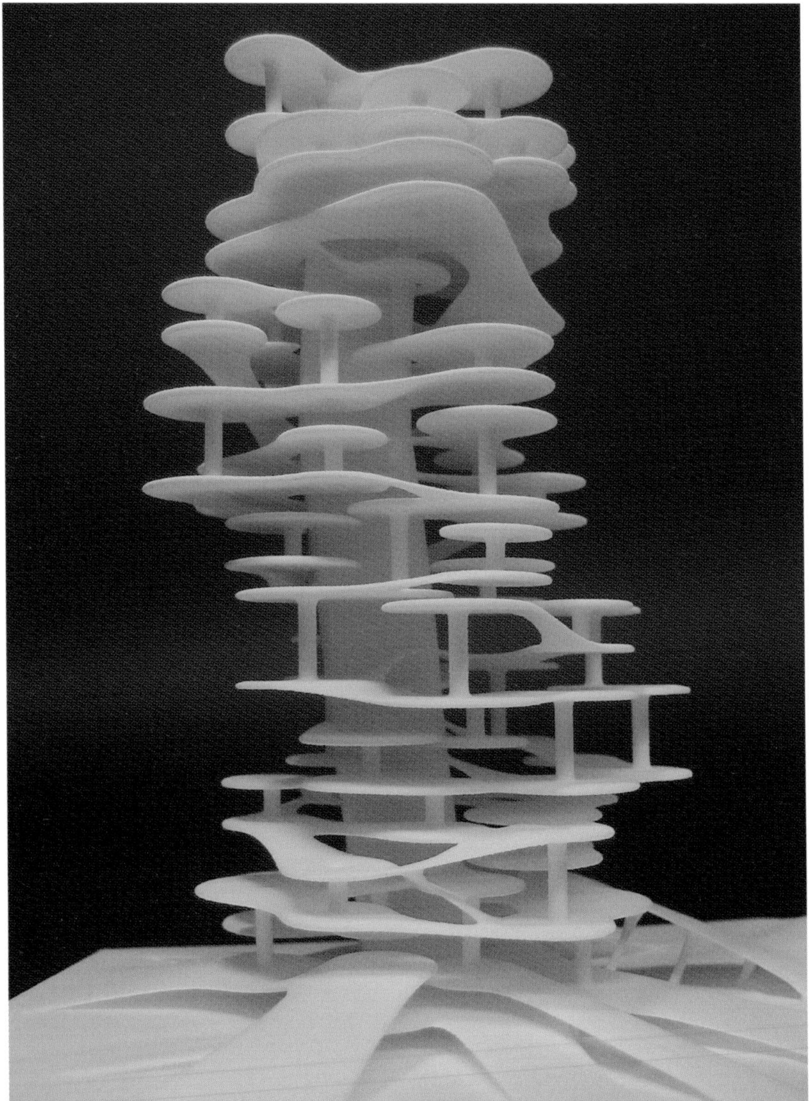

Conclusion

Through designing the process (the algorithm), we found out that there is a very positive aspect to using this kind of approach. Architectural design process can be more flexible and adaptable by using this kind of process, so that architecture can respond more quickly and appropriately to the erratic demands of users in the built and un-built environment.

Here are some more specific points from our reviewing the process. This process was initiated by defining the relation between the parameters and the building organisation as simply and explicitly as possible, but as a result, of the process, we found out that the form of the building is not driven by the parameters but by the interrelation between them. Non-predefined (and implicit) relations between parameters occur while the latter are combined through the overall algorithm of the process. Investigation of this point will be one of our further tasks.

Regarding the failure of automisation of surface-generation, we discovered that, in order to carry out such a process, the architect needs to be more educated in geometry and computer programming and to collaborate more closely with other disciplines. The lack of knowledge on our part in those areas prevents us from completing a fully unified process which contains a feedback process within itself.

Finally, we would like to raise a question here which we had through the whole process and still haven't found an appropriate answer. To how can we translate a subjective value to an objective one? In other words, how can the experience of a human being be numerically translated and computed in an algorithm? This is about the interpretation of diverse lifestyles, relations between neighbours, and how positive or negative values can be estimated within the relation to public or open space for individuals. We believe that this can only be thoroughly answered through more complete research and through collaboration with other disciplines.

ACCOMODATING CHANGE
high-rise as an adaptive system
Lorena Franco

Hypothesis

Is it possible to create a high-rise housing system which is able to adjust in order to meet changes in demand, both at the selling moment and in time, to confront the rigidity of units in a typical high-rise building? How are we to create a system which is able to update itself to the market conditions and the changing needs of its users?

Short summary

Due to the shortage of urban plots in Madrid, the cost of land there can be up to 50 per cent of the selling price of a house. This thesis proposes as an alternative the creation of Virtual Vertical Plots, a typological transfer of horizontal plots into the high-rise building, in order to combine the customisation freedom of the former with the economical benefits of the latter.

The adaptive system proposed is composed by the combination of two subsystems; a structural and a non-structural one. The structural subsystem transfers the pure structural technology of braced frames into a change adaptor device. The non-structural subsystem, transfers sandwich paneling from the aircraft industry as the most efficient system to make changes to the housing units. These two subsystems are topologically related, as the smallest change could affect the overall organisation.

Structure is one of the major issues in the flexibility or rigidity of housing units in a high-rise building.

Here a system is created where, once the building enters the selling phase, it is possible to customise, not only the non-structural, but also the structural elements.

Braced frames because of their configuration variety are a suitable structural system for the implementation of changes. However, it is not possible to achieve the 100 per cent customisation freedom of horizontal plots, as flexibility in the system operates within certain rules and limits.

Methodology

The first stage of this thesis was to undertake a market study in order to understand housing conditions in Madrid. Madrid has one of the lowest emancipation rates in Europe (32.2 per cent). According to the maximum affordable price and selling prices, there is a problem of housing accessibility for young people. A 25 year old person could only afford 33 m^2 and 100 m^2 could only be achieved by the age of 40, which is five to eight years after the household (four members on average) is already established with its consequent programmatic increase. For this reason, young people stay with their parents until the age of 32, or in the worst case they rent, as it is not worth investing money in a property which will not be sufficient for them over the following ten years.

The most revalorised typology are 40 to 60 m^2 apartments, however 100 m^2 is the most requested one. Because of its shortage, land is one of the basic problems of the final housing price. It can represent 50 per cent of the final price, in comparison to the 10 per cent to 24 per cent in other countries like Holland, Canada, Germany, Switzerland or the United Kingdom.

From these studies a transfer of horizontal plots into a vertical organisation could be a solution to housing accessibility. The cost of the land is shared, and starters will be able to buy a property and occupy only what they are able to afford, with the certainty that they will not need to move when their programmatic needs increases (from 40 to150 m^2). At the same time, the value of their property will increase in time. It is also a solution for breaking the rigidity of units in a high-rise building, as only the basic cell will be defined and the rest could be easily customised at the selling point. This could allow for the developer to sell faster, reduce negotiation time with the clients and design time for the architect.

Are Virtual Vertical Plots Feasible? What do they need to be feasible? An economical comparison between horizontal plots and vertical ones demonstrates that the key point for them to be feasible remains in the efficiency of the structure, as it is the extra element.

Braced frames use less material and have simpler connections than moment-resisting frames. Less material makes the structure lighter, reducing foundation and overall costs. At the same time, the very intrinsic bracing rigidity algorithms make it a potential customisable structure which allows change. A part of mathematics called graph theory deals with solutions to the grids bracing problem. With building costs so high, it is desirable to test for the minimum number of bracing which will make the grid rigid so that by removing any one crossbeam, the rigidity of the structure will be destroyed. Mathematician Jack Graves invented a software called Grid Applet which was used to test the different combinations of bracing elements in same size cell grids (http://www. npac.syr.edu/projects/tutorials/Java/education/grid/grid.html). To make a grid rigid, there are several, but limited, possible combinations of the braced elements. Each bracing is topologically related to the position of the others, so it is possible to change the position of one of them by adding a new one to specific locations and then removing the old one without breaking the rigidity of the structure. What is important is to always keep the same number of bracings in a good topological relationship. Tension rods will be used for bracing due to its weight advantages for changing their position in comparison to compression elements.

But what if there is a variation in the cell size of the grid to generate double heights for example? Grid Applet software only works with same cell size grids.

Jack Graves was contacted, and clarified that the relation between the number of edges to be rigid and the number of rods and nodes also work for variations in the grid, but the position of the bracing elements will have to be tested in pin-models which simulate the behaviour of the structure. Several pin-models were made in order to discover the 'floppy' areas generated by the removement of nodes and rods and to establish rules for variation of the cell size.

In parallel to the bracing studies, typological research about what is the best distribution of the units to be ready to accommodate changes was done. Double-height and single-height plots were considered. At this point, it was necessary to determine the dimension of the minimum cell. 4.2 metres was a good dimension for the circulation cores and the programmatic housing functions. Each unit should have direct access towards the circulation core and double side orientation. A catalogue with all possible changes varying from 40 m² to 150 m² (from market studies) was made with its respectve paths of development. From this catalogue, it was important to notice which walls could be relocated and which ones need to be added. As there is the possibility that the units will be surrounded by non-occupied areas, panels should have an insulating property. Panels should be able to work as interior and exterior. On the other hand, whenever the programme increases, additional storage space is needed. So the thickness for insulation is proposed by using the core of the sandwich panel as a storage space in order to solve both problems. Each wall is composed of three panels that are able to be detached and reassembled in combination with other panels. They allow connection in between the spaces. The curvature of the panel goes towards the outside in order to obtain extra space for the interior of the unit. The idea is that panels could also be located in the interior.

The advantage of sandwich paneling is that one is able to engineer according to desired performances. Research on core, skin materials and insulation materials was done. Three types of panels were considered: transparent, translucent and opaque. The materials chosen because of their performance and price were polycarbonate for the translucent skins and glazing, wood skins for the flooring skin, and aluminum for the core. The geometry of the core was decided in terms of the opening performance in the panel and the storage condition. Nanogel insulator was added to translucent and transparent panels due to its high thermal and sound insulation, while still allowing light transmittance. The panel chosen was the one which offered more storage possibilities and whose shape came from the geometrical constraints of the skins.

These principles were then applied to the specific location in Madrid, in order to have an equal qualitative environment away from the highway and so that the apartments will always double-face towards the outside, an east-west orientated slab high-rise type was chosen. The bracing was radicalised to all the structural elements (floors and shear walls) of the building. The traditional structural vertical core typology was eliminated, generating flexibility to the parking facilities in the underground and reducing the non-sellable area. This is because being structural, an area of 7.5 m^2 (1/10th of the height) would be needed, which exceeds the required area for circulation (4.2 m^2). The bracing elements were positioned in the floor plans so that they will allow future vertical changes and double-heights in the units. In the facade, bracing elements are avoided in living room areas. Double-height living rooms and public spaces were introduced both in the facades and in the floor plans, generating variations in the grids. Pin-models were used to test these variations. The possibility of changing the position of the double-heights was discovered in pin-models of the floor plan. Finally, the sandwich/storage panels were incorporated to the units to make the structure habitable.

SYSTEM

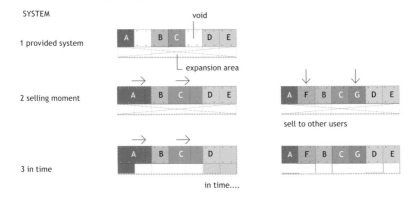

1 provided system

void

expansion area

2 selling moment

sell to other users

3 in time

in time....

ADVANTAGES
· sell faster
· reduce design time
· reduce negotiation time
· sell rights of construction

PROVIDE
· infrastructure
· structure

SUMMARY

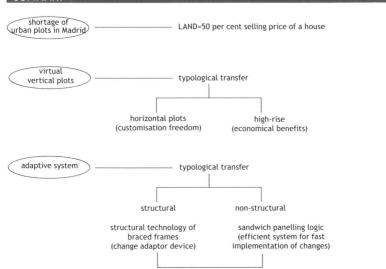

shortage of urban plots in Madrid ———————— LAND=50 per cent selling price of a house

virtual vertical plots ———————— typological transfer

horizontal plots (customisation freedom)   high-rise (economical benefits)

adaptive system ———————— typological transfer

structural   non-structural

structural technology of braced frames (change adaptor device)   sandwich panelling logic (efficient system for fast implementation of changes)

topologically related

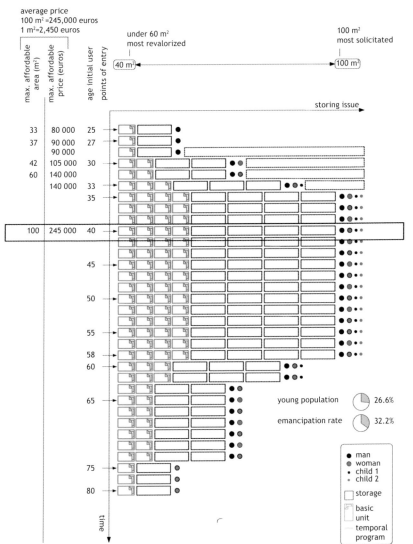

average price
100 m² =245,000 euros
1 m²=2,450 euros

under 60 m²
most revalorized

100 m²
most solicitated

40 m² ← → 100 m²

max. affordable area (m²)	max. affordable price (euros)	age	initial user	points of entry
33	80 000	25	
37	90 000	27	
90 000		
42	105 000	30	
60	140 000		
140 000	33	
	35	
100	245 000	40	
	45	
	50	
	55	
	58	
	60	
	65	
	75	
	80	

storing issue

young population — 26.6%

emancipation rate — 32.2%

● man
● woman
· child 1
· child 2

☐ storage

basic unit

temporal program

time

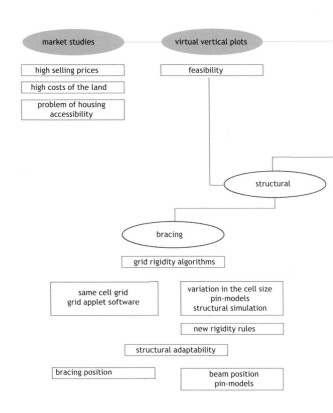

market studies

high selling prices

high costs of the land

problem of housing
accessibility

virtual vertical plots

feasibility

structural

bracing

grid rigidity algorithms

same cell grid
grid applet software

variation in the cell size
pin-models
structural simulation

new rigidity rules

structural adaptability

bracing position

beam position
pin-models

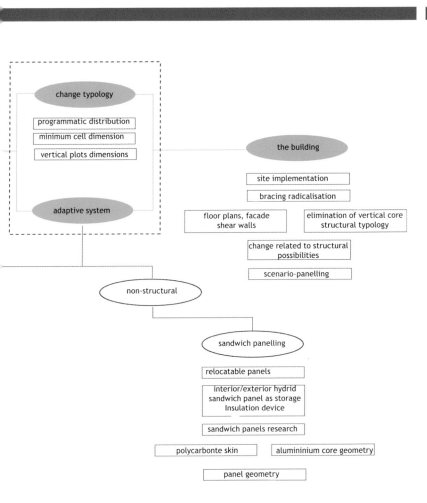

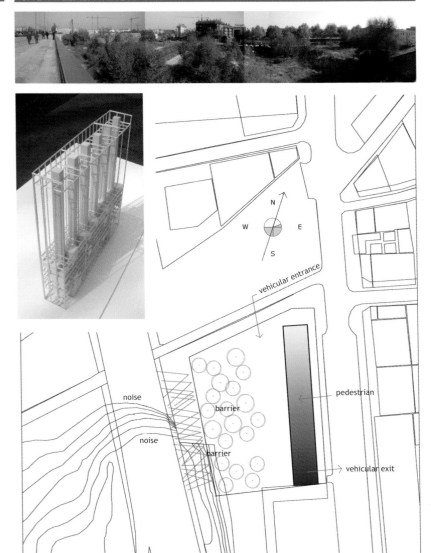

vehicular entrance

N

W E

S

noise

noise

barrier

barrier

pedestrian

vehicular exit

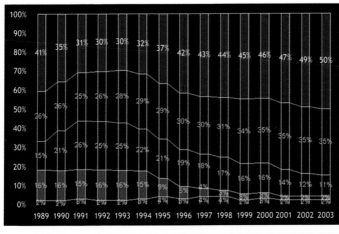

percentage of the cost of land in the final housing price

the whole region of Madrid will run out of land on which to in only 32 years the capital will run out of land in only six years

source: Economist Jose Miguel Naredo

PANEL CATALOGUE PANEL TYPE 1 AND PANEL TYPE 2

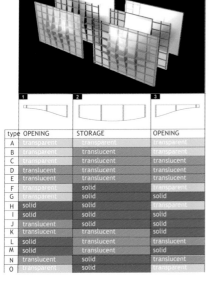

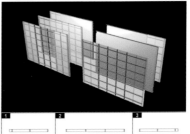

type	OPENING	STORAGE	OPENING
A	transparent	transparent	transparent
B	transparent	translucent	transparent
C	transparent	translucent	transparent
D	translucent	translucent	translucent
E	translucent	translucent	translucent
F	transparent	solid	transparent
G	transparent	solid	solid
H	solid	solid	transparent
I	solid	solid	solid
J	translucent	solid	solid
K	translucent	translucent	solid
L	solid	translucent	translucent
M	solid	translucent	solid
N	translucent	solid	translucent
O	transparent	solid	transparent

OPENING		OPENING
transparent	transparent	transparent
transparent	translucent	transparent
transparent	translucent	translucent
translucent	translucent	translucent
translucent	translucent	translucent
transparent	solid	transparent
transparent	solid	solid
solid	solid	transparent
solid	solid	solid
translucent	solid	solid
translucent	translucent	solid
solid	translucent	translucent
solid	translucent	solid
translucent	solid	translucent
transparent	solid	transparent

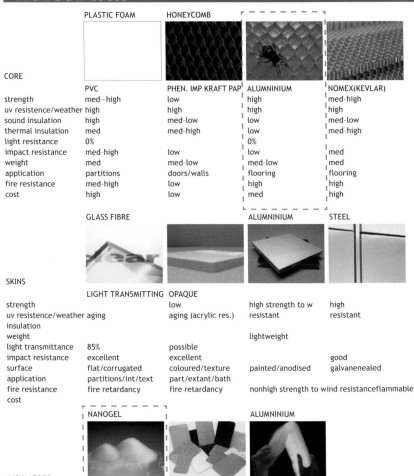

CORE

	PLASTIC FOAM	HONEYCOMB		
	PVC	PHEN. IMP KRAFT PAP	ALUMNINIUM	NOMEX(KEVLAR)
strength	med—high	low	high	med-high
uv resistence/weather	high	high	high	high
sound insulation	high	med-low	low	med-low
thermal insulation	med	med-high	low	med-high
light resistance	0%		0%	
impact resistance	med-high	low	low	med
weight	med	med-low	med-low	med
application	partitions	doors/walls	flooring	flooring
fire resistance	med-high	low	high	high
cost	high	low	med	high

SKINS

	GLASS FIBRE		ALUMNINIUM	STEEL
	LIGHT TRANSMITTING	OPAQUE		
strength		low	high strength to w	high
uv resistence/weather	aging	aging (acrylic res.)	resistant	resistant
insulation				
weight			lightweight	
light transmittance	85%	possible		
impact resistance	excellent	excellent		good
surface	flat/corrugated	coloured/texture	painted/anodised	galvanenealed
application	partitions/int/text	part/extant/bath		
fire resistance	fire retardancy	fire retardancy	nonhigh strength to wind resistanceflammable	
cost				

INSULATORS

	NANOGEL	SOUND LINE	POLY. HONEYCOMB
	LIGHT TRANSMITTING		
sound insulation		0.0037 w/m/k	high strength to w
thermal insulation		0.0033 w/m/k	resistant
light transmittance	20%		
colour		white/black	lightweight
dimensions	5-10 mm	possible	

POLYESTER RIBBON	POLYCARBONATE	POLYCARBONATE	BALSA	FOAMED FILLED
med-low	low	low	high	high
high	uv-stability	uv-stability		med
med	good	good	good	high
med	excellent	excellent	good	high
	excellent	excellent		
med			high	high
med-low			med	med-high
	interior panels	interior panels	interior panels	
low	self-extinguisable	self-extinguisable	low	med
med-low			med	med-high

POLYESTER	POLYCARBONATE	ACRYLIC	MICA	HARDBOARD

FIBRE GLASS REINF

high

excellent
lightweight
excellent
high

non-load bearing

good

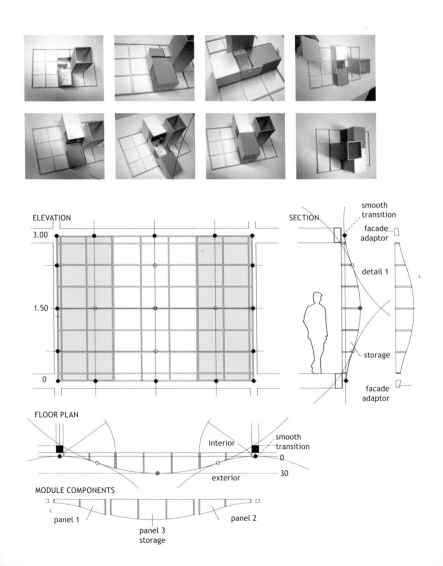

ELEVATION

3.00

1.50

0

SECTION

smooth
transition

facade
adaptor

detail 1

storage

facade
adaptor

FLOOR PLAN

interior

smooth
transition

0

exterior

30

MODULE COMPONENTS

panel 1

panel 3
storage

panel 2

PANEL—STORAGE—INSULATION

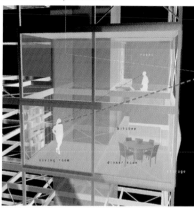

ADDITIONAL PROGRAMMATIC
FUNCTIONS TO THE SKIN

CSKINTETIC

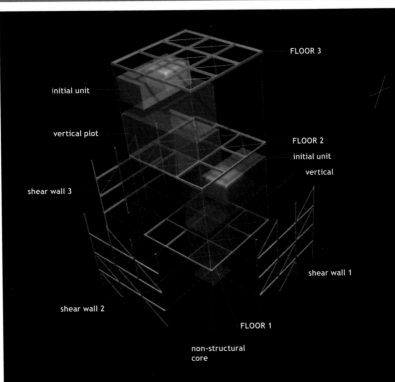

FLOOR 3

initial unit

vertical plot

FLOOR 2

initial unit

vertical

shear wall 3

shear wall 1

shear wall 2

FLOOR 1

non-structural
core

4.20

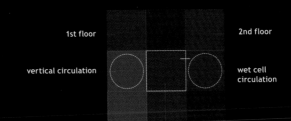

1st floor

2nd floor

vertical circulation

wet cell
circulation

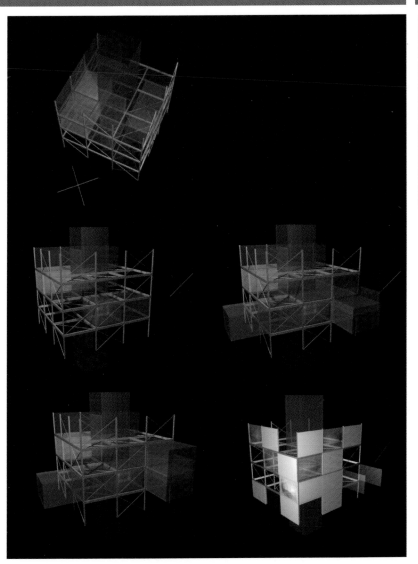

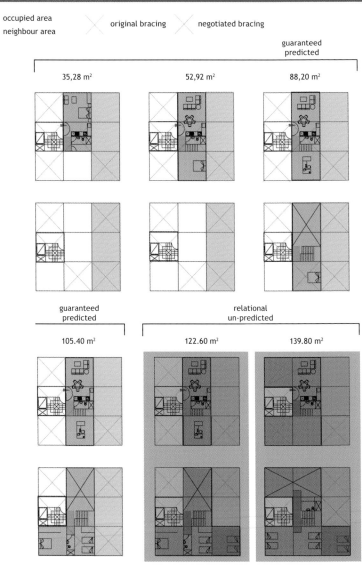

occupied area
neighbour area
original bracing   negotiated bracing

guaranteed
predicted

35,28 m²   52,92 m²   88,20 m²

guaranteed
predicted   relational
un-predicted

105.40 m²   122.60 m²   139.80 m²

what if there is a
variation in the cell
size for generation
of double-heights

new rules for the
position of bracing
elements had to be
discovered through
pin-models

BRACING RIDITY ALGORITHMS

 triangle is rigid   square is floppy the empty row or column principle: if a grid has an empty row or column then it is floppy

  the builder lemma: the grid is rigid if the better builders algorithm fills in all the braces

 =

the side to side conjecture

only brace in its row and its column: floppy if it has a brace which is the only brace in its row and column

the persistent parallel lemma: rigid if the persistent parallels algorithm marks all the egdes

start | these stay vertical | use 1,1 and 1,3 braces to shift the horizontals | use 2,1 brace to shift vertical edges in the 2nd row | use 2,2 brace to shift vertical edges in the 2nd column RIGID | can't proceed floppy

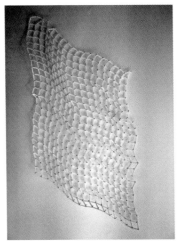

unbraced structure

homogeneous cell size

floppy areas

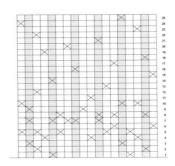

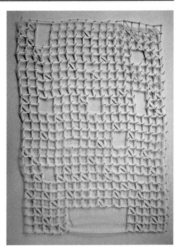

enerated   communal space introduction   deformation controllers—rigid

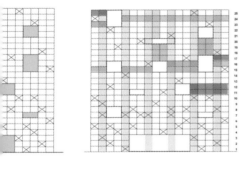

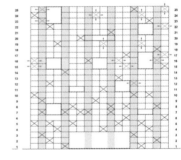

unbraced grid

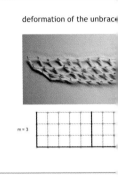

n = 18

m = 3

No. of Edges to be rigid: 2 x 76 - 3 = 149
No. of Rods: 3 x 19 + 4 x 18 = 129
No of braces = 149 - 129 = 20

deformation of the unbrac

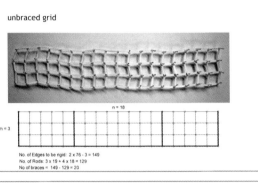

m = 3

cells differentation double-height introduction—floppy areas

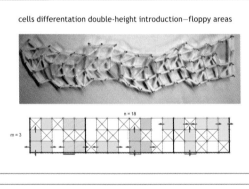

n = 18

m = 3

deformation controllers

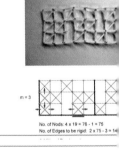

m = 3

No. of Nods: 4 x 19 = 76 - 1 = 75
No. of Edges to be rigid: 2 x 75 - 3 = 14

customisable rods to change position of double-height

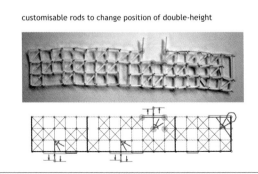

customisable double-heig

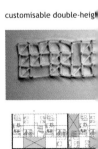

structure

homogeneus cell size—rigid grid

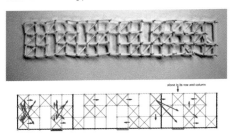

n = 18

m = 3

No. of Edges to be rigid: 2 x 76 - 3 = 149
No. of Rods: 3 x 19 + 4 x 18 = 129
No of braces = 149 - 129 = 20

customisable bracing positions

alone in its row and column

Rods: 67 + 56 = 123
Braces = 147 - 122 = 24

new positions

customisable double-height initials positions

Results

Vertical plots are 39.68 per cent the price of the same metres squared of a horizontal plot. Vertical plots are feasible if using a braced frame structure.

It is possible to make variations in the grid cell size for the introduction of double-heights and public spaces both in the facades and in the floor plans. If the double-height is perpendicular to the length of the floor plan, each side of the structure will behave as an independent grid. On the other hand, if the hole is parallel to the length, less deformation is generated.

There will always have to be at least one bracing element per column, so double- heights could not be used in the whole width of the structure. At least one bracing element that will connect the two parts of the grid is required. Both sides of the hole need to be rigid and rigidity could be tested with Grid Applet Software. Once the building is built, it is possible to customise the position of the bracings and to rotate by 90 degrees the position of the double-heights, without the collapse of the structure. To rotate the position of the double-heights first rotate the connecting beam and connect it to the joint. Then replace the two beams by one single beam piece, make the joint rigid or remove it.

So, a bracing structure is the most suitable structure for the implementation of changes in vertical plots, due to its efficiency, economical performance and configuration variety. Typologically, it is better to intercalate the housing units so that the living room area will be next to the room area of the next unit. This enables negotiation possibilities between the neighbours.

Next to public spaces, it is better to position flat vertical plots, as they can extend horizontally covering the connecting cells of the two parts of the floor plan generated by the introduction of public space.

Conclusion

Vertical plots with bracing structure and sandwich storage panels work as a feasible adaptive system that could solve the problem of housing accessibility for young people in Madrid, as well as the rigidity of the housing market for high-rise buildings. This proposal was evaluated on where it would be too problematic to be implemented in reality with a developer from the Real State Management department of TU Delft. What is problematic for the system is that the value of the units are their flexibility, but whenever neighbours start changing their structural elements, the flexibility of a particular unit starts diminishing. In reality, what is promised at the selling moment has to be able to be achieved regardless of what others are doing.

In order to be implemented, the system will need to have its own economical logic, based on guaranteed flexibility (predicted at the selling moment) and relational flexibility (unpredicted, which depends on the actual condition of the building). Flexibility as an economical value is a new product for the housing market. It has nothing to do with physical space, as one could buy flexibility from somebody who is not even your neighbor. Whether this would be positive or negative would have to be analysed by market experts, however this is what this system is generating.

Technology transfer:
Material Performance: Sandwich panelling Polycarbonate, Aluminium core, Nanogel.
Technology transfer: Bracing, sandwich panelling.
Structural study: Bracing.

INDUSTRY TRANSFERS 395

HOW IS MATERIAL INFORMING ARCHITECTURE?
how is the family of fibre-reinforced polymers informing high-rise building?
Andrea Fiechter

Industry transfer/technology transfer

Composite plastics are usually associated with applications in small-scale structures like furniture, cars, plane parts and small ships.

Within the field of architecture, we find some early examples of fibre-reinforced polymer (FRP) applications, such as Monsanto House, which generated huge interest even outside architectural disciplines. Problems, in particular with the durability of the resin, in the formative years of FRP development prevented the material from being widely used within architecture. The shipbuilding industry has used FRPs since the mid-1950s, at first for relatively small parts and a series of sails and motor-yachts.

Recent developments have resulted in structures on a different scale. The newly completed Mariella V sailing yacht and the Vispy class corvettes with a length of 70 plus metres are today's biggest FRP structures. The industry is confident that it can push the envelope even further and expects them to exceed the 100 metre range within five years. The size of these structures is comparable to the size of modern buildings, and makes the FRP shipbuilding industry a possible source for a technology transfer.

Material

The FRP laminate and FRP sandwich is informed through its structural and physical properties, the related fabrication methods, applicable building regulations, weather-resistance, duration and formal language.

The FRP is 'fabricated' the moment it is applied. It is custom-made and tailored to fit specific needs and known for its high tensile properties in combination with a low density. Using FRP, dead loads may be reduced by up to 50 per cent. These weight-savings reduce the vertical loads and, more significantly, reduce the bending moments caused by horizontal forces (wind, earthquakes) resulting in a much lighter vertical structure. The hand lay-up production with the use of 'forming core material' allows a non-standardised prefabrication and non-standardised mass production.

The level and size of prefabrication shifts from building elements to the scale of building parts and through the different working conditions on site the building process is shortened. The thickness of the skin is significantly reduced because of the good thermal insulation results of the foam cores. However, the limited thermal storage capacities have to be considered. To prevent the combustibility of the FRP, the resin and core material selection range is limited. Fire-resistance can be achieved through reactive coatings, additives and selected resins.

Project

Unit/Structure
The FRP has good tension properties and average pressure properties.

Geometries where the FRP structure works mainly under tension are favoured. The use of minimal surfaces reduce the appearance of bending moments and the forces work in mainly a linear direction. The parameters for choosing the particular surface were: the spatial definition, a high surface to opening ratio, and the possibility of horizontal connections. The chosen 'Schwarz P Surface' with 'handles' suits these parameters best. The basic unit can be combined to different derivates. Further deformations of the unit and its combinations are possible.

Compartment
The high vertical loads that arise in a high-rise building are too big to be handled by FRP sandwich constructions. The loads have to be divided to prevent the sandwich-laminate from de-lamination. Considering the higher live loads in comparison to ships, compartments of four floors are possible. The use of a primary structure out of steel or full laminate (with higher pressure capabilities) handles the forces.

The compartment is a variable combination of units and derivates. For each particular arrangement, the structural properties of the surface have to be considered. These are able to support up to four units vertical and one and a half units angular.

Fabrication
The prefabrication happens in three stages. Production in the factory is limited to the 10 x 4 x 2 metres trough size of the milling machine. These elements are combined to units of a maximum transportation size of 18 x 3 x 5 metres. At a temporary workshop the units get assembled to compartments of four. With the use of the primary structure, the compartments are lifted into their final position.

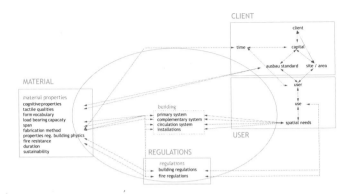

CLIENT

client

time → capital

ausbau standard   site / area

user

use

MATERIAL

material properties
cognitive properties
tactile qualities
form vocabulary
load bearing capacty
span
fabrication method
properties reg. building physics
fire resistance
duration
sustainability

building
primary system
complementary system
circulation system
installations

spatial needs

USER

REGULATIONS

regulations
building regulations
fire regulations

cognitive properties	user related, personal but in generall similar to plastics	
tactile properties	user related, personal but in generall similar to plastics	
form vocabulary	the possibility of 3-D milling and the use of the core material to be used as a 'mould' gives an almost absolute formal freedom unsurpassed by any other present building material beside a perfect 90 degree angle any form is possible fibres in general, but mostly the high modulus fibres, have a bending angle	
load bearing capacity		
span		

fabrication method

pre-fabrication → lay-up → hand lay-up / robotic fibre placement

transportation / size / weight → vacuum bagging → hand lay-up / robotic fibre placement

→ prepregs → hand lay-up / robotic fibre placement / size limitof available autoclave / up to ø6m l: 35m

onsite-fabrication / tempered curing (20-30°C) / shed / "dustfree" → lay-up

building physics

thermal properties
- thermal insulation → depending on core material pvc, pu-foam, etc. good aluminum honeycomb bad → no additional thermal insulation needed
- thermal "storage" → bad, low density of core → no passive energie usable / use of thermal plate as floorplate
- thermal expansion → very small thermal expansion (no expansion) → to consider when combining with materials with high thermal expansion

sound absorbtion
- "air" sound → neutral: hard, smooth surface → furnishing the rooms
- "step" sound → bad → use of 'swimming' floorplate
- "body" sound → good sound conductor → disconnect source with dampers

electric insulation
- conducting fibres → good insulation →
- non-conducting fibres → very good insulation (problematic regarding lightning) → use of conducting fibres to spread the electric 'shock'

fire resistance

not resistant / gases are highly toxic

→ active fire fighting → halon (and other gases) fire exguishener / at most likely fire sources / water sprinkler spread in the structure

→ passive fire fighting → covering the frp structure with non-burning and thermal insulating materials

fibre particles inhaled are very dangerous

most resins starts 'dropping' around 230°c

duration

experience-45 years:
weather resistant
waterproof (osmosis prevention)
uv-resistant
fatigue resistant
colour renewed after five to ten years

sustainability

high grey energy consumption
for production of resin and fibres
recycling not solved/research in process
resin is toxic, toxic damps during curing
fibres (lose) can cause
lung "problems" and cancer

Picture (Frontpage/Cover) of *Professional Boatbuilder*, Number 87, February/March 2004
Photograph by Neil Rabinowitz.

To the left is a 29 metre custom motoryacht nearing complettition, and on the right a 34 metre awaiting tanks
and transom installation at Norduland Boat Company in Tacoma, Washington.

CASE STUDY—FIBRE-RESIN RELATIONSHIP

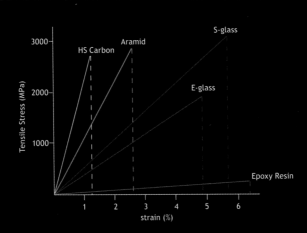

CASE STUDY—CORE MATERIALS

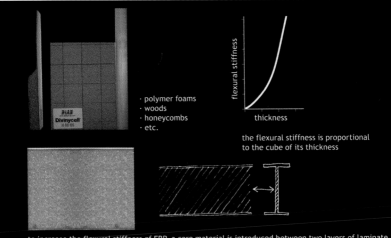

· polymer foams
· woods
· honeycombs
· etc.

the flexural stiffness is proportional to the cube of its thickness

to increase the flexural stiffness of FRP, a core material is introduced between two layers of laminate

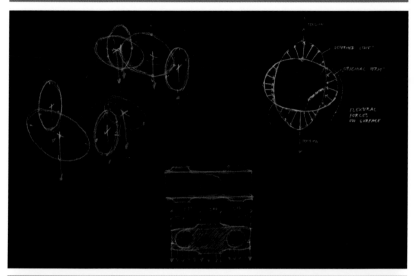

CASE STUDY—FIBRE REINFORCED POLYMERS

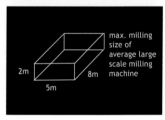

max. milling size of average large scale milling machine

2m

5m

8m

sandwich laminate

FRP—Sips Live —Loads—1-1.5 kN/m²

maximal size of non-moulded sandwich elements limited to 8m/5m/2m

high tension properties 170-500 N/mm². limited compression properties 117-284 N/mm² (regarding high rise). good flexural properties 143-425 N/mm²

the high live loads (2kn/m²; high regarding ship structures) of housing limits the number of self-supporting floors to four

the high live loads (2kN/m²; high regarding ship structures) of housing and the limitation of the core thickness up to six to ten cm the maximum beam is between five to seven metres

through the core in the FRP sandwich has embeded thermal insulation properties´, 'thermal bridges' and skin surface ratio can be neglected.

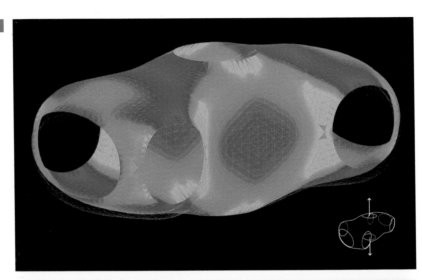

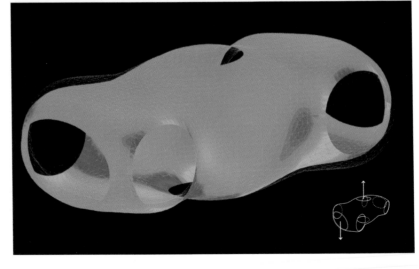

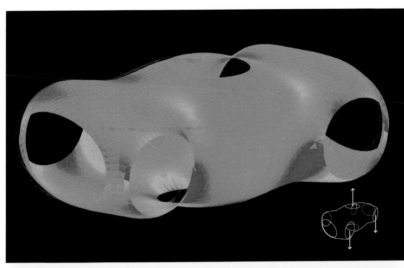

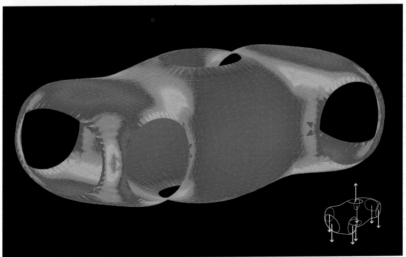

CORE SYSTEM

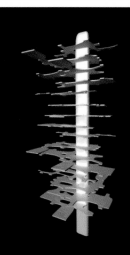

STRUCTURE

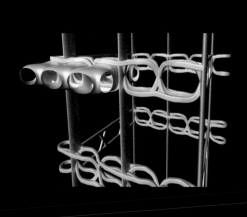

MODEL

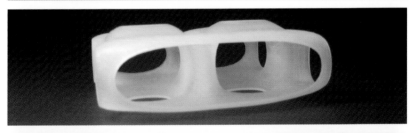

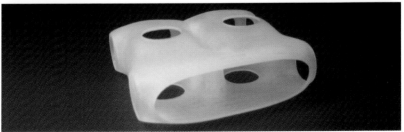

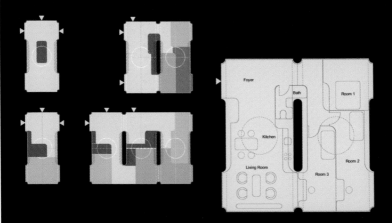

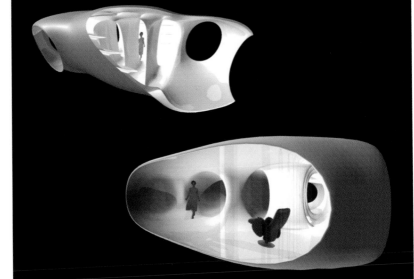

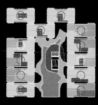

floor in-between 1

2

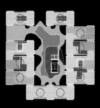

3

4

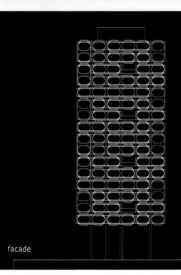

facade

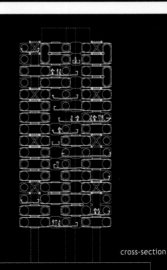

cross-section

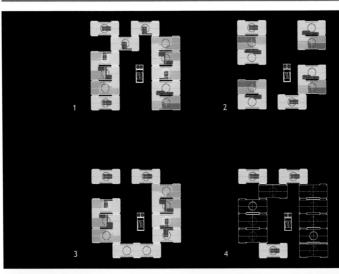

PRIVACY ALONG INTERIOR FACADES ACCORDING TO UNIT FUNCTIONS

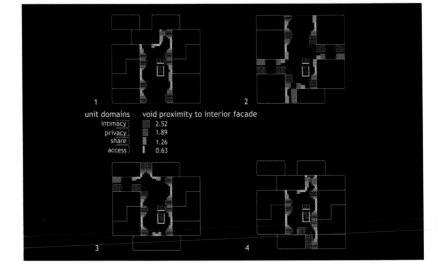

unit domains | void proximity to interior facade
intimacy | 2.52
privacy | 1.89
share | 1.26
access | 0.63

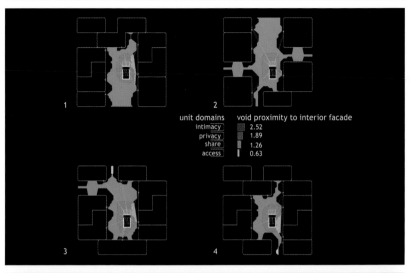

unit domains | void proximity to interior facade
intimacy | 2.52
privacy | 1.89
share | 1.26
access | 0.63

1   2   3   4

SURFACE DIFFERENTIATION OF EXTERNAL SPACE

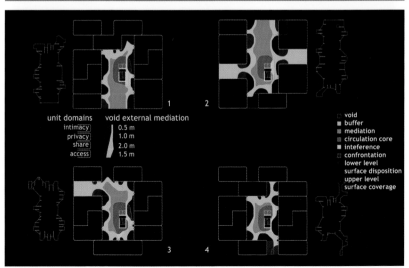

unit domains | void external mediation
intimacy | 0.5 m
privacy | 1.0 m
share | 2.0 m
access | 1.5 m

void
buffer
mediation
circulation core
inteference
confrontation
lower level
surface disposition
upper level
surface coverage

1   2   3   4

LOST FORM
lost form as a method for generating body skeletons
Yorai Gabriel

New techniques for casting complex objects used in the car and heavy machinery industries, combined with developments in the field of porous materials and disposable moulds, provide us with the opportunity to establish an agglomeration of varied shaped lofts with greater ease.

Lost form research investigates the potential of combined technologies and production techniques used to generate invertebrate bodies, to achieve spatial complexity and diverse units of organisations in a building. It explores new potentials for the housing industry while radicalising the dwelling environment, breaking away from conventional typologies of stacking habitat units in high-rise projects.

Shaping processes of buildings

The preliminary assumptions of this research relates to architecture as a landform. As such, the built environment is an organic entity which is established through mediated processes between the inhabiters and their abilities to construct their ideas. The first intention here was to provide a tool which involves the dweller in the forming of their space, unlike the current system of a rigid spatial frame subjected to individualisation through sub-division or population. Lost form technique relates to space as a shape and allows the user to experience the actual shape of the resulting space.

Radical housing

Most high-rise projects today are built using techniques which are a century old, and this affects the possibilities of what they can offer. Today, through technology, we can increase the potential for different living. We can incorporate dwellers within the design process and present to them a clear representation of their desires in terms of spatial definition. We can increase the capacity for spatial differentiation in a high-rise building. And we can also generate complex organisations which provide elaborate potential for their programmatic use. We can push further architectural ideas related to a building's integrity by involving all functions, desires and components participating in the housing environment into one process, fully related to the construction process.

Individualisation through mass production

This project is designed to be a radical scenario for the use of technology in a society which emphasises individualisation through common industrial processes.

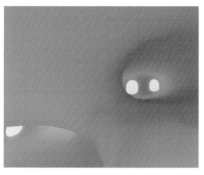

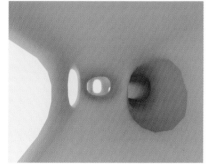
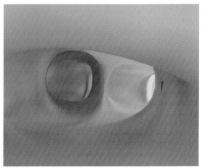

Aluminium mono-blocks created using the lost foam technique

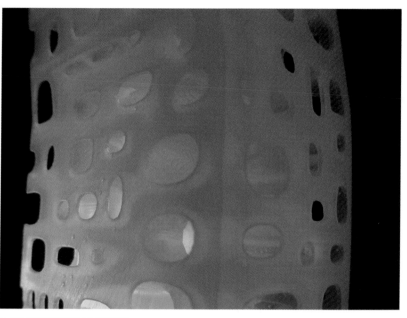

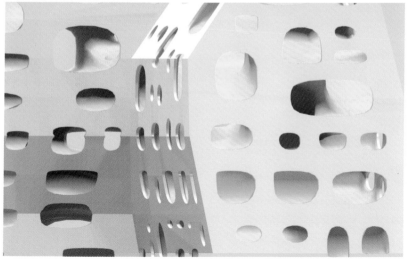

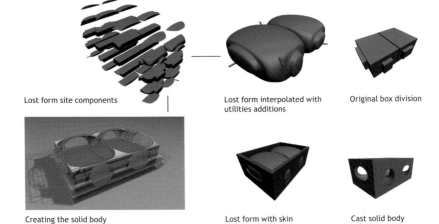

Lost form site components

Lost form interpolated with utilities additions

Original box division

Creating the solid body

Lost form with skin

Cast solid body

The 'interpulated' form of the unit is cut to small blocks when shipped to the site. Put together with the external blocks of the exterior shape, the cement is then poured in layers to allow quick drying.

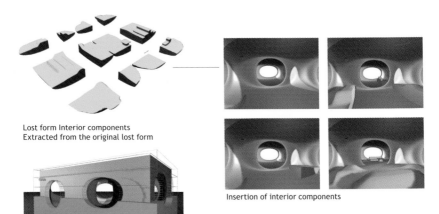

Lost form Interior components
Extracted from the original lost form

Insertion of interior components

Once the concrete dries and the foam blocks are carved out, interior elements made of polystyrene can be placed inside the solid body for furnishing.

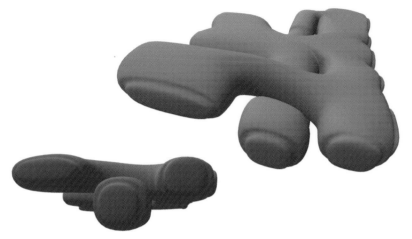

Complex lost form

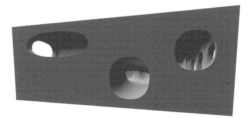

Complex lost form inside moulded material

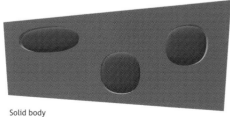

Solid body

Lost form method uses the shape of space as a representative trigger, not its perimeters

The lost form mould can achieve various topological characteristics and allow for different types of internal organisation for the dwelling units.

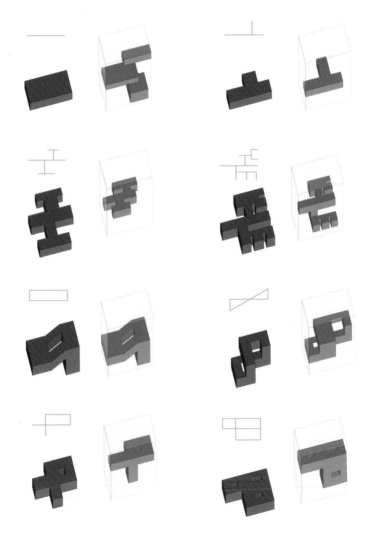

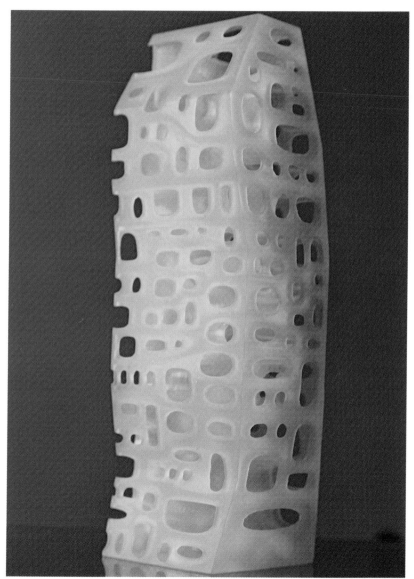

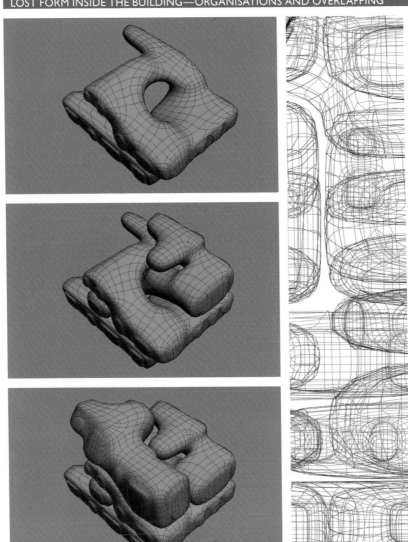

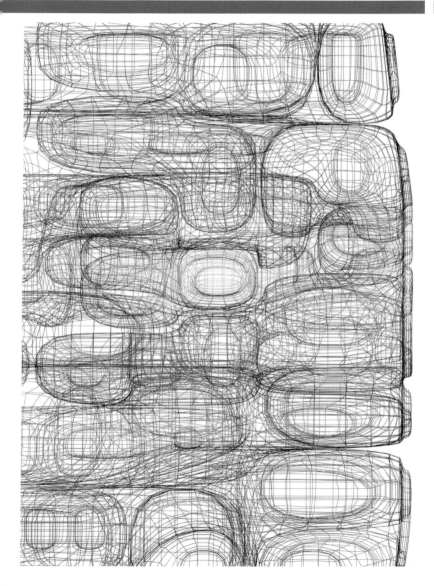

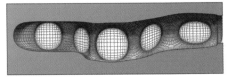

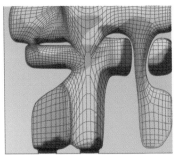

section 1

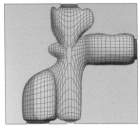

section 2

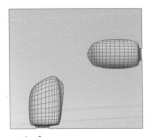

section 3

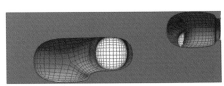

section 4

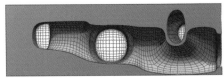

section 5

section 6

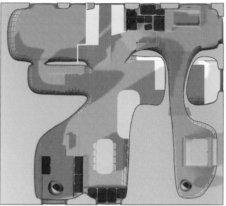

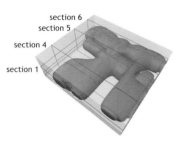

section 6
section 5
section 4
section 1

section 1—proposed interior organisation

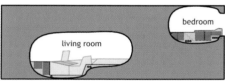

living room

bedroom

section 4

Interior spaces with foam blocks
furnishing the space

Water system and other utilities
are integrated into the foam blocks
achieving storage space and allow for
distribution in the entire dwelling unit

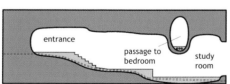

entrance

passage to
bedroom

study
room

section 5

Foam based interior additions

Pipes, water and electricity

Storage space integrated in
Foam base

Interior modules are also cut from the
digital representation of the lost form

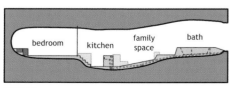

bedroom   kitchen   family
space   bath

section 6

ACKNOWLEDGEMENTS

Material Research
With the contribution of:
· Marco Sardella, Architect, PhD at ITACA Department, University La Sapienza of
Rome and Professor at LUDI, University of Industrial Design La Sapienza of Rome
Special thanks to:
· Els Zijlstra, Architect, Head of Materia, Statenweg 63c, 3039 HD Rotterdam, P.O.
Box 28131, The Netherlands
· Antonio Schiano, Material Engineer at Material ConneXion, Milan, Italy
· Tommaso Coppola, Researcher, Centro Sviluppo Materiali S.p.A.,Via di Castel
Romano 100, 00128 Roma, Italy
· Marc Rayan, second year student at Berlage Institute

Maria Mandalaki, Housing Senses
Advisors:
· Rogier Van der Heide, Associate Director, Arup Lighting
· Caroline Raines from Square One research Pty Ltd
· Maarten van der Niet: Sound and Light design company
· Light design software: Relux Informatik AG
Companies:
· CoverTex GmbH. Berghamer Str 19, D-83119 Obing
Tel +49 862489690 Mr. Benoit Fauchon, Export Sales Manager
· FOILTEC Verarbeitung von Folien und Textilien GmbH, Steinacker 3,
D- 28717 Bremen
Tel: +49 421693510, Fax: +49 4216935119
· Buitink Technology
Advanced Lightweight Structures, Nieuwgraaf 210, NL-6921 RR Duiven
Ms. Ruth Simons
Tel: +31 263194181, Fax +31 263194191

Pieterjan Vermoortel, Vertical City
   Engineering Advisor:
   · Salvatore Bono (collaborator Buro2 , Renzo Piano)

Noa Haim, Vertical Kibbutz
   Engineering Advisor:
   · Hugo Mulder (Arup, Amsterdam)
   Advisors:
   · Peter Trummer
   · AB Technun, Tel Aviv, arch. Gadi Almog and arch. Mira Yehudai
     (former Kibbutz Planning Department)

Eriko Watanabe, Tree Twister
   Engineering Advisor:
   · Hugo Mulder (Arup, Amsterdam)
   Advisor:
   · Vedran Mimica
   Model:
   · Hiromi Haruki

Kiwoong Ko and Alexandros Vazakas, Demand versus Geometry
   Model
   made with Selective Laser Sintering technology:
   · by Materialise NV, Technologielaan 15, 3001 Leuven Belgium

Lorena Franco, Accommodating Change
  Engineering Advisor:
  · Hugo Mulder (Arup, Amsterdam)
  Real State Managemet Advisor:
  · John Heintz (TU Delft)
  Advisor:
  · Peter Trummer
  Bracing Rigidity Advisor:
  · Jack Graver, Mathematician, Syracuse University

Andrea Fiecther, How is Material Informing Architecture?
  Engineering Advisor:
  · Hugo Mulder (Arup, Amsterdam)
  Material Research Advisor:
  · Philipp Westphal, SP Technologies, Southampton, UK
  Printing of model:
  · RP^2, Hagemuntweg 35, 4879 Etten-Leur, NL

Yorai Gabriel, Lost Form
  Printing of model:
  · RP^2, Hagemuntweg 35, 4879 Etten-Leur, NL

This book was made with editorial support from the Berlage Institute:
  · Jennifer Sigler, Lynn Suderman, Verdan Mimica.

728
ARR

R63263

Designed by: Rossana Atena
Re-design by: aleatoria
Additional research: Maisie James
                     Safiya Waley
Translation by: William Bain (p12-13)
                     Lucille Banham (p16-21)

berlage institute
postgraduate laboratory of architecture

Berlage Institute, Postgraduate Laboratory of Architecture

Sponsored by: Empresa Municipal de Vivienda y Suelo de Madrid, Área de Gobierno
de Urbanismo, Vivienda e Infraestructuras, Ayuntamiento de Madrid

madrid EMPRESA MUNICIPAL DE VIVIENDA Y SUELO
ÁREA DE GOBIERNO DE URBANISMO,
VIVIENDA E INFRAESTRUCTURAS

Eco-Valle

Mediterranean   COMISIÓN EUROPEA
Verandahways   Programa Life